The Equality State
Government and Politics in Wyoming
Fifth Edition

by

Larry Hubbell, *Editor*
Richard Engstrom
Michael Horan
James King
Robert Schuhmann

Department of Political Science
University of Wyoming

eddie bowers publishing co., inc.
P. O. Box 130
Peosta, Iowa 52068

Exclusive marketing and distributor rights for
U.K., Eire, and Continental Europe held by:

Gazelle Book Services Limited
Falcon House
Queen Square
Lancaster
LA1 1RN
U.K.

---

eddie bowers publishing co., inc.
P. O. Box 130
Peosta, Iowa 52068 USA

e-mail: eddiebowerspub@aol.com

ISBN: 1-57879-055-7 • Fifth Edition

9 8 7 6 5 4 3 2

Table of Contents

CHAPTER 1

WYOMING'S FIRSTS AND LASTS

As the forty-fourth state, Wyoming entered the Union in 1890, more than 100 years after the birth of the Republic and the adoption of the Constitution. Nevertheless, Wyoming is known for many political firsts. The Wyoming territorial government in 1869 gave women the vote and the right to hold political office. Hence, women served on grand and petit juries in 1870, and Esther Hobart Morris became the first woman justice of the peace. In 1894, Wyoming elected the first woman to a state office. The first woman to be inaugurated governor of any state was Nellie Tayloe Ross in 1925. Although the political representation of women in Wyoming languished for many years after these firsts, today women hold significant numbers of state and local offices.

As a result of these political firsts, Wyoming has adopted the motto, "The Equality State." Many explanations have been offered for the adoption of women's suffrage by the first territorial legislature: the work of leaders of the suffrage movement; an effort to lure more women to settle in the state; a political joke (Larson, 1965: 89-94; Chapman, 1952: 54-68). Regardless of the reason, the grant of suffrage is consonant with Wyoming's frontier spirit and dominant libertarian philosophy. Individualism, conservatism and distrust of the federal government, big business and other big organizations pervade the state.

CONTEXT OF WYOMING POLITICS

To understand Wyoming politics, it is first necessary to examine the context.

Demographics

Wyoming has the smallest population of any state and yet its land area is ninth largest. With five people per square mile, only Alaska is less densely populated. There are 112 counties and 83 metropolitan areas in the United States which have larger populations. Wyoming is largely a rural state. Approximately 30 percent of its residents live in metropolitan areas as compared to the national average of almost 80 percent. After growing more than 40 percent during the 1970s, thanks to the energy boom, the population of Wyoming remained fairly stable in the 1980s. In 2001, Wyoming had a population of approximately 494,000. While Wyoming's population increased 8.9 percent between 1990 and 2000, several of Wyoming's neighbors had much larger populations increases during the same period: Colorado +30.6%, Utah +29.6% and Idaho +28.5%

Wyoming is a state with a very small minority population. The African American population is less than one percent. Native Americans comprise another two percent while the Hispanic population is six percent. Although Wyoming is a rural state, it does not have a large farm population. In 1999, the farm sector employed approximately 12,200 workers. As in the United States as a whole, the number of farms and ranches has declined drastically. In 1930, there were nearly 18 thousand farms or ranches in Wyoming. In 2000, the comparable figure was around 9,200.

Economy

Throughout its history, Wyoming's economy has been dependent upon mineral extraction and agriculture. Both have been highly susceptible to boom and bust. Wyoming's economy is much like that of many Third World nations in its dependency upon several commodities and its inability to control the price of these products. For example, Honduras, a Central American country, is dependent upon bananas; Wyoming on oil, gas and coal. Honduras has little or no control over the price of bananas, which is set in a world market. Similarly, Wyoming has essentially no control over the demand for and consequent price of its basic commodities. Exacerbating the problem is the state's small population base, which translates into little national political clout. Overwhelmingly, Americans prefer low energy prices; thus, any national policy which might reduce dependence on foreign energy or increase the price of domestic oil is not politically feasible. In a democratic nation, the low cost of gasoline in Los Angeles or Boston is significantly more important than the unemployment rate in the state with the least population.

The first boom period began when the Union Pacific snaked its way across the state in 1867 and 1868. The demand for coal and cattle fueled the economy following the coming of the railroad, but coal demand leveled off, and a series of severe winters devastated the cattle industry. Both World Wars increased demands for Wyoming agricultural and mineral products, but in the post-war eras Wyoming's economy did not prosper. Between 1960 and 1970 the population grew by only 2,000 people. The Arab oil embargo in 1973 resulted in the sharpest increase in the state's economic base as well as its population. Less than a decade later, the rapid decline in world oil prices and the unwillingness of the federal government to support oil prices led to the most precipitous decline of the economy and the population. The market for uranium also foundered in the early 1980s. Personal income in the state ranked among the highest in the nation at the beginning of the 1980s, but by the end of the 1980's the rate of personal income increase was among the lowest in the nation.

The mineral extraction industry suffered in the 1980s, but in many aspects, the plight of the agricultural sec-

A Union Pacific train entering Green River in 1869. 120 years later the company is moving its work force out of Wyoming. *American Heritage Center, University of Wyoming.*

tor was nearly as severe. Wyoming's sheep, lamb, and wool production is among the highest in the United States, but, as in the past, the cattle industry produced by far the greatest revenue. During the past several decades, Wyoming's farm income has fluctuated. In 1979, Wyoming farmers and ranchers received a net farm income of $93.9 million. In 1986, income fell to $29.8 million. In the 1990s, net farm income varied within a range of a loss of $18 million in 1996 to a profit of $240 million in 1993. In 2000, net farm income increased to $114 million.

In the 1980s and beyond, airline deregulation also had a significant impact on the state's economy. Although the cost of air travel between Denver and New York, or San Francisco and Washington, D.C., became significantly less expensive, most major airlines have abandoned Wyoming's small cities. Large airlines have been replaced by less predictable and more expensive commuter airlines. The federally-operated train service, AMTRAK, deserted the state in the early 1980s for a potentially more lucrative Colorado route. It returned in the summer of 1991 to cities in southern Wyoming but once again abandoned service in the mid 1990s. However, major bus companies have resumed service to many Wyoming towns and cities. Even the company so instrumental in the founding of Wyoming, the Union Pacific Railroad, consolidated operations and reduced its Wyoming work force.

During the 1990s, Wyoming's economic performance has been mixed. For the past several years, Wyoming's unemployment rate remained relatively low. In 2001, while the national unemployment rate was 4.8 percent, Wyoming's rate was only 3.9 percent. However, per capita income at $27,372 in 2000 was roughly 93 percent of the national average. .

Despite the increase in bankruptcies in recent years, Wyoming, unlike most states, had a budget surplus in 2002-2003. Furthermore, the state has an attractive quality of life. The state has the nation's best air quality. Wyoming's violent crime rate in 1999 was the nation's 7th lowest and it had the 8th lowest murder rate. In 2000, 90 percent of Wyoming's population over 25 had attained at least a high school education, which was the sixth highest level in the nation. Finally, Wyoming's poverty rate between 1998 and 2000 was 11.1 percent, below the national average of 11.9 percent.

Mass Communication

Mass communication is another important aspect of the Wyoming political landscape. To a significant degree, many Wyomingites know as much or more about politics in surrounding states as they do about politics in the Equality State. Denver, Rapid City, Billings and Salt Lake newspapers and tele-

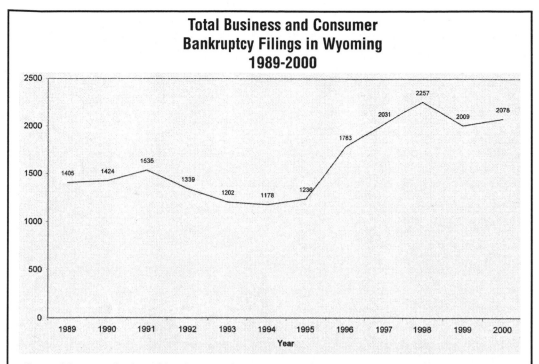

Total Business and Consumer Bankruptcy Filings in Wyoming 1989-2000

Figure 1 is a graph of total business and consumer bankruptcy filings in Wyoming since 1989. The trend increased dramatically during the mid 1990s, but since 1998 has come off its high.

Figure 1

vision are viewed by a large percentage of the population. A citizen of Laramie is more likely to watch a Denver television station and subscribe to The Denver Post than to watch a Wyoming channel or read a Wyoming newspaper. A Wyoming candidate may be sorely tempted to advertise on a Salt Lake, Billings or Denver television station, although the cost may be prohibitive. There is no question, however, about which Wyoming television channels and newspapers dominate the state. A 1987 Wyoming Heritage Foundation survey found that 59 percent of Wyomingites

get most of their information about the state from newspapers, 23 percent from television and 16 percent from radio. By far, the dominant newspaper in the state is The Casper Star-Tribune. Forty-five percent of the Heritage Poll respondents indicated that they relied most upon this paper (Heritage Foundation Public Opinion Poll, 1987). Seventy-two percent believe it is generally fair and unbiased. Two other newspapers, the Laramie Boomerang and the Rock Springs Rocket Miner, were relied upon by six percent of the population. The Star-Tribune is a highly independent newspaper which clearly gives better coverage to state politics than its competitors. Its coverage of events and personalities, its editorials and political cartoons have repeatedly outraged the Republican establishment although Democrats are frequently the targets of its barbs.

There are two principal television stations in Wyoming: Casper's KTWO, relied upon by 43 percent, and Cheyenne's KGWN relied upon by 16 percent according to the Heritage poll. Both devote considerable air time to Wyoming politics, but neither is nearly as confrontational as the Casper Star-Tribune.

Political Culture

Political cultures vary considerably among American states. A rather diffuse concept, political culture in general refers to widespread attitudes, beliefs and practices that influence people in a state or region. What is the dominant Wyoming political culture?

The most obvious feature of Wyoming political culture is its conservatism. Overwhelmingly, Wyomingites identify themselves as conservative. For more than twenty years the Wyoming Election Year Survey (WEYS) has asked respondents whether they consider themselves to be conservative, liberal or middle-of-the road. Figure 2 shows the disparity between the number of conservative and liberal identifiers. Since 1980, between 40 and 50 percent of Wyomingites have identified themselves as conservative. The proportion of liberal identifiers has hovered around 20 percent. (See Figure 2.)

Conservatism has a variety of meanings and is manifested in an assortment of ways. For example, Wyoming government has historically been slow to adopt policy innovations. One study found that only two other states were slower to adopt new ideas into law than Wyoming (Walker, 1969). Wyoming has also been traditionally very fiscally conservative. Unlike the federal budget, the Wyoming state budget by constitutional fiat has been balanced unfailingly.

Most conservatives are very reluctant to increase taxes, believing that individuals should be given priority in spending their earnings and that government spending is almost always inefficient and wasteful. Not increasing taxes became almost a moral dogma with conservatives during the 1980s, largely because of pledges by Presidents Reagan and Bush not to increase taxes. The Republicans' 1994 campaign manifesto, "The Contract with America," reiterated this abhorrence of taxes. Interestingly, nearly 84 percent of Wyomingites declared that they believed state and local taxes were reasonable just prior to

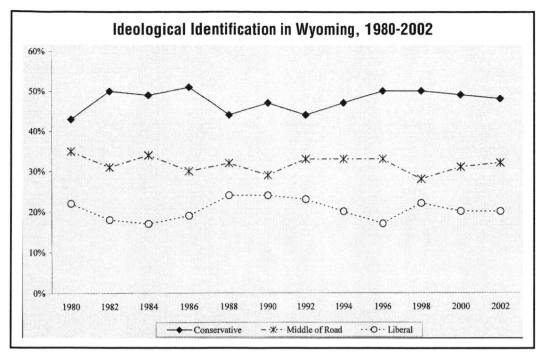

Ideological Identification in Wyoming, 1980-2002

Conservative — *** · Middle of Road · · O · · Liberal

Figure 2

the 1994 general election (WEYS, 1994). Moreover, nearly three-quarters of those responding to the 1994 Wyoming Election Year Survey indicated there were circumstances in which they would favor tax increases. (These percentages have not changed by more than a couple of points in subsequent surveys.) However, most citizens undoubtedly agree with the state's Republican leadership that has, in recent years, been adamantly opposed to almost any form of tax increase. Thus, although Wyoming state tax rates are among the very lowest in the United States, legislators are leery of voting for tax increases.

Nevertheless, in the 2003 legislative session, a bill that authorized a 48 cent increase in the cigarette tax was approved by the legislature and signed by the governor.

Distrust of the federal government has long been an element of Wyoming political culture and, as this belief has become a central tenet of American conservative ideology, this lack of faith has reached new highs in Wyoming. For example, among the most effective arguments against increasing the drinking age during the 1988 session of the legislature was that the federal government was "blackmailing" the state.

Wyoming Attitudes Toward the Federal and State Governments		
Survey Item	Federal Government	State Government
Agree that government wastes a lot of money.	68%	27%
Trust government to do what is right only some or none of the time.	74%	46%
Agree that government is run for the benefit of a few big interests.	63%	36%

Table 1

Table 1 contains answers to three questions about the federal and state governments asked of Wyoming residents. The first queried respondents about whether government in Washington or in Cheyenne wasted a lot of money, some, or not much. Two-thirds of the sample indicated that the federal government wastes "a lot." Another asked Wyomingites how often they could "trust the government in Washington (or Cheyenne) to do what is right." More than seven out of ten Wyomingites indicated that the federal government could be trusted only some or none of the time. A third item asked respondents whether they believed government was run for the benefit of a few big interests. Over 60 percent of the respondents agreed (WEYS, 2002). Although demonstrating a lack of faith in the federal government, these figures are actually higher than in previous surveys. Confidence in government is related to confidence in public officials, and President George W. Bush had the confidence of Wyomingites much more than either of his predecessors.

In contrast, attitudes toward their state and local government are much more favorable. Large majorities are satisfied with the services provided by their local government, and they seem more likely to trust the state government to do what is right. All three survey questions presented in Table 1 show Wyomingites having greater trust in the state government than in the federal government. Still, only about half of the state's citizens believe the government in Cheyenne can be trusted to do what is right all or most of the time (WEYS, 2002).

Gun control is a highly salient issue among Wyoming conservatives. Almost every week the <u>Casper Star</u> publishes letters from readers excoriating those who would regulate firearms. Figure 3 indicates the high degree of agreement that gun control laws are anathema to Wyoming citizens. Over three-fifths of Wyoming citizens oppose a "strong gun control law" (WEYS, 2002). Given the vehemence of those opposed to gun control, it is perhaps surprising that nearly one out of three Wyomingites favor just such regulation.

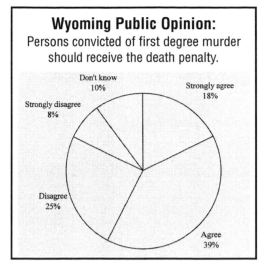

Wyoming Public Opinion:
Persons convicted of first degree murder should receive the death penalty.

Figure 4

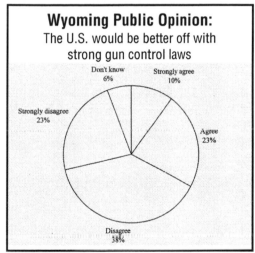

Wyoming Public Opinion:
The U.S. would be better off with strong gun control laws

Figure 3

Wyomingites are also overwhelmingly conservative when it comes to the question of whether or not to impose the death penalty for murder. Almost 60 percent of Wyoming citizens favor the death penalty (Figure 4). Given this high level of support, it is surprising that the death penalty has been carried out in only one case during the last 25 years.

Conservatism places a distinct emphasis on individualism. Wyoming's "mascot" of the lone cowboy illustrates this belief in individualism. Whether Wyomingites are more individualistic than citizens of other states is arguable, but as can be seen in Figure 5, nearly three-fourths believe themselves to be more self-reliant than other Americans (WEYS, 1984). Certainly, individualism is an important component of Wyoming political culture.

The emphasis on individualism is evident when we consider public attitudes on affirmative action programs and welfare. Affirmative action is intended to compensate for the effects of discrimination against women and minorities in the workplace but is often seen as allowing people to advance because of personal characteristics rather than individual achievement. When

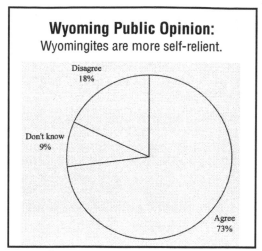

Wyoming Public Opinion:
Wyomingites are more self-relient.

Disagree
18%

Don't know
9%

Agree
73%

Figure 5

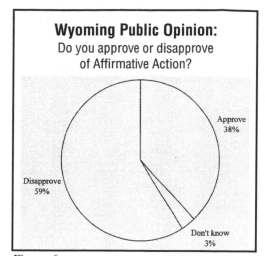

Wyoming Public Opinion:
Do you approve or disapprove
of Affirmative Action?

Approve
38%

Disapprove
59%

Don't know
3%

Figure 6

asked about affirmative action in 2002, nearly three-fifths of Wyomingites expressed disapproval (Figure 6). The citizens surveyed were almost equally split between those supporting the notion that people receiving welfare payments were "taking advantage of the system" and those believing such people truly need assistance (Figure 7). The basic message of these opinions is the same: people advance through individual effort rather than reliance upon government programs.

As with all political ideologies, conservatives do not agree on every tenet of their doctrine. For instance, conservatism in many southern states and in Wyoming's neighboring state of Utah is characterized by an emphasis on social control. Tolerance for beliefs and behavior inconsistent with the majority standards is frowned upon. Wyoming conservatism, however, is more of a

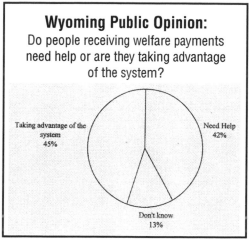

Wyoming Public Opinion:
Do people receiving welfare payments
need help or are they taking advantage
of the system?

Taking advantage of the
system
45%

Need Help
42%

Don't know
13%

Figure 7

live-and-let-live variety. The individualistic spirit and libertarian political philosophy that pervade the Wyoming culture are shown by staunch hostility to government intervention in private moral decisions. Wyoming citizens are libertarians in the sense that they espouse freedom of choice. As an example, a plurality of Wyomingites support the position that abortion is a matter of personal choice while very few oppose abortion in all circumstances (Figure 8). In the 1994 general election, Wyoming soundly defeated a measure on the state ballot that would have made

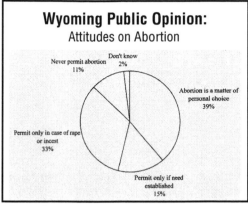

Figure 8

it more difficult to receive an abortion. Equally significant, Wyoming citizens are staunch supporters of civil liberties. Evidence for this proposition can be found in a set of questions asked several times by the Wyoming Election Year Survey.

No other liberty is as central to American political liberties as is freedom of speech. However, many Americans, while agreeing with the central principle, find it difficult to permit members of out groups the right to speak. In 1982, Wyoming respondents were asked whether those against churches or religion, communists, and members of the Ku Klux Klan should be allowed to give speeches in the

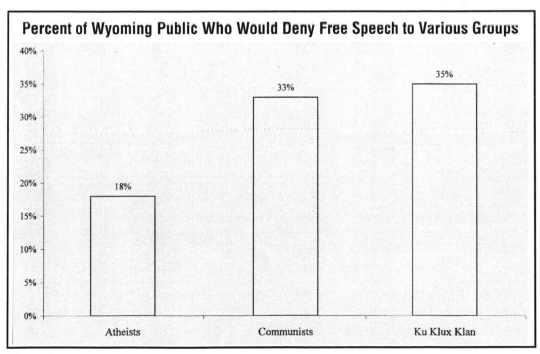

Figure 9

respondent's community (WEYS, 1982). Those Wyomingites who would deny freedom of speech are a distinct minority.

Finally, as Wyoming's nickname would indicate, there is a rather strong sense of egalitarianism in the state, a value generally not associated with conservatism which places much greater emphasis on equal opportunity. Wyomingites do not perceive great social differences among themselves. This is reflected in answers to an item in the 1984 Wyoming Election survey. Government Research Bureau interviewers asked respondents whether they agreed or disagreed with the following item: "Wyomingites are less aware of social differences than other Americans." Nearly seven in every ten indicated that Wyomingites are less aware of social differences than other Americans. However, the sense of egalitarianism does not extend to acceptance of government policies to "force" equality, such as those reducing income differences (WEYS, 1984).

The equality nickname resulted from Wyoming's pioneering efforts in granting women equal political rights. Prominent conservatives like Rush Limbaugh and Phyllis Shlafly eschew feminism. Like conservatism, feminism has many meanings, but a strong belief in political equality for women is present in all conceptions of feminism. What attitudes do Wyomingites hold on this issue? Attitudes toward women's rights in "The Equality State" are quite favorable and, interestingly, have become more positive during the last decade. Wyomingites reject the stereotypes making politics a male domain. They do not accord superiority to men as political decision makers in domestic or foreign affairs (WEYS, 1984, 1998).

Wyoming Support For Common Sex Stereotypes		
Survey Item	1984	2002
Agree that men are better suited emotionally for politics than are women.	28%	14%
Agree that male political leaders are better able to stand up to foreign leaders than women.	33%	33%
Agree than men are better decision makers about war and peace than women.	32%	24%

Table 2

Wyoming, then, has a conservative political culture. Wyomingites tend to identify as conservatives and strongly hold many conservative political issues. On the other hand, they strongly support full political equality for women, strongly support freedom of speech and would be described as libertarian conservatives rather than social conservatives.

CHAPTER 2

THE WYOMING CONSTITUTION

The Wyoming Constitution was written over a 25-day period in September, 1889. Delegates were elected on a partisan ballot from the ten then-existing counties. Fifty-five delegates were chosen but only 49 attended the convention which was held in Cheyenne. Nearly a majority of the delegates came from New York, Pennsylvania, Ohio, and Illinois. Thirty-one of the 49 participating delegates were Republicans. Thirty-four delegates were selected from the southern tier of counties. The constitutional convention delegates were very well educated, with over 40 percent of them college graduates. By way of occupation, lawyers were the dominant group, both in terms of delegates (18) and in terms of the number of speeches given. There were no female delegates. Although ranching was the dominant industry in 1890, only eight delegates were ranchers. Interestingly, 40 percent of Wyoming's Founding Fathers moved to other states sometime after the convention (Walter, 1987).

The delegates approached their task under the pressure of coming up

Francis E. Warren, territorial governor, called for a constitutional convention in 1889. *American Heritage Center, University of Wyoming.*

Figure 1

with a document which could win public approval and satisfy a majority of Congress without taking any more time off from personal occupations than was absolutely necessary, thus it is not difficult to understand how the result of the constitutional convention of 1889 came to be a pastiche of familiar concepts affected by the circumstances of the state's history, political culture, and physical environment.

THE ELEMENTS OF THE WYOMING CONSTITUTION IN HISTORICAL CONTEXT

What were the principal ingredients of this constitutional mix, and in what respect are they primarily reflective of the *Wyoming* experience rather than representative of most state constitutions? How do they manifest themselves in the language of the document and its implementation in the operative processes of government?

Wyoming has had only one constitution and one constitutional convention since 1889, mirroring a tradition of political and legal stability found in only a minority of the states today (Book of the States 2002). The document contains 31,800 words, more than triple the length of the United States Constitution. Its length is exceeded by only 16 other states.

The Wyoming Constitution (published as an appendix to this book), like its counterparts in each of the other 49 states, allocates political authority within and between the state and local governments, and deals with matters of paramount concern to the welfare of the

people of the State which lie beyond the scope of the United States Constitution. Similarly, like the constitutions of other states, the Wyoming document recognizes personal rights (as well as group interests) which are omitted from the federal document. Although the Wyoming Constitution is legally subordinate to the United States Constitution, there is no question that its provisions are otherwise the supreme law of the State and take precedence over contrary provisions of state statutes, administrative regulations, and common law.

In terms of broad contents, its 21 articles, much like other state constitutions, contain a preamble or statement of purpose, a declaration (bill) of rights, provisions creating the structure of state and local government, and specific financial limitations and mandates affecting the revenue-raising authority of government on all levels. It also contains provisions on broad topical areas, including: the well-being of the community, a grab-bag of miscellaneous stipulations apparently thought unsuitable for placement elsewhere in the text, and, finally, provisions whereby the document may be formally amended or completely revised. The text is written in a dry, businesslike, and frequently legalistic style of other late-nineteenth century constitutions. The style was no doubt facilitated by the readiness of the men who wrote it to draw liberally upon—even replicate—arrangements

The members of the Wyoming Constitutional Convention pose in front of the Capitol Building. *American Heritage Center, University of Wyoming.*

Figure 2

they found in the copies of constitutions of similar states which were distributed to the authors at their 1889 convention (Peterson, 1940: 104; Larson, 1977: 247).

Those constitutional arrangements were grounded on doctrines long embedded in the American political culture and taken for granted by the convention delegates: popular sovereignty, political equality, republicanism, separation of powers, checks and balances, civilian supremacy over the armed forces, natural rights (including private property), judicial independence, trial by jury, bicameralism, local self-government, allegiance to the Union, and obedience to the Constitution of the United States.

These doctrines are not necessarily expressed in the same language as the federal Constitution. The Wyoming document implicitly accepts the right of revolution, a matter which the framers of the federal Constitution preferred to leave couched in the more ambiguous language of the preamble. The Wyoming Declaration of Rights incorporates some protections (such as "safe and comfortable prisons") against a potentially overbearing government which have no parallels in the federal Bill of Rights. Where corresponding freedoms are found, they are occasionally stated in broader (such as the right to bear arms in self-defense) or more restrictive terminology. Separation of church and state, which the United States Supreme Court has construed the no-establishment-of-religion clause of the First Amendment to require, is given specific form in the Wyoming Constitution's prohibitions against appropriation of public funds to religious organizations. Similarly, the Wyoming Constitution is clear in its prohibition against religious instruction in the public schools of the State, also a problematic issue in the federal Constitution.

Equality, which was forthrightly proclaimed in the Declaration of Independence, but left out of the original United States Constitution under the pressure of the slavery question, is emphatically, if not repeatedly, set forth in the Wyoming Constitution. It is first framed as a broad philosophical principle, then subsequently applied to political, legal, and civil rights, without regard to race, sex, religion, or (in the case of property rights) resident aliens.

Many aspects of the Wyoming Constitution are understandable in light of the circumstances of the American, and specifically Wyoming, political culture and physical environment of the late nineteenth century, or what one convention delegate referred to as the "[q]uestions arising from the evils or the necessities of the day and generation in which we live[.]" (Constitutional Convention Debates, 1893: 348) (statement of George W. Baxter). The State's pioneering enfranchisement of women was the continuation of an experiment born

JUDGE WITH PRISONER

A JURY TRIAL? ARE YOU ONE OF THOSE TROUBLE-MAKERS WHO'S BEEN READING THE CONSTITUTION?

COUNTY JAIL

Figure 3

in territorial days, in turn a result of the scarcity of women, hopes of recruiting settlers, and growing pressure for female suffrage in other parts of the West. By 1889, the results of this experiment were viewed favorably enough by Wyomingites to justify the conclusion that women's suffrage was right as a matter of principle (Larson, 1977: 84-89, 248-49; Constitutional Convention Debates, 1893: 344-59).

The provisions of the constitution guarding against religious instruction in the public schools of the State and the appropriation of state money to religious institutions are consistent with the secular orientation of the territorial population. These provisions were not unlike similar prohibitions written into the laws of other states during the period to squelch the efforts of Roman Catholic groups to secure public aid for parochial schools.

Historians of nineteenth-century America have shown how the spate of constitution-making in America between 1860 and 1900 (38 constitutions were written in 18 states between 1860 and 1875; 19 more were written in 18 states from 1875 to 1900) reflected a public mood to curb the power of local government to borrow heavily for public improvements, a practice which had brought many cities to the point of bankruptcy in the wake of the depression of 1873 (Sturm, 1982: 57, 66-68). In Wyoming, this mood is evident in the state constitution's specific limitations on the ability of counties, municipalities, and school districts to create indebtedness.

The Wyoming founders were also interested in authorizing public regulation of the more notorious practices of private firms. The Union Pacific Railroad, in particular, was a dominant feature in the economic livelihood of many, and owned huge amounts of rich coal lands along its rights-of-way. In constitutionalizing the right to bring wrongful death actions, mine inspection and safety requirements, an eight-hour day in mines, a ban on female and child labor in "dangerous" mines (repealed in 1978), and a prohibition on importing private police forces, the convention delegates clearly had in mind certain employment practices of the Union Pacific and its mining operations in the years before statehood. These perceived abuses had also been the targets of territorial legislation. The political vulnerability of the railroad, as well as the revenue needs of the State, were important factors in writing into the constitution (rather than leaving it up to the legislature) a tax on coal lands or upon the value of the gross product thereof (Bakken, 1987: 59-60, 64; Larson, 1977: 251-53). It became the duty of the legislature to protect and assist other economic interests, such as the stockgrowers and the vaguely worded term "labor".

Sectional conflict, including fear of political domination by the southeastern area of the State, led convention delegates from the western and northern counties to insert into the constitution a provision guaranteeing each county at least one seat in both houses of the legislature, regardless of population (Bakken 1987: 45; Larson, 1977: 250-51).

The position of the legislature is perhaps the most telling example of the interaction between theory and practice in the Wyoming Constitution. Modern representative democracies by and large vest decisions regarding public policy in the legislative branch, whose members are chosen directly or indirectly by the electorate. In contrast to the national government, where Congress legally may exercise only those powers delegated to it by the federal Constitution, state legislatures inherently are vested with the full power to pass laws on any topic, subject only to the substantive and procedural limitations found in the state and federal constitutions. The Wyoming Supreme Court has held this principle to be implied in the state constitution, even if it is not explicitly stated. Experience with corruption and financial profligacy in American legislatures after the Civil War, however, suggested the necessity of prescribing additional restrictions upon legislative behavior in the state constitution, beyond those already provided by checks and balances, bills of rights, and the ballot box (Press & VerBurg, 1983: 168-73; Bakken, 1987: 45, 53). The Wyoming Constitu-

tion epitomizes this tendency in its numerous procedural specifications for enactment of bills, in its various restrictions upon the legislature's power to tax, borrow, and spend, and in the many provisions obliging (rather than simply authorizing) the legislators to pass certain kinds of laws.

CONSTITUTIONAL CHANGE

The Wyoming Constitution, as it was handed down by its framers, is not the same one that exists today. While many of its original provisions remain intact, others have undergone a process of evolution in much the same way that the state and its people have changed over the past century.

The document itself contains two modes whereby it may be formally amended, or even totally replaced: legislative initiative, or proposed revision by a constitutional convention called by the legislature with popular approval. Proposals of either kind must be ratified by a majority of the electors (i.e. a majority of the persons voting in the *election*, and not merely a majority of those voting on the proposed *amendment*). As a matter of practice, the former method has been used exclusively, precedent for the convention route being confined to the original 1889 assembly. Seventy-one separate amendments have been adopted (out of 116 submitted to the voters) since the Constitution went into effect July 10, 1890. Fifty-five of the 71 amendments have been adopted since 1960. (It has also been the practice in this state to incorporate amendments into their logical place in the text of the constitution, rather than listing them separately at the end of the document, as is the case with the United States Constitution). While assessments in this regard are likely to differ, the amendments most significant in terms of altering the scheme of government created by the original Wyoming Constitution are those: revising how judges are chosen, retained and disciplined (Art. 5, sects. 4-6); providing for "home rule" authority for cities and towns (Art. 13, sect. 1); and adding an optional 20-day budget session for the legislature (Art. 3, sects. 6-7). Also of importance have been a series of amendments enabling the state to build an economic infrastructure in the form of highways, water projects, and airports (Art. 16, sects. 9-11), and increasing the taxing and borrowing authority of state and local government for spending on public education (Art. 7, sect. 2; Art. 16, sect. 5).

It is true that the Wyoming Constitution, as do all documents of its genre, also changes in ways other than through formal revision. Judicial interpretation, so clearly vital in adapting the meaning of the United States Constitution to changing circumstances, plays a part in keeping state fundamental law up to date, although perhaps less so than on the federal level. The Supreme Court of Wyoming, while no radical innovator in state constitutional jurisprudence, frequently has spoken of the importance of adapting constitutional provisions to evolving times and circumstances. Moreover, the court has taken a more prominent role in the shaping of public policy through state constitutional interpretation in recent years. Perhaps the most outstanding example of this was the series of decisions of the court between 1971 and 2001 which ruled that the legislature's duty in Art. 7, sect. 1 to provide for a "complete and uniform system of public instruction" meant a fair, complete, and equal education <u>appropriate for the times</u> (emphasis added). In 1995, the court declared the then-existing system of financing Wyoming's public schools to be so inequitable as to be completely unconstitutional. The court directed the legislature to replace this system with one that would satisfy the legislature's obligations in Art. 7.

Statutory amplification of fundamental law is an important change-agent as well. While the Wyoming Constitution seems more preoccupied with restricting rather than enhancing the powers of the state legislature, surely such laws as the Wyoming Industrial Siting Act and the mineral severance tax law

From the Casper Star-Tribune, February 27, 2001, page A9

Figure 4

of 1969 reinterpreted the legislature's constitutional police and taxing powers to cope with the strains placed upon the state's resources as a result of the boom in energy development experienced during the 1960s and 1970s. The Court Consolidation Act of 2000 likewise implemented the legislature's constitutional authority over the lower courts to modernize the structure, jurisdiction, and personnel matters of local tribunals of justice. The tradition according to which the Speaker of the Wyoming House of Representatives serves only one term and then retires from the House is purely a matter of informal practice followed by both parties in the House, but exemplifies how custom can affect constitutional arrangements, even though the result arguably is to weaken the institutional position of the legislature vis-a-vis the governor.

Change can also be accomplished by ignoring constitutional provisions whose validity is thrown into doubt by federal law or court decision, or which are inconvenient, or overlooked.

CRITICISMS OF THE WYOMING CONSTITUTION

The Wyoming Constitution has taken its own lumps in addition to the criticisms directed at state constitutions generally. Referring to the Wyoming constitutional convention's heavy borrowing from the constitutions of nearby states, Professor T.A. Larson, Wyoming's premiere historian, characterized the document as a product of the cut-and-paste method of constitution-making, with little originality beyond the provisions dealing with irrigation and water rights (Larson, 1977: 246-47, 253). The diffusion of executive authority among five elected officials, including the governor, has been faulted for blurring political responsibility and hindering efficient management in the administration of state affairs (Richard, 1974: 65, 77-79). The numerous constitutional specifications regarding legislative procedure, as well as the short amount of time for legislative sessions, have been cited as obstacles to the ability of government to meet the needs of a society undergoing rapid economic change. The constitution's stricture against gubernatorial threats to wield the veto power has been attacked as inane (Jordan, 1990: 114-122), and the prohibition against logrolling in legislative voting seems out of touch with the informal norms of practical politics.

No purely objective judgement as to the validity of these criticisms is possible, because too much depends on the perspective and experiences of the observer. What is an obstacle to progress in the eyes of one may be a design to safeguard freedom in the eyes of another. If a constitution is the method by which "a generation of citizens attempt to nail down what is important to them[,]" (Press & VerBurg, 1983: 190), there may well be differences of opinion among those citizens about what is important enough to rate constitutional mention, and the content of such debates is bound to shift with the passage of time.

The Wyoming Constitution is largely a stitching together of borrowings from other states. It often strays into areas that are more appropriately legislated. One searches in vain for the well-turned phrase in a torrent of restrictions, duties, and advice which is more reflective of the ideas of better than a century ago than of today. In a nation which has been described as "a land of constitutions[,]" (Grant & Omdahl, 1989: 94), there seems little reason to single this one out for praise.

Yet, the Wyoming Constitution has come to occupy its own place in the State's life. If it has failed to impress itself upon the popular consciousness, it is still respected as fundamental law by those in charge of public affairs in the State. If it is wanting in innovation, much that is borrowed undergirds the general structure of law and politics common to America as a whole. The framers' selective replication of constitutional provisions from elsewhere was not guesswork, but reliance upon ideas and processes that had been tried and found workable in places culturally and geographically proximate to Wyoming. In this sense, the lawyers, businessmen, politicians, and stockgrowers who dominated the constitutional convention were not dreamers, but people who believed practical experience was the best guide in their labors.

Where conditions required departure from past practice, as in the case of state ownership of surface water rights, the framers tempered the individualism of the law with a dose of socialism (though they would have rejected the use of that term).

If these hard-headed delegates legislated in the constitution, they knew exactly what they were up to, and wrote in such provisions because they thought they were important enough not to leave up to the unbridled discretion of future legislatures. Like the federal constitutional convention of a century earlier, sectional rivalry and compromise affected the outcome. If some of the results seem wed to interest group maneuvering or the popular mood of the times, it would be unrealistic to suppose any constitution could exclude these influences (Grant & Omdahl, 1989: 96-97, 109-110).

Finally, in its provisions for change, both formal and informal, the constitution has been flexible enough to accommodate the needs of a state whose population has increased tenfold, and become far more urbanized and economically dependent upon forces beyond its control. Population growth, industrialization, or political crisis may, at some time in the future, cause Wyomingites to reconsider whether a constitution fashioned over a century ago can persist without wholesale revision, but until now that document has served them well. It has worked. It has been a lasting legacy.

CHAPTER 3

POLITICAL PARTICIPATION:
INDIVIDUALS, PARTIES AND GROUPS

Political participation among Wyoming citizens takes several forms. Each person can act as an individual to express political ideas and preferences, or the individual can join with like-minded citizens to achieve common goals. In this chapter we examine participation on the part of citizens, participation by political parties, and interest group participation. Studies of Americans have discovered conflicting evidence concerning their levels of political participation. In some ways, Americans seem more attuned to politics and the democratic ideal of participation than citizens of other nations. They discuss politics more and are much more likely to join interest groups (Almond and Verba, 1965). On the other hand, voter turnout in American elections falls far short of levels achieved in other western democracies (Wolfinger, et al., 1990).

INDIVIDUAL PARTICIPATION

The levels of participation among Wyomingites are above national and regional averages. Figure 1 provides data on the level of electoral participation for Wyoming, the states that border Wyoming, and for the United States as a whole during the 2000 general election. As the figure demonstrates, citizens in Wyoming vote more often than people in the United States generally, and more often than citizens from most of the other states in a region with relatively high voting rates.

The act of voting is, of course, the most basic form of individual participation in a democracy. Article 6 of the Wyoming Constitution spells out the qualifications and disqualifications for voting. It specifies that all United States citizens who are 21 or older, regardless of sex, may vote, provided that they are not insane, convicted of infamous crimes or unable to read the constitution of the state. However, the literacy requirement was rescinded by the Federal Voting Rights Act of 1970, and the age requirement was dropped to a minimum of 18 by the 26th Amendment to the United States Constitution. Figure

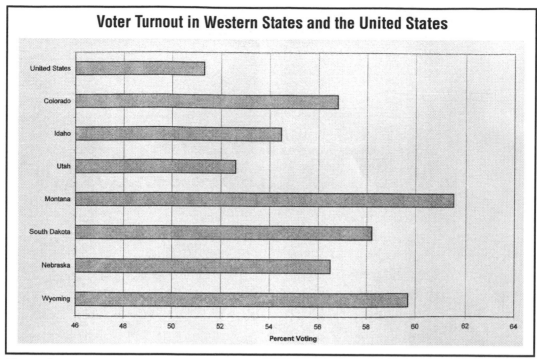

Voter Turnout in Western States and the United States

Figure 1

1 shows that fewer than six out of every ten eligible Wyomingites, and only slightly more than half of eligible Americans, chose to vote in the 2000 general election. To those who believe that democracy works best when all citizens participate in the process, these figures are disturbing.

There are various explanations for low participation rates. Frankly, many citizens simply do not discern the value of participation. As we have seen in Chapter 1, many Americans do not trust or have confidence in the government they elected. Moreover, many citizens probably reason that one vote would have little impact on the final result.

Other Americans do not participate because they perceive so little difference among the parties and candidates. Why give money or work for a candidate if all candidates are basically the same? This contention is certainly fallacious in many, if not most, circumstances but the perception remains.

Much alienation from political participation is the result of not understanding the political system. Politics and the political process are complicated, and complexity may well lead to feelings of political ineffectiveness. Education is one factor that eases these feelings. It has an impact on individuals in many ways. For one thing, education in the United States is related to civic duty, the belief that the good citizen is a political participant. As an example, Wyoming citizens were asked during the 2002 electoral campaign a series of questions designed to measure how important they believed voting to be. Those with college educations were substantially more likely to believe that the act of voting was important than were those with only a high school degree (WEYS, 2002).

Why do Wyomingites generally participate more in politics than other Americans? A partial answer must relate to Wyoming's political culture and its small population. Residents of the Mountain states traditionally hold a higher sense of civic duty and thus participate more than those in other parts of the nation. This is evident from a comparison of surveys conducted in Wyoming and the nation as a whole in conjunction with the 1992 election. Respondents were asked to agree or disagree with the statement: "If a person doesn't care how an election comes out he or she should vote in it." Nationally, 45 percent disagreed while 75 percent of Wyomingites disagreed, indicating a stronger belief that citizens should vote under any condition. In addition, because of the size of the state, Wyomingites are more likely to know their political leaders personally, and personal knowledge generally reduces political alienation and increases political effi-

cacy. Both factors correlate with higher levels of political participation.

CITIZEN INITIATIVES AND REFERENDA

The Wyoming Constitution does not limit citizens to merely voting for candidates or contacting public officials in support of policies, but allows them to directly create legislation. In 1968, the Constitution was amended to include the initiative and referendum process by which citizens can propose, enact, and reject legislation. An attempt by citizens to write a new law through the petition process is termed an "initiative." A "referendum" occurs when the effort is aimed at vetoing an enactment of the state legislature. While the definitions of initiative and referendum are different, the practical implications are the same. The process allows the state's citizens to write their own laws by collecting signatures on petitions and winning approval of the voters.

Wyoming's provisions are so rigorous that, until recently, few petition drives were successful. The Wyoming Constitution (as amended in 1998) requires that the signatures on initiative and referendum petitions total 15 percent of the number of votes cast in the previous general election in each of two-thirds of the counties. To be adopted, an initiative or referendum must receive a majority of all votes cast in the election. All voters abstaining on an initiative or referendum are counted as voting against the proposal. These provisions make Wyoming's initiative and referendum process among the most demanding—perhaps the most demanding—in the nation (Magleby 1984: 38-39).

Proposed initiatives and referenda have dealt with a wide variety of issues, including abortion, gambling, liquor, taxation, and natural resources. The most common topic, however, has been government reform. Many have attempted to change the way government does business, including limits on the number of years elected officials may serve and procedures within the state legislature. The first initiative to obtain the necessary signatures was voided on the grounds that legislation previously enacted accomplished the same objective (Horan 1991: 30). Thus, Wyoming voters got their first opportunity to vote on initiatives in 1992 when three propositions reached the ballot.

Two features of Wyoming's initiative process make it controversial. First, the Constitution permits the state legislature to amend or repeal a statute enacted by ballot proposition after two years. The discord surrounding limits on the number of terms elected officials may serve illustrates the controversy that can result if the legislature tinkers with an initiative. In 1992, Wyoming

voters overwhelmingly approved term limits for members of Congress, state legislators, and state executive officials. Under the provisions of the initiative, state senators are limited to three four-year terms while state representatives have a maximum of three two-year terms. Thus, a senator can serve a total of 12 years but a representative only six. Believing that members of the two chambers should be permitted equal time in office, several state legislators proposed modifying the term limits law to grant representatives six two-year terms. The Wyoming legislature in 1995 accepted their arguments and equalized the limits on senators' and representatives' terms over objections from term-limits advocates. Supporters of term limits responded by launching another petition drive aimed at restoring the original six-year restriction on representatives. They succeeded in reaching the ballot but the referendum failed to win a majority of the votes cast in the 1996 election, leaving the Legislature's modification of the term limits statute intact.

The second controversial feature of the state's initiative and referendum process is the requirement that a majority of all voters participating in the election is necessary for passage, rather than a majority voting on the proposition in question. In effect, a voter who chooses not to vote on an initiative or referendum in an election is counted as if he or she had voted against the proposal. The

1996 term limits referendum is a case in point. Slightly more than half (53.7%) of those voting on the referendum supported it. With a total of 215,844 Wyoming citizens voting in the 1996 general election, 107,923 "yes" votes were required to adopt the referendum. The 104,544 "yes" votes fell short of the required number and, as a consequence, the measure failed.

The recent popularity and success of the initiative and referendum process in Wyoming are striking. More petitions have been filed with each passing decade. One explanation for this is the creation of consulting firms that specialize in organizing and conducting petition drives. A political group facing the daunting task of collecting tens of thousands of signatures can now get help in drafting the petition, and in recruiting or hiring workers to circulate it. (Several propositions reaching the ballot benefited from services such as these.) A general dissatisfaction with government may be another reason for the recent popularity of the initiative in Wyoming. Those who feel their interests are not being represented by elected officials see the initiative as a means of having their voices heard. Whatever the reasons, it is doubtful that the initiative's popularity will soon wane. Once the public's response to unpopular laws was to "throw the rascals out" in the next election. Now, the response is for voters to try writing their own laws through the initiative process.

POLITICAL PARTIES

Political parties provide an important link between the citizen and government in several ways. First, political parties are rallying points for various ideological perspectives. To the voter, this is of considerable import because a party label is a reasonably good indicator of a candidate's issue positions. For another, parties help recruit candidates for public office and provide campaign assistance to these candidates. Finally, political parties help organize government. For instance, the majority party in the Wyoming legislature decides which legislators will be committee chairs and house and senate leaders. Certainly, political parties do not exclusively perform the functions described above. Interest groups, for example, generally provide greater financial assistance to political candidates than do political parties. Further, a party label may not always provide an accurate indication of policy preferences. Still, as imperfect as they are, American political parties do provide the voter with considerable information and help translate individual desires into governmental policy. If nothing else, the political party controlling state or national government can be blamed for failure and thrown out of office.

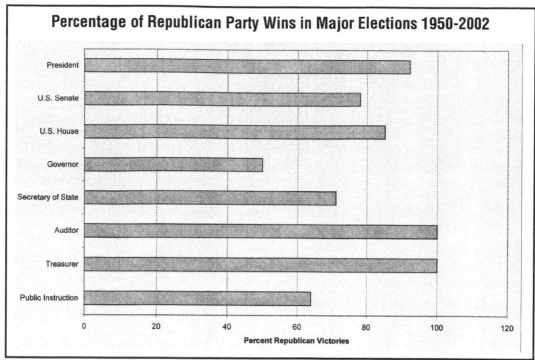

Percentage of Republican Party Wins in Major Elections 1950-2002

Percent Republican Victories

Figure 2

The first Wyoming state election occurred in 1890. Republican candidates won all state offices and both houses of the legislature, beginning an almost continuous dominance of the state by the Republican Party. The modern political era has not been much kinder to Democrats. Figure 2 illustrates this, showing the percentage of elections for various offices won by the Republicans since 1950. The Democratic Party has not done poorly in gubernatorial elections, winning half of the contests. On the other hand, no Democrat has won election as auditor or state treasurer.

As dominant as the Republican Party has been historically, its strength has increased during the past 20 years. Figure 3 shows that more than six out of every ten Wyomingites register as Republican. This is the highest percentage of Republican registration in the United States, although not every state requires registration by party. After being nearly equal to Republicans in the 1970s, Democrats now find themselves at a two-to-one disadvantage in voter registration.

The Republican advantage is not limited to the greater number of registered voters. Republicans tend to vote more frequently than do Democrats, and they tend to support their party's candi-

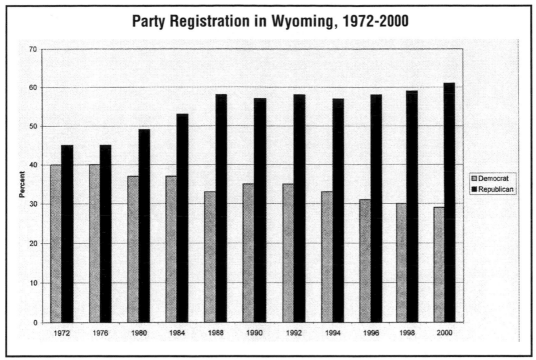

Party Registration in Wyoming, 1972-2000

Figure 3

dates more consistently (Miller and Shanks 1996: 148). An obvious question at this point must be: How do Democrats ever win in Wyoming? There are several explanations. First, a significant percentage of Wyomingites do not identify with either political party. Independents are more likely to split their ballots than are partisans. Second, even though Republicans tend to be loyal to their party's candidates, this loyalty falls short of perfection. A final reason for occasional Democratic success is the tendency for Wyomingites to reelect incumbents. In state legislative races about 93 percent of incumbents win reelection. Since 1970 only one incumbent for statewide office, U. S. Senator Gale McGee, has been defeated. Thus, if a Democrat can win because of some issue or personal factor, the chances are quite high that the electorate will return him or her to office. On the whole, however, Republicans have a huge advantage in Wyoming and win the vast majority of elections. The advantage of being an incumbent should only strengthen Republican hegemony.

Party organization in Wyoming is much like that in other states. At the base of the party organization are the precinct officers. Wyoming law provides for a precinct committeeman and committeewoman in each of the state's several hundred precincts. These persons are elected by voters within a precinct. Voters registered as Republican can vote for the Republican precinct candidates and Democrats can vote for only Democrats. Rarely are precinct offices contested, and in many precincts there are no candidates. Precinct officers elect a county chair, and these individuals, in turn, become part of the state central committee that is responsible for choosing a state party chair.

As was indicated earlier, there is not a strong connection between party officials and elected government officials. The primary reasons for this are the direct primary and the civil service. In the 1800s, political party organizations were responsible for choosing candidates to run for office. But political reformers found fault with this procedure, arguing that a closed elite controlled nominations; therefore, the average citizen was excluded from government office. The direct primary was the result. In most states, including Wyoming, all nominations are decided in a primary election. Not only does the primary election shift nomination decisions to the voters, but Wyoming law forbids the political parties from endorsing one primary candidate over another. Thus, both the Democratic and Republican Party organizations have little say in who runs as a Democrat or Republican for Governor, U.S. Senator

and so on. Obviously, elected governmental officials may feel little allegiance to the party organization, since the party neither selects nor prevents anyone from running as a Republican or Democrat.

The state government bureaucracy is further removed from party influence because of personnel rules in state law. In the past, if a party won the governorship, often many government workers of the other party were fired and replaced with bureaucrats from the governor's party. In Wyoming, the governor and other elected state executives can hire and fire their immediate staffs, but beyond the immediate staff, it is illegal to fire someone for political reasons. In fact, unless there is very strong evidence of wrongdoing, it is exceedingly difficult to remove any state government worker. Again, state government officials have little or no reason to be responsive to political party officials.

Frankly, since party officials do not control nominations and their ability to influence government decision makers is very limited, their activities have a rather narrow focus. Prior to general elections, precinct committeemen and committeewomen may actively campaign for their party by identifying supporters and ensuring that their supporters reach the polls. During presidential election years, the Republican Party allows only precinct officials to vote in county caucuses for the various presidential candidates. The Democratic Party, however, allows all registered Democrats to participate in a county convention, and thus Democratic precinct officials have no extraordinary influence. During general elections, the county and state party officials may also actively provide support for the party's candidates.

POLITICAL INTEREST GROUPS

Although political interest groups have a rather negative image in the United States, they play a major role in connecting the individual to government. It is a rare Wyomingite who does not belong to some interest group, a group that may lobby in Cheyenne.

Over the years, the powerful interest groups of the state have been tied closely to its economic interests, and the strength of group influence has depended greatly upon the problems and issues of the times. The first powerful interest in Wyoming was the Union Pacific Railroad. Generous land grants from the federal government made the Union Pacific a powerful landowner in the Wyoming Territory, and the railroad made strenuous efforts to protect its interests. The economic diversification of the state has reduced the influence of the Union Pacific, but it remains an active participant in Wyoming politics. It forcefully opposed measures that would allow the construction of coal slurry pipelines, permit triple trailers on Wyoming highways, and increase taxes on the railroad's vast property holdings.

Another old and powerful interest group has been the Wyoming Stockgrowers Association. Cattle ranching has always been an extremely important economic force in Wyoming, and the Stockgrowers have wielded considerable influence in state government. Together with the Woolgrowers Association, the Farm Bureau Federation and the Farmers Union, they represent Wyoming's agricultural interests. Although these agricultural groups generally assume conservative and fiscally austere positions on most issues, they have convinced the state legislature to institute low interest loan programs available to farmers and ranchers. The agricultural community has also assiduously supported and defended state programs to protect state water resources for farm and ranch use. On other issues, it is quite difficult, if not impossible, to discern a distinctive pattern in the agricultural vote.

The power of the mineral extractive industry has been significant since the Union Pacific began mining coal in Wyoming. During the state's constitutional convention, the industry managed to scuttle a severance tax. The mining industry has consistently argued that severance taxes place Wyoming minerals at a competitive disadvantage. Still, Wyoming has one of the highest severance taxes in the nation. Another example of the influence of the oil and petroleum industry can be found in the voting behavior of the state's congressional delegations. Whether Republicans or Democrats, Wyoming's members of Congress have consistently favored policies at the national level that benefited the oil and gas industry. Since the state is so dependent upon these industries, even the most liberal politician would hesitate before advocating policies that might decrease employment and reduce tax revenue. One should not, however, conclude that the mineral extractive industry, particularly oil and gas, has veto power over state policy; there are important opposition groups that have succeeded in passing legislation to regulate and tax the industry (Clark and Walter, 1987: 135).

Wyoming has several important environmental groups. The Wyoming Wildlife Federation is the largest and maintains a high profile on conservation issues. The Sierra Club has a Wyoming chapter active in lobbying the legislature. The Wyoming Outdoor Council (WOC) was established in 1967. During its early years, it coordinated the activities of environmental groups in the state. Today, the group not only engages in legislative lobbying but also plays a role as industry watchdog, testifying frequently at hearings of the Department of Environmental Quality and the Industrial Siting Council. Despite the efforts of this group, environmental issues have lost ground in recent sessions of the legislature. For example, four positions were cut from the Industrial Siting Administration. Presently, WOC is engaged in a variety of lobbying efforts including land use and water quality.

The Powder River Basin Resource Council is another influential environmental interest group. This group was organized primarily by ranchers who feared the encroachment of the mining industry upon precious water supplies. Recently, it has been concerned with protecting the ranchers' rights to surface water, which miners wish to use, and has also been focused on mine reclamation.

In recent years, public employees have also dramatically increased their lobbying efforts. The Wyoming Public Employees Association (WPEA), which counts as members 53 percent of all state employees (one-third of whom are in Cheyenne), has actively sought improved benefits and increased salaries for state employees. When the state had substantial budget surpluses, WPEA was quite successful in its demands, but economic hard times have reduced its power. However, because of the large concentration of public employees in

Cheyenne, the WPEA has been central to the election plans of Cheyenne legislators.

The Wyoming Education Association (WEA) is another group that has increased its influence during the past decade. It also benefited from the state's prosperous economy during the 1970s, when state aid to local school districts increased markedly. Much of the influence of the WEA is due to its visibility, for teachers are distributed throughout the state and are very likely to exercise their franchise; nevertheless, as the state's economy has deteriorated, so also has the influence of the WEA.

Several governmental bureaucracies have exercised considerable influence. For example, the University of Wyoming influences the legislature. The university has the advantage of being the only four-year school of higher education in the state; roughly one-half of the legislators in any session have attended the university as students. Yet, it has not always met with success in the legislature. Before the energy boom, the university was not well funded largely because of the state's lack of prosperity, and when the boom years gave way once again to recession in the 1980s, university budgets were frozen until the economic decline bottomed out.

Two other governmental interest groups should be noted: the Game and Fish Commission and the Highway Commission. Both are independent of direct gubernatorial control, and their budgets do not come from the state's general fund. They regularly monitor the legislature in an effort to preserve their autonomous control over their funds, and they are often involved in heated legislative squabbles. Game and Fish battled with agricultural interests regarding the privatization of game animals. The Highway Commission supported raising the drinking age in Wyoming by arguing that state gasoline taxes would have to increase drastically to replace lost federal funds.

The Great Depression brought the Wyoming Taxpayers Association into being. It is a watchdog of governmental activity, protecting citizens, but most especially businesses, from "wasteful" expenditures. It is still one of the most active and effective lobbying groups. The Taxpayers Association maintains close surveillance of the state government bureaucracy and is quick to point out what they believe to be profligate practices. With almost no exceptions, it opposes increases in state government spending and vehemently opposes even a suggestion that Wyoming should increase taxes.

Another consequential lobby has been the Wyoming Truckers' Association. During the 1950s, it was one of the most powerful in Cheyenne, and some legislators claimed that it was the only group that could dictate its own taxes (Larson, 1965: 521). In recent years, the truckers have strongly supported a provision in state law that would allow triple trailers. Although many in government favored this proposal, opposition from a variety of groups, including the Union Pacific Railroad, has stymied the changes.

Another business that has been important in lobbying the legislature is the Wyoming Liquor Dealers' Association. Wyoming is a state that controls the sale of alcoholic beverages through the Liquor Commission, which has a monopoly on wholesale liquor. The retail dealers have tried to influence both the legislature and the Commission regarding the control of licenses and regulation of liquor sales.

Professional associations such as the Wyoming Bar Association and Wyoming Medical Association also wield power over state policies. They participate on such issues as licensing and policing members of the professions. They often come into conflict with members of other professional associations. Recently, the medical profession has battled the lawyers over the medical profession's desire to impose limitations on liability in medical malpractice lawsuits.

A relative newcomer among interest groups is the Wyoming Heritage Society. Founded in 1981, the society represents a coalition of every aspect of Wyoming's economy including agriculture, ranching, timber, oil and gas, tourism, retail, mining and service. It consists mainly of relatively moderate Republicans and a few Democrats as well. It provides a forum for prominent individuals to express their views on economic, regulatory, and environmental issues through the publication of position papers. The Wyoming Heritage Foundation is a conservative think tank that gathers information and sponsors seminars for state officers.

Until the advent of the federal Women, Infants and Children (WIC) program, human services and welfare program had no strong advocates. A Domestic Violence Group was also formed to support state funding for SAFE Houses for victims of spousal or child abuse. In 1987, a group called WYOCAN was formed to speak out on welfare issues. These advocates pressured the legislature to raise the state's standard of need for families needing assistance. In the 1990 legislative session, the standard was raised to a level that reflects more nearly the amount of money required to meet a family's basic health and nutritional needs. However, recent efforts to cut federal aid to the states for social programs have threatened these gains.

Finally, the League of Women Voters is an active interest group in the state. In the past, it was one of the few public interest groups that regularly lobbied at the legislative sessions. The League has lobbied the state legislature for laws regulating water quality and use, supported laws to regulate industrial plant siting, and strongly supported ratification of the Equal Rights Amendment.

The partisan ties of Wyoming interest groups have been similar to those elsewhere in the West. Republican strength has been concentrated in the Farm Bureau Federation, the Wyoming Stockgrowers Association, and other employer groups. The Democrats have been allied mainly with the labor unions and workers' associations (Larson, 1965: 507-8), though the rural nature of the state has usually prevented labor unions from being influential. Their emphasis on united action runs contrary to the individualistic culture of Wyomingites, and the relative weakness of their ally, the Democratic Party, has not protected them. They suffered a major defeat in 1963 when Wyoming became the 20th state to adopt a right-to-work law, a provision that bans the use of union shops requiring all employees to join the union in order to keep their jobs. This legislation was pushed by a state-wide organization backed by the Farm Bureau Federation, Associated Contractors, Wyoming Truckers' Association, the Retail Merchants, and the Grange (Larson, 1965: 537). Efforts by the Democrats to repeal the law have met with total failure.

LOBBYING ACTIVITIES

Interest group activity in Wyoming is generally most overt during the legislative session. Regulation of interest group activity is not stringent. All who represent the interests of others at the legislature must register as lobbyists with the Legislative Service Office, giving their names and the organizations or persons they represent. A small registration fee is charged, and lobbyists must wear identifying badges. Failure to register results in a $200 fine (Wyoming Statutes, sections 28-7-101 and 28-7-102). Efforts to strengthen interest group regulations by requiring disclosure of lobbyists' financial activities failed during recent sessions of the state legislature. Interest groups and organizations of all kinds are banned from making direct contributions to election campaigns. However, this prohibition is easily circumvented. Groups wishing to support candidates must form political action committees (PACs), a relatively easy process requiring only two members. There are no limitations on the amounts that a PAC can contribute (Wyoming Statutes, sections 22-25-101 and 22-25-102).

One of the greatest sources of interest-group influence in the legislature has been the membership itself. Many of the state's most powerful interests are represented in the occupations and or-

ORGANIZATIONAL MEMBERSHIPS HELD BY WYOMING LEGISLATORS

	1979 House	Senate	1991 House	Senate	1999 House	Senate
Stockgrowers Association	26%	13%	21%	7%	13%	13%
Farm Bureau	21	23	19	7	13	10
Chamber of Commerce	29	30	27	27	25	20
Veterans' Groups	13	33	26	27	12	13
League of Women Voters	11	3	5	3	na	na
Heritage Society	na	na	na	na	7	7

Table 1

ganizational memberships of the legislators. Partially because of malapportionment of legislative districts and because ranchers are held in high esteem by the Wyoming population, the agricultural industry has always been overrepresented in the legislature, especially the Stockgrowers Association. In the early 1960s, members of the association regularly held one-half of the senate seats and about one-fourth of the house seats. At present, fewer than ten percent of the state's work force is engaged in agriculture, yet about 25 percent of the legislators are ranchers and farmers. Table 1 lists the group membership of legislators in three recent sessions.

The registration of lobbyists provides one source of data on interest group activity. Table 2 shows the groups registered in recent years. Although it is difficult to place each organization in a single category, certain trends are apparent. Until the 1991 session of the legislature, the total number of lobby groups increased greatly. More business and banking groups appeared in Cheyenne. Groups representing clients needing services stepped up their lobbying efforts to increase funding for their programs, and the number of environmental groups grew. Local governments and educators also increased their lobbying to protect their budgets. The number of groups in a category should not be confused with level of influence, however. After all, only two railroads (Union Pacific and Burlington Northern) were registered during the 1995 session, but the rail industry remains a powerful force influencing Wyoming government.

Interest Group Registrations in Recent Legislative Sessions

	Number of Individual Interest Groups		
	1979	1988	1995
Business/Industry	57	124	94
Energy/Mining	52	48	51
State/Local Government	16	38	13
Agriculture	14	18	6
Medical/Health/Social Service	12	20	23
Education	11	23	9
Professional Groups	9	15	16
Police & Firemen	9	9	5
Citizen Groups/Religion	8	29	16
Labor Unions	6	13	10
Banks & Financial Institutions	6	18	8
Liquor Retailers	6	11	6
Political Reform	5	10	10
Environment	4	10	13
Fraternal/Social Organizations	4	3	2
Railroads	3	3	2
Recreation/Tourism	3	28	7
Aging/Senior Citizens	3	3	1
Miscellaneous	22	0	9
Total	250	423	301

Sources: Miller, <u>State Government: Politics in Wyoming</u>, p.72; Lobby Registrations 1988, 1995.

Table 2

Since 1950, no interest group has consistently dominated Wyoming politics. If an issue arose that directly impinged on a group's economic interests, the group would be very active during one or two terms of the legislature and then fade from public notice. In the late 1980s, the Wyoming Liquor Dealers' Association was very active when the national government pressured the state to raise the drinking age to 21. The industry, backed by lobbying efforts of University of Wyoming students, prevented the legislature from making the change for several sessions, but facing the loss of federal highway funds, the industry lost the issue in 1988.

In 1979, legislators themselves saw the mineral lobby as the most influential group; yet, one year later, it was badly defeated when the severance tax was increased. Legislators in the 1983 session indicated that the agricultural lobby was the most powerful, but by 1986, a liability crisis hit the state. In that year, legislators felt that those most concerned with liability insurance, the medical profession, had become the most influential group. Table 3 shows the five groups that were rated by the legislators as most influential during several sessions. The most powerful group varied from year to year, but certain interests—such as the mineral lobby, agriculture, and the WEA—appear consistently. It is easy to understand the influence of the mineral lobby and agriculture for these industries play important roles in Wyoming's economy. Some people might wonder about the prominence of the WEA, but this is really not very surprising. Teachers' organizations rank among the most influential interest groups in virtually every state (Thomas and Hrebenar, 1990: 142).

In recent years, many legislators with agricultural backgrounds have opposed measures that would benefit either the mining industry or the environmental movement. This opposition is especially evident in regard to measures concerning water rights. For instance, the Republican Party has generally favored providing a proposed coal slurry pipeline with access to water. Agricultural interests argue that the State is too arid to allow such exportation of water. The agriculture lobby is supported in its

---

INTEREST GROUPS PERCEIVED AS MOST INFLUENTIAL BY LEGISLATORS

1979
1. Mineral lobby
2. Retail liquor lobb
3. Wyoming Education Association
4. University of Wyoming
5. Wyoming Truckers

1983
1. Agriculture
2. Wyoming Education Association
3. Mineral lobby
4. Insurance
5. ABATE*

1986
1. Medical profession
2. Mineral lobby
3. Water development lobby
4. Trial lawyers
5. Insurance

1994
1. Mineral lobby
2. Wyoming Education Association
3. Agriculture
4. Wyoming Association of Municipalities
5. Medical Profession

*A group formed to oppose a law mandating the wearing of protective helmets by motorcyclists

Table 3

opposition to the pipeline by the Union Pacific and Burlington Northern Railroads, as well as by Democratic legislators.

Despite rumors of unsavory tactics by lobbyists in earlier days, Wyoming has not recently experienced any reported corruption by interest groups. The lobbyists' free spending more or less ended with the post-Watergate concern for ethics in government. Now, both lobbyists and legislators are more cautious in their contacts; lobbying the legislature and the governor must proceed in a professional manner and not with pressure tactics. Attempts to impose stricter standards for lobbyist reporting have failed to secure either legislative approval or the necessary signatures to place an initiative on the ballot. On the whole, Wyoming legislators and citizens see little value in restricting lobbyists or legislators further.

Wyoming legislators have been asked to rate the effectiveness of various lobbying techniques. Personal presentations, working with committees on bill revisions, testimony at hearings, and contacts from constituents in favor of the lobby were ranked as the most effective techniques. On the other hand, interest group contributions to legislators' campaigns for reelection were rated as the least effective way to influence votes. Yet, PAC contributions to legislative campaigns have grown in recent years. In 1990 legislative races,

PACs spent approximately $200,000, almost twice the amount of individual contributions. PAC contributions that year averaged $3,436 per senate race and $2,478 per house race (Pelkey, 1991a and 1991b). In 1994, PAC contributions accounted for 60 percent of expenditures by victorious legislative candidates (Drake, 1995).

Interest groups have not always relied solely on the legislative process to achieve their goals. For example, environmentalists, frustrated by the defeat of their instream-flow bill in the legislature, then turned to the initiative procedure in the hope that Wyoming voters would support their views. However, before this initiative came to a vote, the legislature was pressured to pass a compromise instream-flow bill. The railroads, in 1992, sponsored an initiative banning the use of triple trailers in Wyoming, which won voter approval. Further, interest groups also devote considerable attention to personnel in the executive branch. PACs contribute large amounts to the campaign chests of governors and other officials. Lobbying of the administrative agencies is also important to assure that policies are carried out or ignored to the benefit of the group. Finally, interest groups are concerned about the attitudes and opinions of the general public. Educational and propaganda programs are developed to inform the public of the implications of state policies.

Although some data seem to indicate that interest groups are of crucial importance in the Wyoming political process, there are other factors that work against interest group domination. First, the libertarian culture of the state creates an atmosphere in which numerous groups can compete, but it also creates an ethic that considers dictation by any one group or set of groups illegitimate. Business groups have financial resources that give them power, but they are counterbalanced by environmental groups sharing a bond of common values with the general public. The libertarian thread in Wyoming makes the people suspicious of big government, big labor, and big business.

Related to this independence from group domination is the transitory nature of the Wyoming Legislature. Legislators cannot be dependent upon their political office for their livelihood. This lack of economic dependence lessens the potential hold an interest group might exert on a policy maker. Moreover, there are legislators in both houses who refuse to accept campaign funds from PACs.

Finally, Wyoming's legislature has institutional features that might limit the influence interest groups can have over policy in the state. These features of the legislature (discussed in the next chapter) make Wyoming an unattractive target for interest group money. The short legislative session, stringent rules that slow the passage of bills, and the limited resources legislators have to research, draft, and submit legislation all combine to limit the return on investment interest groups would be able to receive from political contributions (Engstrom 2002: 121-123).

Thus, interest groups are very important to legislators primarily because they provide information not easily available from other sources. But, there is no evidence that any interest group or alliance of groups has a veto over more than a narrow range of issues. The legislature may depend upon its interest groups, but the relationships formed are quite open and seldom long-lasting.

Many techniques are available, therefore, to the citizens of Wyoming to participate in the political process and influence the policy decisions of their government officials. They may devote a great deal of time, energy, and money through such activities as joining interest groups or party organizations; or they may merely follow events in the news media and vote for candidates of their choice. Many Wyomingites do none of these things. What difference does it make whether or not citizens participate in politics? How much impact do their activities have on political decisions? To answer these questions, we must examine governmental structures and look at the legislature in action to see how laws are made.

CHAPTER 4

THE WYOMING LEGISLATURE:
A LOT FOR A LITTLE

Wyomingites have an ambivalent view of their state legislature. Note Figure 1, which provides the results of a question in the 2002 Wyoming Election Survey. Respondents were asked to assess the performance of the legislature in recent years. Only two percent thought the legislature was doing an excellent job while roughly two-fifths believed the legislature was performing at a good level.

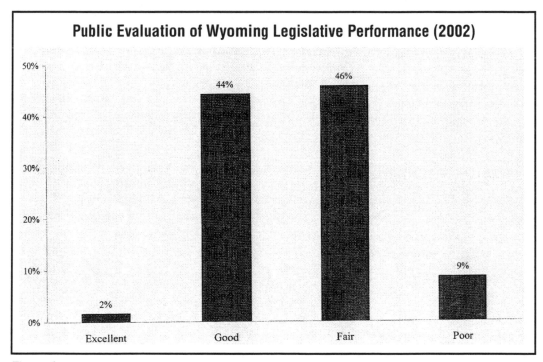

Figure 1

A Wyoming state legislator might very well be discouraged by these results. The legislator's lament could be:

You ask me to take time off from my regular job and spend one or two months in Cheyenne. You pay us less than almost any other legislators in the United States. I don't have an office. I don't have a personal staff. I must make hundreds of decisions in a very short time. How could you expect us to do a better job given these conditions?

However, these are just the characteristics of the legislature that the majority of Wyomingites and, for that matter, most legislators would least prefer to change. Wyomingites endorse the concept of part-time legislators who have "real" jobs, who must reside in their home counties most of the time and who must make decisions with little professional staff assistance. In this chapter we will examine Wyoming's "citizen legislature."

The Wyoming Capitol Building. The building was built in 1888, two years prior to statehood. The Senate is on the left and the House on the right. The Governor and other state elected officials are also housed in the Capitol building. *Picture courtesy of the Wyoming Travel Commission.*

THE LEGISLATURE AND THE CONSTITUTION

Article 3, Section 1 of the Wyoming Constitution states: "The legislative power shall be vested in a senate and house of representatives which shall be designated the legislature of the State of Wyoming.'" This statement seemingly gives the Wyoming legislature a broad grant of power, but Wyoming's founding fathers were suspicious of legislatures. They were suspicious because, especially since the Civil War, many state legislatures had become the means by which special interest groups had robbed the public treasury and bent laws to benefit their own private greed. Thus, Article 3 of the Wyoming Constitution does not specify legislative power as much as it limits legislative power.

This fear of the legislative branch is illustrated in Article 3, Section 27, the most lengthy section in Article 3. Here the Constitution prohibits the legislature from enacting "special or local" laws. These are laws that apply to specific individuals or localities. For example, a law stating that John Doe should be given an exclusive right to hunt on Elk Mountain would apply to one person and would, therefore, be a special law. Laws of this kind were employed in other states to pilfer the public treasury. The framers did not want this to happen in Wyoming. In all, Article 3, Section 27, lists 32 such prohibitions.

Other limitations are more important than the "special laws" provision. Article 3, Section 6, declares that the legislature may not meet for more than 60 days every two years. Originally, the session length had been set at 40 days every two years, but in 1972 a constitutional amendment added a budget session to be held in even numbered years. When the Wyoming Constitution was written, most state constitutions had similar limitations on the duration of legislative sessions, but during the last few decades these restrictions have been modified to increase the length of sessions or have been totally removed. Proponents of a more active legislature argue that it is absurd to limit sessions to such a short amount of time. How can the legislature successfully meet the many challenges facing Wyoming if the people's representatives are limited to no more than 60 days every two years? And how can the legislative branch serve as a countervailing force to the executive and judicial branches if the law-making body can perform its duties only two months out of 24? Clearly, Wyoming's short sessions give those favoring the status-quo considerable advantage; even short delays by committee chairs or majority party leaders can spell the death of legislative proposals.

Regardless of the legitimacy of these arguments, there is little support either within the legislature or among the electorate to lengthen legislative sessions. For instance, in the 1986 Wyoming Election Survey, voters were asked whether the Wyoming legislature should have longer sessions. Nearly 60 percent were content with the present short sessions. Seven out of 10 of this group agreed that longer sessions would result in the legislature spending more money and that the short sessions forced legislators to keep in touch with their constituents. Thus, suspicion and fear of the legislature does not appear to have abated since the writing of the Constitution.

Many legislators are not enthusiastic about lengthening the session, either. Almost all Wyoming legislators have full-time occupations. Longer sessions would force legislators to choose between their occupations and the legislature. In addition, many argue that the short sessions do impose a discipline on the legislators, forcing them to confront even the most contentious political issues. Many question whether lengthening the sessions would improve legislative decisions.

Distrust of the legislative branch is further illustrated by legislative procedure rules placed in the Constitution. Article III, Sections 20-26 states among other things that:

1. all bills must be referred to committees;
2. a bill must receive a majority vote of all those elected to the legislature prior to becoming law;
3. an appropriations bill must be introduced at least five days before the end of the session;
4. a bill must have only one subject (this provision prevents riders that are so frequently used in the U.S. Congress);
5. all bills must have a specified enacting clause; and
6. bills and votes must be published.

Today, most political scientists would find fault with these rules. Constitutions should be reserved for the most important principles of government and the mundane rules of the legislature are not of such import.

One provision of the Constitution's legislative section has resulted in continuing controversy. Section 46 states that a legislator with a personal or private interest in a bill shall disclose his or her interest and not vote. The meaning of this provision is more ambiguous than one might expect. For example, should someone who works for the railroads be able to vote on a bill that would outlaw triple trailers for trucks? Should a rancher vote on a bill designed to provide low interest loans to ranchers? Should a school teacher be able to vote on increased state funding of schools? In 2002, the issue of conflicts of interest arose concerning Senator Bruce Hinchey (R-Casper), who was named president of the Petroleum Association of Wyoming, and Representative Bill Stafford (R-Chugwater), the director of government relations for Basin Electoral Power Cooperative. Some observers believed these legislators should not vote on legislation concerning petroleum or electric power, respectively (Morton 2002). But in Wyoming the decision to declare a conflict of interest is left to the individual legislator and, in general, only the most obvious conflicts are declared. Efforts to tighten conflict of interest provisions of state statutes, both through both the legislative and initiative processes, have been unsuccessful in recent years.

Fear of legislative abuse is further illustrated in the prohibitions against aid for the construction of railroads and appropriations to individuals or groups not under state control. Finally, the Wyoming Constitution contains an unusual provision forbidding the universal legislative practice of logrolling (Article 3, Section 42). Logrolling occurs when one legislator promises his or her vote on a bill in return for a colleague's vote on another bill. In simplest terms: I'll vote for your bill if you'll vote for mine. According to the Wyoming Constitution, legislators involved in such dealings are guilty of bribery. Enforcement of this provision is difficult, however.

In sum, the legislative portion of the Wyoming Constitution is quite similar to other state constitutions written in the late 1800s. The framers were convinced that the legislative branch could be easily corrupted. Therefore, they believed that dozens of constitutional restrictions were essential.

APPORTIONMENT

An enduring controversy in American politics concerns the proper way to allocate legislative seats. At the national level, the Constitution allocates seats in the House of Representatives on the basis of population. Senators, on the other hand, are allocated equally to the states. Thus, Wyoming, with fewer than 500,000 inhabitants, has the same number of Senators as does California with a population of over 34 million. This gives citizens of Wyoming over 60 times more representation in the U.S. Senate than California citizens have.

Apportionment of seats was one of the most contentious issues at the Wyoming Constitutional Convention. In 1890, about 70 percent of the population resided in the southern tier of counties. Most of the delegates from these counties argued that both the Wyoming House and the Wyoming Senate should be apportioned on the basis of population. Delegates from the northern counties, however, contended that each county should receive equal representation in the Senate. The southerners won the dispute. The Constitution specifies in Article 3, Section 3, that both houses of the legislature shall be allocated on the basis of population. However, as a concession to the small counties, it was agreed that all counties should be guaranteed at least one senator and one representative. If the population of a county grew faster than that of another, the rapidly growing county would receive additional house and senate seats.

The Wyoming Constitution also declares that following the U.S. census, which is conducted every 10 years, the legislature should "revise and adjust" the apportionment of senators and representatives (Article 3, Section 48). This provision is unequivocal. The legislature shall reapportion the state after every census. But population growth in Wyoming has not occurred equally in all counties. Natrona and Laramie counties have grown much more rapidly than Crook or Niobrara, for example. Following the 1940 census, legislators from the less populated counties realized that their percentage of votes in the legislature would decline significantly if this constitutional dictate was observed. Thus, they vehemently opposed reapportionment even though the result was that the citizens in Casper and Cheyenne had less representation than those from Sundance and Lusk.

The larger counties continued to grow in population more rapidly than the smaller counties and the legislature again ignored the Constitution following the 1950 and 1960 census. Under the ideal of majority rule, 50.1 percent of the state's population should be necessary to elect a majority in the legislature. In 1960, 28 percent of the state's population could elect a majority in the Senate and 34 percent could elect a majority in the House. A Senator from Laramie County represented about 30,000 people while one from Teton County represented about 3,000. The trend toward malapportionment was by no means confined to Wyoming. Nationally, urban growth had been much more pronounced than rural growth, and rural interests had thwarted attempts to increase urban representation. Finally, in the early 1960s, the U.S. Supreme Court decided that state legislatures could not ignore large population discrepancies among districts. In a series

of cases culminating in <u>Reynolds v. Sims</u> (1964), the Supreme Court set forth the principle of one person, one vote and ruled that both houses of state legislatures must be apportioned on the basis of population.

These cases did not go unnoticed in Wyoming. The legislature attempted to reapportion itself in 1964 and in 1965 but partisan wrangling prevented a resolution. Finally in 1965, the federal district court exhausted its patience with the legislature and declared that Wyoming was violating the U.S. Constitution. Since the legislature was unwilling to meet its constitutional obligations, the court reapportioned the state. Larger counties were allocated more senators and, perhaps most important, the court ruled that it was impossible to give each county a senator without drastically increasing the size of the Senate. Therefore, 17 senatorial districts were created out of the 23 counties. County-based representation was retained for the House of Representatives.

Wyoming experienced very little growth in the 1960s, and apportionment was carried out after the 1970 census with little controversy. The 1970s were different as the energy boom caused the population of Wyoming to grow by over 40 percent, and as usual, growth was not uniform. The population of Sweetwater County, a mineral-rich county, more than doubled while that of Niobrara County did not grow at all. Retaining

Niobrara's one representative and adhering to the one-person, one-vote principle would have meant increasing the size of the Wyoming House of Representatives to 81. For reasons of cost and the size of the House chamber, the legislature decided to ignore once again the constitutional principle of one person, one vote. The House was apportioned on the basis of population with the exception of Niobrara, which was given its own seat. The legislature justified its decision on the grounds of preserving the integrity of county-based representation. The League of Women Voters challenged the legislature's decision, contending that the one-person, one-vote principle established in <u>Reynolds v. Sims</u> had been violated. The citizens of Niobrara County were extremely upset about this challenge. They argued that Niobrara would effectively be denied representation if the county were forced to join another larger county since the majority in the larger county would usually elect a representative from that county.

The U.S. Supreme Court surprisingly rejected the League of Women Voters' complaint. The Court declared that (1) Wyoming's malapportionment was constitutional because the state was pursuing the legitimate objective of maintaining the integrity of a political subdivision, and (2) the malapportionment was entirely the result of the "consistent and nondiscrimi-

natory application of a state policy," namely using counties as legislative districts (<u>Brown v. Thomson</u>, 1983). No state in the Union had a greater percentage population difference between its largest and smallest districts.

The debate over apportionment resumed following the 1990 census. Again, the forces for county-based representation dominated the reapportionment process and allowed Niobrara County to retain its House seat under the first plan approved by the legislature. This plan was challenged immediately in federal district court by private citizens in underrepresented counties. The litigants chose a much wider basis for their suit than was used in 1981 and asked the court to set the entire plan aside so that most of the variation in district population size could be eliminated. Attorneys hired by the legislature argued that the 1991 plan was similar to those upheld in previous decades and that malapportionment was less severe in Wyoming than in other states In <u>Gorin v. Karpan</u> (1991) the federal district court rejected these arguments, however, and ordered the legislature to create a new plan.

After a week of impassioned debate between Republicans and Democrats, the legislature approved a plan that attempted to preserve the county-based representation system while reducing the population deviation among districts. Governor Sullivan vetoed the plan on the grounds that it lacked "clarity, consistency, rationality or fairness" (Pelkey 1992:A1). An attempt in the House to override the veto failed by one vote in a straight party vote. The legislature then approved a plan creating all single-member districts for the first time in Wyoming. There are now 60 House districts and 30 Senate districts with two House districts embedded in each Senate district (Horan and King 1999).

For 30 years various Wyoming political leaders had proposed that the large county districts be broken into subdistricts. The advantage of subdistricting is that voters in counties such as Natrona or Laramie would only have to decide between two candidates rather than among 18. Certainly, it is a rare voter who can make an informed choice when confronted with 18 candidates. Subdistricting also ensures that legislators come from different parts of a county. In the past, it was possible that all Natrona county legislators could live within a few blocks of one another in southern Casper. Traditionally, the greatest opposition to subdistricting came from the Democratic Party. Many Democratic leaders believed the majority Republican Party would draw district lines in such a manner that Democrats would have less chance of winning. However, Democrats ultimately led the charge for creating single-member districts based on equal population without reference to county lines.

The redistricting following the 2000 census was accomplished with relative ease. An interim committee of the Legislature held hearings across the state in 2001 but found little support for returning to the county-based multi-member districts (Luckett 2002a). When the legislative session opened, the discussion focused on the precise boundaries of certain districts and the question of whether all senators should stand for election in 2002. The legislature decided that only the 15 districts where the incumbent's four-year term ended in 2002 would be contested in November (Luckett 2002b, 2002c). Thus, the process completed with little of the controversy or acrimony that accompanied the two previous efforts.

LEGISLATIVE ELECTIONS

Elections are the centerpiece of a democracy primarily because elections allow citizens to remove political leaders. Although Wyomingites are not overwhelmingly positive about the performance of the legislature, few incumbent legislators are defeated in elections. One study of elections to state legislatures showed incumbent representatives in Wyoming having a 97 percent probability of being re-elected (Carey et al. 2000). Figure 2 presents data on the fate of incumbent legislators over the past two decades. The advantages of incumbency were most evident in 1990 when 60 legislators out of 61 seeking reelection were returned to office. There is nothing especially unusual about the incumbents' success in recent elections, as similar trends are evident in other states (Tucker and Weber 1992). Only at the height of the Great Depression did Wyomingites remove more than 20 percent of the legislature through elections (Cawley et al. 1991:63).

Most legislators leave office not through defeat but through voluntary retirement, either to leave public service or seek another office. The only recent elections with significant retirement were those in 1982 and 1992, when over one-third of the legislators did not seek reelection. These anomalies can be at-tributed to reapportionments. The new apportionment of legislators among counties in 1982 and the change to single-member districts in 1992 either put legislators at an electoral disadvantage or offered opportunities to run for higher office under the new system.

Term limits may be an important factor in future legislative elections. Under the provisions of the 1992 initiative and the 1995 legislative amendment, both representatives and senators are restricted to 12 years in office. The effects of term limits are not yet clear as no legislator has been ineligible to seek reelection. However, one study of legislative tenure in the 1980s found that no senator elected in 1981 remained 12

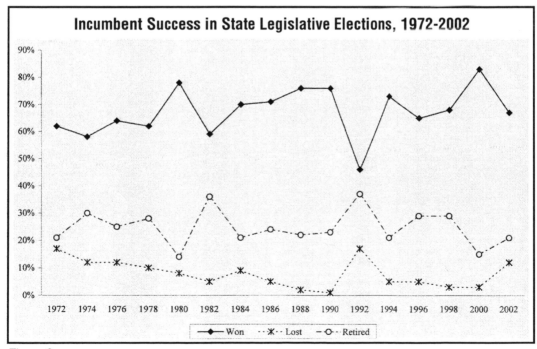

Figure 2

years later (King 1993:12-13). Thus, it appears that the limits imposed by the 1992 initiative may be more symbolic than real. The constitutionality of term limits is also open to question. One interpretation is that the initiative imposed a qualification for service in the state legislature beyond those specified in the Wyoming Constitution. This would amount to amending the Constitution by statute, a procedure that is unacceptable (King 1993:15-16). The courts will ultimately decide if the term limits adopted in 1992 are valid.

WHO ARE THE LEGISLATORS?

With few exceptions, Americans do not elect legislators who are representative of the mainstream of society. Instead, legislators tend to be older, from higher socio-economic groups, and male. This generalization holds true for the U.S. Congress and all state legislatures, including Wyoming's.

The extent to which Wyoming's legislators differ from the state's population as a whole is evident from the data presented in Table 1. First, the vast majority of legislators are 45 years of age or older but less than half of the state's adult population have reached that age. This difference is not especially surprising. Younger people are more occupied with establishing them-

selves in their careers and beginning their families. It is the people who have reached or passed middle-age who have the luxury of time to devote to legislative service.

Similar differences are found when we compare legislators' educations with those of the general public in Wyoming. Although most residents of the state completed high school, only one out of four Wyomingites over 25 years of age has earned a bachelors or graduate degree from a college or university. In contrast, roughly more than two of three legislators hold college degrees. In addition, many of those without college degrees have taken college courses.

More than three-fourths of Wyoming's legislators hold either business or professional occupations, such as law, teaching, and medicine. Slightly more than one-half of Wyoming's people hold jobs in these occupations. Agriculture, particularly ranching, and mineral extraction industries are often referred to as staples of Wyoming's economy and are well represented in the legislature, with 27 percent of representatives and 33 percent of senators deriving their livelihoods from these areas. In contrast, only 11 percent of the population as a whole is employed in agriculture or mineral extraction. Notably, Congress and most state legislatures, including Wyoming's, have few members engaged in blue collar occupations. Why is this the case? First,

CHARACTERISTICS OF WYOMING'S POPULATION AND LEGISLATORS

Characteristic	House	Senate	Adult Population
Age 45 years or older	87%	90%	36%
College graduate	67%	77%	22%
Employed in white collar occupation*	78%	80%	54%
Employed in agriculture (ranching, farming, forestry) or mineral extraction*	27%	33%	11%
Female	15%	17%	50%

*These occupations are not mutually exclusive. An executive of a logging company would be consider a member of both categories.

Table 1

ranchers, businessmen, doctors, lawyers and, to a lesser extent, teachers are in high prestige occupations, prestige which may translate into votes on election day. Second, in general, persons in these occupations earn more than the average Wyomingite and have greater flexibility allocating their time. Both factors are important for prospective legislators. The average worker might not be able to afford the pay cut that a trip to the legislature would mean and, in all likelihood, the worker's employer would be reluctant to allow him or her to leave a job for a one- or two-month legislative session. Finally, the ability to win elections and operate successfully as a legislator requires a specific set of skills, particularly communication skills. These are similar to the skills needed to complete college and graduate degrees.

Women comprise one-half the population but hold only 20 percent of Wyoming's legislative seats. The percentage of women legislators in Wyoming is considerably more representative of the population than in Congress but recent trends are not encouraging. After years of being above the national average Wyoming dipped below the norm. In 1985, Wyoming ranked third among states in the percentage of women legislators. The Equality State now ranks 37th (see Figure 3). The change in ranking is due both to advances made by women legislative candidates in other states and a decline in the fortunes of female candidates in Wyoming.

Political scientists have offered a variety of reasons for the substantial underrepresentation of women in legislative bodies. First, tradition is an important explanation. As we have seen, some occupations are much more common in the legislature than others. Few women have traditionally been found in these occupations. The legislative role itself has not been one frequently occupied by women. In the past, women who ran for public office deviated from commonly held norms. These norms are rapidly changing but they do remain a drag on equal representation for women.

On the other hand, why do some states provide greater equity in the representation of women? In general, women's representation is greater in states with citizen-oriented (rather than professional) legislatures, that value participation in the political process by all elements of society, and that use multi-member districts for choosing legislators. The last of these reasons has been particularly important in Wyo-

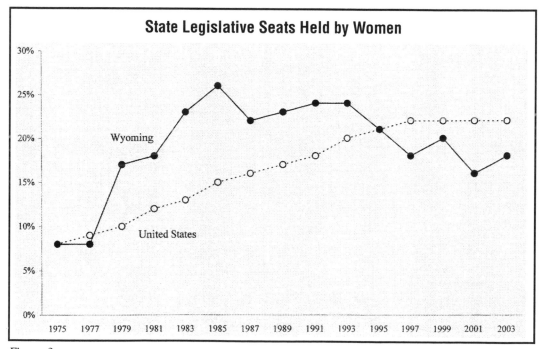

Figure 3

ming. Between 1981 and 1990 only one female legislator, Marlene Simons of Crook County, represented a single-member district. Voters seem more willing to vote for women when they have more than one vote to cast, and women are more likely to run in multi-member districts where they campaign for a seat rather than against an opponent (Darcy et al., 1994:160-167). An analysis of trends in election results indicated that the conversion to single-member districts contributed heavily to the recent decrease in female representation in the Wyoming House of Representatives (Horan and King 1999).

Prior to the 1984 election, Wyoming residents were asked to respond to the following item: "Men are better suited emotionally to politics than most women." Two-thirds of the sample rejected this proposition, but nearly 30 percent agreed (there was no difference between males and females answering this question). When the question was repeated in the 2002 Wyoming Election Survey, only 14 percent agreed (again, responses by men and women were nearly identical). Certainly this reflects a greater acceptance of women in the political arena, but because of lingering bias, being a woman is usually a political disadvantage.

In terms of representing Wyomingites, do the dissimilarities between the legislature and the populace described above really make a difference? There is no conclusive answer to this question.

We do know that the less well educated, those in blue collar occupations and women have somewhat distinctive political opinions on some issues. For instance, the less well educated and those in manual occupations are less negative about government welfare programs and somewhat less willing to support cuts in government programs of all kinds. Women are more supportive of social welfare programs, more willing to see government reduce income differences between rich and poor and much more positive about gun control than are men. However, whether these differences would be reflected in the legislature is problematic. Social and economic factors may have an influence on political ideology but are not determinative. Still the socio-economic biases in the legislature probably enhance already dominant trends. The agricultural sector is not hurt by an overrepresentation of farmers or ranchers nor is the legislature's fiscally conservative approach endangered by an overrepresentation of businessmen, professionals or men.

THE LEGISLATIVE LABYRINTH

All state legislatures perform a variety of tasks such as overseeing the operations of the executive branch, confirming or rejecting gubernatorial nominations, proposing amendments to the

State Constitution, ratifying amendments to the federal Constitution, and deciding whether governmental officials will be impeached and removed from office. However, the primary function of legislatures is to make laws and appropriate governmental funds. The process by which a bill is passed is reasonably similar throughout the United States and is characterized by a set of rules that give those opposing passage a substantial advantage. Approval at several stages of the process is required to pass a bill. One failure at any given stage almost always results in the death of a piece of legislation.

In Wyoming, the process of enacting legislation begins with the <u>first read-</u><u>ing</u>. The title of the bill is read and the President of the Senate or the Speaker of the House refers the bill to a standing committee. The choice of standing committee can be of substantial importance, for one committee may be willing to support a bill while another committee may kill it. The chamber can overrule its leader's decision by majority vote but it rarely does so. During budget sessions, which are 20 day sessions held during even numbered years, each house is asked whether nonbudgetary bills shall be considered. Only if a nonbudgetary bill receives the support of two-thirds of the members will it be dealt with in the budget session.

Members of the House of Representatives confer on pending legislation.
Compliments of Casper Star-Tribune.

The fate of most bills is decided during <u>committee consideration</u>. A bill is almost certain to die if it receives a committee report of "do not pass" or "without recommendation." Most legislators take the committee's recommendation seriously. Moreover, all bills with a "do pass" recommendation will be considered prior to one with a negative recommendation in the Committee of the Whole. Each legislative body can remove a bill from a committee by a majority vote, but almost never does so.

When bills are reported out of committee, they are placed on General File. The majority leader decides when bills will be considered by the <u>Committee of the Whole</u>. This parliamentary procedure is used to facilitate consideration of bills by the entire chamber. Debate rules are less stringent at this stage. Members may talk as long and as often as they wish. Votes are not recorded. Frequently, amendments are offered during the Committee of the Whole. In most instances, a bill need only receive a majority of those present and voting in the Committee of the Whole. Many times, this is the stage at which the most serious floor debate takes place.

The <u>second reading</u> of the bill comes the day following consideration by the Committee of the Whole. Amendments may be offered during the second reading but the practical purposes of this stage are to satisfy the con-

stitutional requirement for three readings of each bill and to alert legislators that the <u>third reading</u> will occur the next day.

All bills must pass the <u>third reading</u> by a majority vote of all members, not just those present and voting as at earlier stages. An absence is tantamount to a "no" vote. Debate may be cut off by a majority vote in the Senate and by a two-thirds vote in the House. Opponents of most major pieces of legislation will attempt to kill a bill by offering an amendment to delete the enacting clause required by the Constitution. All third reading votes are recorded. Legislators may speak only once on a bill unless no other legislator wishes to speak, in which case the legislator may take a second speaking turn.

Assuming the other chamber has passed the same bill but in a somewhat different form, it must go to a <u>conference committee</u>. Members of the conference committee will try to reach agreement on a common bill. If agreement is reached, the conference report goes back to both houses for approval. If either house rejects the conference report, a new conference committee must be formed. The Speaker of the House and the President of the Senate appoint three members each to the conference committee, two who favor the bill and one who opposes it. Again, the choice of conferees may very well decide the fate of a bill. The short session means that conference committees have added power to determine the fate of bills.

A bill passing all of these tests is sent to the governor. The governor may veto any piece of legislation. In addition, the governor has an item veto on appropriation bills, which allows him or her to veto any specific appropriation without vetoing an entire bill. The legislature may override a veto by a two-thirds vote but has rarely done so; the first override of a governor's veto occurred during the 1991 session. The governor's power is enhanced in Wyoming because most of the important legislation is passed near the end of the session, and the governor has 15 days after passage to decide whether to sign or veto bills. If the governor vetoes after the session has ended, the legislature has no chance to override.

During a nonbudgetary session, between 500 and 800 bills are introduced. About one-third of these bills eventually become law. The percentage of bills passed in the 40-day sessions is quite high compared to Congress, which meets almost continuously. The 1995 general session of the Wyoming State Legislature was especially productive, with 221 of the 555 bills and resolutions introduced being enacted. This 40 percent passage rate far exceeds the five or six percent passage rate for a typical session of Congress.

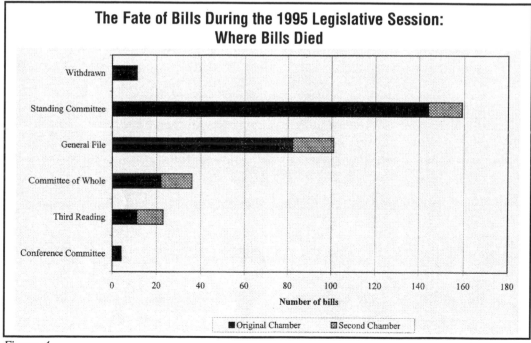

Figure 4

What happens to the remainder of the bills introduced in the Wyoming legislature? Figure 4 shows at which stage bills die. An analysis of the bills introduced during the 1995 general session show that one-quarter never leave the committee of the chamber in which they are introduced, while another three percent die in the standing committee of the other chamber. Thus, nearly three out of every 10 bills introduced are killed in one of the standing committees. The second most dangerous stage of the legislative process is when the bill is placed on General File. Here 18 percent of all bills introduced and 26 percent of those coming out of a standing committee are never brought to the floor. This demonstrates the power of the Majority Leader. Short legislative sessions make it possible for this party leader simply to keep a bill on General File until it is too late in the session to bring it to the floor. Finally, as noted in Figure 4, only about four percent of the bills are defeated at the third reading stage when a vote of the entire House and Senate is required.

LEGISLATIVE LEADERSHIP: POSITIONS AND POWERS

The Wyoming Constitution requires the House to elect one of its members as Speaker, and the Senate to elect one of its members as President. In practice, the choice is made by the majority party, which since the mid-1970s has been the Republican Party. In Wyoming, no legislator from the minority party has ever served in one of the leadership positions discussed in Figure 5.

A description of formal powers often gives a misleading picture of the actual operation of the legislature. For instance, some Wyoming House Speakers view themselves almost as functionaries, that is, they are not particularly partisan nor do they strongly advocate specific policies. Others believe they should employ their formal powers to promote the majority's legislative agenda and that the majority leadership should present a program that might rival that of the governor. In many states the activists become legislative leaders and remain in their positions for several sessions. On the other hand in Wyoming, the Republicans have a tradition of leaders serving only one term. This tradition is strongest in the House where the Speaker is expected to serve one term and then not run again for a House seat. This practice has both positive and negative features. The tradition does ensure that many legislators will share the leadership function and that no one person will become a legislative autocrat. On the other hand, ever changing leadership also ensures that the legislative branch will remain a fairly weak institution as compared with the executive branch.

LEADERSHIP POSITIONS IN THE WYOMING LEGISLATURE

HOUSE	SENATE

Speaker of the House   *President of the Senate*

Major Powers:
1. Decides when a legislator may speak during debate on a bill.
2. Decides to which committee a bill is referred.
3. Decides composition of conference committees.
4. Has major role in deciding who shall chair a standing committee and the committee assignments of majority party members.

Speaker Pro-Tem   *Vice President of the Senate*

Major Powers: Presides over chamber in the absence of the Speaker or President.

Majority Leader   *Majority Leader*

Major Powers: Is in charge of scheduling the order in which bills are considered by the legislature. This is particularly important given Wyoming's short legislative sessions.

Whip   *Whip*

Major Powers: Acts as an assistant to party leadership. Plays important role in informing leadership of members' policy sentiments and the members of leadership's opinions on bills.

Figure 5

LEGISLATIVE COMMITTEES

Almost since the inception of the Republic, the U.S. Congress has used legislative committees. Committees are essential if a legislative body is to accommodate its work load but also committees can increase legislative effectiveness by developing policy expertise. Each house of the Wyoming legislature has 12 standing committees. These are listed in Figure 6.

Each member of the legislature serves on one or two committees. Prior

STANDING COMMITTEES IN BOTH THE HOUSE AND SENATE

Agriculture, Public Lands & Water Resources

Appropriations

Corporations, Elections & Political Subdivisions

Education

Journal

Judiciary

Labor, Health & Social Services

Minerals, Business & Economic Development

Revenue

Rules & Procedures

Transportation & Highways

Travel, Recreation, Wildlife & Cultural Resources

Figure 6

to the start of a session, legislators request a committee assignment of the party leadership. Clearly, some committee assignments are regarded as better than others; therefore, the party leadership must consider such factors as seniority, expertise and particularly in recent years, party loyalty. A seat on the Joint Appropriations Committee (JAC) is the most coveted and the members of the committee are some of the most knowledgeable, articulate, partisan and combative individuals in all of the legislature. The chairs of the JAC rival the Speaker and the President of the Senate in terms of legislative influence, although such influence varies with the political skills of the chairs.

The chairs of the standing committees play a very important role in the legislative process. Assuming that the chair has the support of a majority on the committee, it is within the chair's discretion to schedule public hearings and committee meetings to discuss a piece of legislation. The chair decides who will present the committee's position on the floor and often serves on conference committees or is influential in deciding who does.

Between 1911 and 1974, congressional committee chairs had almost dictatorial powers. They were chosen by the seniority principle (the member of the majority party who had the longest continuous service on a committee would be chosen as chair), which was seldom violated. Single-handedly these leaders could thwart the will of the majority of Congress. Seniority is of substantial importance in choosing Wyoming committee chairs, but there is little evidence that these chairs have enjoyed the influence of congressional chairs. For example, a majority vote of the committee will overrule a chair. It is, therefore, rare for a chair to act regularly in an arbitrary and capricious manner, or at least in a way that alienates a majority of committee members. When a committee chair fails to schedule a public hearing for a bill, undoubtedly that chair has the confidence of the committee's majority.

As noted, the most prestigious committee in the Wyoming Legislature is the Joint Appropriations Committee. This committee is composed of members from both the House and the Senate. During budget session years, the JAC meets for several weeks prior to the convening of the entire legislature. The governor's budget proposal is carefully examined as are budget proposals emanating from the legislators themselves. The governor and the heads of various state agencies are asked to defend their requests during the committee hearings. This is a time of great anxiety for many administrators who frequently are required to justify the very existence of their agencies or to explain some minuscule expenditures which may have occurred in the past one or two years. In recent years, one of the more controversial practices of the JAC has been the insertion of footnotes in appropriations bills that demand that an agency manage a program in a specific fashion.

The Joint Appropriations Committee has dominant influence over the size and content of the state's budget. It is influential for several reasons. First, the members unquestionably have more knowledge about the extremely complex budget than the great majority of part-time lawmakers, and knowledge is power, particularly in the legislative process. Second, the majority leadership normally selects members to the JAC who generally reflect the dominant policy sentiments of the majority of their party and who are respected by their colleagues. Thus, it is surprising when either house overrules committee decisions. Whatever the reasons, the Joint Appropriations Committee has become a commanding force in the legislature, one that can successfully challenge the governor on a regular basis.

LEGISLATIVE STAFF AND OVERSIGHT

Wyoming legislators depend almost exclusively upon the Legislative Service Office (LSO) for staff assistance. The LSO was created in 1971 and presently employs 24 full-time individuals plus part-time staff added during the legislative session. The organization is divided into three sections. The Budget and Fiscal section conducts budget analyses and works very closely with the Joint Appropriations Committee. The Program Evaluation division conducts systematic reviews of state government programs and functions to determine whether they are achieving the intended results. Finally, the Legal Services division does research primarily for the standing committees but, as time allows, for individual lawmakers. Lawyers in the Legal Service division also write bills at the request of legislators.

A major portion of LSO activities is concerned with the operation of the executive branch. Is an agency operating efficiently? Is a division spending money as the legislature intended appropriated money to be spent? Are administrators enforcing the law as the legislature proposed? These questions are the substance of legislative oversight. The legislature decides which part of the executive branch it wishes to investigate and the LSO attempts to carry out this mandate.

Compared to Congress or most state legislatures, staff assistance and oversight of the executive branch are meager in Wyoming. A 1996 report by the National Council of State Legislatures show Wyoming ranking 50th in full-time legislative staff and 49th in part-time staff. This is a concern to some observers, who believe the relatively short legislative sessions and the lack of staff makes it difficult for the legislature to fulfill its responsibilities and increases outside influence. "With severe time deadlines and a mountain of work, the ability to really spend quality time on key issues appears to be strained on the part of most legislators," noted political commentator Bill Sniffin. "Obviously, as legislators' time is strained, lobbyists gain power" (Sniffin 2003).

LEGISLATIVE DECISION MAKING

The task that is set before Wyoming legislators is an enormous one. During Wyoming's short legislative sessions, members vote hundreds of times on often highly arcane subjects, some of which may have enormous effects on the citizens of Wyoming. In the 1995 general (40-day) session, 555 bills were introduced. Representatives and Senators made decisions about these bills at the committee stage, in the Committee of the Whole, on second reading, on third reading, and in conference committees. Moreover, they were asked whether a gubernatorial veto should be overridden. Given this enormous task, how do legislators make up their minds?

Most Americans believe that, for the most part, legislators should reflect constituent opinion. However, this belief is more a value than a reality. For the vast majority of decisions the legislators are asked to make, the constituents simply do not have an opinion. For instance, Walter and Baker (1973) found that barely one-quarter of Wyoming residents could identify four issues discussed in the 1972 legislative session. One-third could not identify a single issue that had been discussed in the recently completed legislative session. In addition, nearly 40 percent could not give the name of one state legislator from their county.

Most legislators and citizens realize that there is a knowledge gap. Table 2 gives the results of 1986 surveys of the legislators and the general public. Both groups were asked to estimate how often citizens knew about legislative issues that concerned them. Clearly, there is a recognition on the part of both that the general public does not assiduously follow most legislative votes.

was whether or not to increase the drinking age to 21. The 1986 Wyoming Election Year Survey revealed that nearly 70 percent of Wyomingites favored the increase. But the legislature was closely divided largely because those opposing the increase were more committed to their position than those favoring the increase. In Albany County, home of the University of Wyoming, students

PERCEPTIONS OF CITIZEN KNOWLEDGE OF LEGISLATIVE ISSUES (1986)			
	Almost Always Informed	Sometimes Informed	Seldom Informed
Legislators	13%	67%	19%
Citizens	28%	50%	21%

Table 2

But, even if the general public did closely follow legislative sessions, constituent opinions cannot always be a guide because constituents do not speak with one voice. On major issues, the public is likely to be split. What guidance does a legislator receive when constituents are divided on an issue? Frequently, the deciding factor is intensity of opinion. Legislators tend to take notice of groups that are highly concerned about legislative issues even though the group may be in the distinct minority. For example, during the 1987 and 1988 sessions, one of the most controversial items before the legislature

were so active that the entire legislative delegation opposed the drinking age increase in spite of the fact that two-thirds of the Albany county citizens favored an increase.

Even if the constituents do have a definite opinion and the legislators are aware of the opinion, should we expect legislators to vote against what they believe is right? This question was asked of both legislators and the general public in 1986. Note that only one in 10 legislators feels compelled to vote with the constituency in the presence of conflicting opinions. Note also that constituents are not very sympathetic to this stance.

WHEN CONFLICT BETWEEN CONSTITUENTS AND LEGISLATOR, HOW SHOULD THE LEGISLATOR VOTE?

	Do what legislator Believes best	Support constituents	Depends
Legislator	33%	10%	56%
Citizen	10%	40%	50%

Table 3

Finally, citizen influence in the legislature depends upon how actively those citizens pursue their interests. Do Wyomingites believe they can influence the legislature? Table 4 sheds light on this question. The 1986 Wyoming Election Year Survey included these two questions: "Suppose a law were being considered by the state legislature you considered to be very unjust or harmful. If such a case arose, how likely is it that you could take the time to get in-

volved?" and "How likely is it that you would succeed?"

These data indicate that about two out of three Wyomingites might become politically involved over a legislative issue even though a large majority believe they would not succeed in their efforts. Citizens do contact Wyoming legislators quite frequently. In 1983, legislators were asked: "Based on a daily average during the session, how often do your constituents contact you

CITIZEN EFFICACY TOWARD THE WYOMING LEGISLATURE (1996)

	Very Likely	Somewhat Likely	Not Too Likely	Not Likely at All
Would Get Involved	25%	40%	20%	12%
Would Succeed	5%	32%	32%	20%

Table 4

in person, by phone and by letters?" The average number of daily personal contacts was two; phone contacts was three; and the average number of letters received was five.

Political parties play a central role in organizing the Wyoming legislature. The majority Republican Party holds all leadership positions in the House and Senate and on all committees. Thus, one might expect that political parties would play an important role in legislative voting behavior. At one level, this expectation would be correct. No other legislative characteristic is as good a predictor of vote as party affiliation. Furthermore, the leadership of both parties do their best to promote party cohesion. One of the most frequently used techniques is the caucus. For example, House Republicans meet frequently as a group to discuss issues and to develop a party position. The caucus is not binding, that is, Republicans who do not agree with the majority are not forced to vote with the majority on the floor. However, considerable peer pressure is brought to bear on dissenting members and these members are forced to justify reasons for not voting with the party.

Nevertheless, as compared to other states, Wyoming political parties are not a commanding presence in the legislature. First, political parties do not actively recruit individuals for the legislature. The 1986 legislative survey revealed that the political parties had been instrumental in recruiting only one out of 10 lawmakers and less than 16 percent of the legislators asserted that the party had been very helpful in their election to the legislature. In the same survey, legislators were presented with the following item: "Even if a legislator disagrees with his party on a bill, he has an obligation to support his party." Only seven percent of the legislators agreed with this statement. Legislators were also asked how likely it would be that they would seek voting information from party leadership. Less than one in five replied that he would be very likely to seek party leadership advice.

The most telling evidence concerning party influence comes from actual legislative voting behavior. One frequently used indicator of party influence is the percentage of time that a majority of Republicans vote against a majority of Democrats. In some New England states this can reach 90 percent. In Congress, about one-half the votes are party votes. But in Wyoming, only about one-third of the votes are party votes. There are several reasons for the lack of party voting. First, Wyoming socially and economically is a very homogeneous state. Republicans and Democrats come from similar districts. Therefore, social and economic differences do not divide the parties as they do in other states. Second, party voting is not high in any of the Rocky Mountain states. Thus, we suspect cultural factors are at work. Voters in Wyoming and the region have repeatedly demonstrated a tendency to elect candidates without regard to party label. This disregard of party label is likely reflected in legislative thinking. Finally, the consistent minority status of the Democratic Party mitigates party influence. The Republican Party generally has such a large majority there is not much incentive for them to remain cohesive. On the other hand, even if the Democrats vote as a block against the majority Republicans, they are destined to be defeated.

The President of the United States actively attempts to influence voting in Congress. The <u>governor</u> of Wyoming also tries to exert influence but success varies. For obvious reasons, Republican governors have been more successful than Democrats. However, Democratic governors can be quite influential. Perhaps the best example would be Governor Ed Herschler's fight to increase the severance tax. Most legislative Republican leaders opposed an increase but with a united Democratic Party and large number of defections from the Republican Party, Governor Herschler won a significant increase in this tax. Legislators were more likely to look to Governor Herschler for leadership than to Governor Mike Sullivan.

The 1995 legislative session was the first in 20 years with Republicans in control of the governor's office as well as the legislature. Many anticipated a smooth relationship between the executive and legislative branches and envisioned a session of great accomplishments. Republican legislators balked, however, when Governor Jim Geringer, himself a former state senator, surprised them with a last-minute supplemental budget request. In the end, the legislature approved most of Geringer's requests for additional funding but the message conveyed to the new governor was clear: communication and cooperation are two-way streets. Future surprises by the governor would not be as well received.

The conflict between Geringer and legislature escalated in 1997 over differing interpretations of the governor's item veto power. The focus of the dispute was a comprehensive education reform bill passed by the legislature during a special session. Some provisions of the bill altered existing statutes concerning the structure and financing of public education, while others appropriated new funds. Geringer adopted a literal reading of the Constitution, which allows the governor to disapprove specific items of "any" bill making appropriations. The legislature argued in response that the item veto power enabled the governor to veto specific appropriations but that his power did not extend to substantive portions of the bill. The Wyoming Supreme Court ultimately sided with the governor and accepted a broad interpretation of the veto power (<u>Management Council of the Wyoming Legislature v. Geringer</u> 1998). The practical effect of this decision is that the legislature must be more careful in the future to pass separate bills defining policy and appropriating funds. The legislature and governor became embroiled in a subsequent dispute when Geringer vetoed a resolution proposing a constitutional amendment that would diminish the governor's line-item veto power. Once again the Wyoming Supreme Court sided with the governor, ruling that the Constitution's require-

ment that "every order, resolution, or vote, in which the concurrence of both houses may be necessary . . . shall be presented to the governor" for his approval or disapproval included resolutions proposing constitutional amendments (<u>Geringer v. Bebout</u> 2000). Proposals to amend the relevant sections of the Wyoming Constitution to limit the governor's veto power in both these instances were placed before the state's voters in 2002 but neither received the majority needed for adoption. Thus, Governor Freudenthal entered office in January 2003 with the veto power intact.

Gov. Jim Geringer delivers his 1999 State of the State address to a joint session of the Wyoming Legislature in the House chamber. *Compliments of The Casper Star-Tribune.*

Lobbyists play a vital role in their explanations of policy issues to state legislators. Legislating is a part-time avocation for Wyoming Representatives and Senators. Unlike members of Congress and legislators from other states, they do not have their own personal staffs to do research. In addition, because of the abbreviated session, legislators have little time to do research. Therefore, virtually every legislator must turn to lobbyists for information. In a 1979 survey, 96 percent of the Wyoming legislators indicated that lobbyists helped rather than hindered the legislative process. According to the 1983 survey, legislators were contacted an average of 3.3 times each day by interest groups. This does not mean the lobbyists distort the legislative process. For the most part, lobbyists represent significant groups in the state, and it would be difficult to argue, given the variety of interest groups that descend upon Cheyenne each spring, that any one pressure group dominates the legislature. Legislators must have information and as long as they do not have the time or staff to gather that information, lobbyists will remain a dominant force in the Wyoming legislature.

Political scientists have long known that legislators look to their colleagues for voting cues. Since it is impossible to fully study every piece of legislation, why not look to a colleague whose opinion you respect? For in-

stance, it is quite rational for fiscally conservative Republicans to look to the chair of the Joint Appropriations Committee for voting information. Eight out of every 10 Wyoming legislators indicate they are very likely to follow the lead of legislators they respect (1983 GRB surveys). In this way, Wyoming legislators are like their counterparts in other states. Lacking the time or resources to become experts on all issues that come before them, legislators seek advice from knowledgeable colleagues who share their general perspectives (Ray 1982; Songer et al. 1985).

In sum, Wyoming legislators come to Cheyenne with their own opinions about issues. Their job is immense and they are only part-time lawmakers who must decide hundreds of issues in a small amount of time with very little staff help. Constituents, party leaders, the governor, lobbyists and respected legislators provide the information that makes their lawmaking task possible.

For centuries, the legislature epitomized democracy. It was the representative body that expressed the will of the people. On the other hand, executives were viewed with suspicion. Strong executives were feared for their ability to curtail individual freedom. Constitutions in America were originally written to give the major powers of government to the legislatures. Over time, the strength of legislatures has declined relative to that of the executive branch. Trends in all of the states and the nation have increased the powers of the executives. As shown above, constitutional limitations on Wyoming's legislature have placed it at a disadvantage. In the next chapter we will examine how Wyoming's executive branch is organized.

CHAPTER 5

THE EXECUTIVE BRANCH:
WHO'S IN CHARGE?

The executive branch is clearly the largest and most complex part of Wyoming state government. In addition to the governor and other elected officials, it contains the bureaucratic agencies. Ninety-eight percent of the people who work for the state are here. It is also the branch that accounts for most of the expenditures for government and governmental services.

In this chapter, we will consider the basic structure of the executive branch. We will begin with an overview of the elected officials. We will then examine the bureaucratic structure and finances of state government.

THE STRUCTURE OF THE EXECUTIVE BRANCH

In Wyoming, the people elect five administrative officials: Governor, Secretary of State, Auditor, Treasurer, and Superintendent of Public Instruction. (Wyoming Constitution: Art. 4, Sects. 3 and 11). The election of several administrative officials in most of the states is different from the federal government, where only the president and vice president are elected. We call the governor <u>chief</u> executive, but the governor is not all-powerful. The other four elected executives have their own authority under the Constitution and law. The governor is not their supervisor; in fact, no one is their supervisor. One goal of reorganization efforts in the 1990s was to enhance the administrative authority of the governor.

All five elected executives serve four-year terms. Each executive elected statewide is subject to a two term limit. These are partisan offices, which means that candidates usually run as members of political parties. While most incumbents of the five offices have been Republicans, Democrats have been more successful in winning election as governor than any other office. (See Chapter 3 regarding partisan strength.) Turnover in the offices of governor and treasurer has been much greater than turnover in the other offices. Why is this so? Until 1982, treasurers could not immediately succeed themselves. They might (and several did) run again at a later date. Perhaps the Wyoming Constitution writers feared that managing large amounts of state money would tempt some state treasurers. In Wyoming's history, three governors died in office and five resigned to take a seat in the U.S. Senate. The governor with the longest tenure of office was Democrat Ed Herschler, who held three consecutive terms from 1975 through 1987. (Wyoming Secretary of State, 1995)

Does Wyoming have too many elected executives? Table 1 permits us to compare Wyoming with the other 49 states. Taking all 50 states together, voters elect administrative officials to leadership positions in 269 agencies. Wyoming figures are slightly less than average: five agencies and five officials compared to a national average of 3. Some people believe that having only an elected governor (or a combined governor/lieutenant governor package) is a good idea. Nevertheless, only four of the 50 states do this. They argue that a short ballot makes the voter's task easier. Also, one official is clearly in charge of the executive branch.

STATE AGENCIES HAVING ELECTED ADMINISTRATIVE OFFICIALS: THE FIFTY STATES

AGENCIES WITH ELECTIVE ADMINISTRATIVE OFFICIALS	NUMBER OF STATES
1	4
2	2
3	1
4	5
5	10
6	19
7	6
8	4

Taking all 50 states together, voters elect the top administrative officials to 269 agencies (mean per state = 5.3 agencies; median = 6 agencies)

Source: THE BOOK OF THE STATES 2002 (Lexington, Kentucky: Council of State Governments, 2002), Table 6.2.

Table 1

One of the interesting features of Wyoming government is that the five elected officials sit jointly on several state boards and commissions. All five officials are members of the Farm Loan Board, Capitol Building Commission, Liquor Commission, Board of Land Commissioners and the State Loan and Investment Board. The governor, secretary of state, state auditor, and state treasurer form the Canvassing Board; and the governor, secretary of state, and state treasurer form the Board of Deposits. In addition, the five elected officials serve individually as members and/or *ex officio* members of various other state boards. For example, the governor and superintendent of public instruction are members of the University of Wyoming Board of Trustees.

What kinds of people have been selected to serve as state officers? How representative are they of Wyomingites in general? During the territorial period, the officials were appointed and came from outside the state. Some early governors had been career officers in the U.S. Army, reflecting the fact that Wyoming was organized as a territory soon after the Civil War when former General U.S. Grant was President. The secretaries of state were mainly lawyers or politicians while many of the auditors and treasurers had been businessmen with banking interests. The superintendents of public instruction held that post by virtue of holding another state office—at first, auditor, then state librar-

ian. Since statehood, the dominant occupations of state officials have been ranching, business, and law. The exception here is the post of Superintendent of Public Instruction. The overwhelming majority of people elected to this position have come from the field of education.

Reinforcing the state's motto, women have held each of the five elected state offices at one time or another. The first woman state official was Minnie Slaughter who was *ex officio* superintendent of public instruction from March 14 until October 11, 1890. She became state librarian as the result of the illness and the resignation of her father, John Slaughter, in 1890 and remained librarian until 1892 (Trenholm, 1974: Vol. 1). Wyoming had the very first woman elected state official, Estelle Reel, who became Superintendent of Public Instruction in 1895. Wyoming also had the first female governor, Nellie Tayloe Ross, who was inaugurated in 1925. From 1975 to the present, three women have served as Secretary of State: Thyra Thomson (1975 - 1987); Kathy Karpan (1987 - 1995); and Diana Ohman (1995 - 1999). Two women have been State Treasurer: Shirley Wittler (1979 - 1983); and Cynthis Lummis (1999 - present). In addition, three women have been Superintendent of Public Instruction: Lynne Simmons (1979 - 1991); Diana Ohman (1991 - 1995); and Judy Catchpole (1995 - 2003).

Gov. Nellie Tayloe Ross is signing her oath of office, surrounded by her proud family. Chief Justice Charles T. Potter is standing far right. *Picture is courtesy of the American Heritage Center, University of Wyoming*

GOVERNOR

The governor is the most visible and probably most powerful individual in the Wyoming government. As the chief executive of the state, some people think that the governor must also run the state. While there is some truth to this belief, the actual role and powers of the governor are a bit more complicated.

Article 4 of the State Constitution defines the basic structure and function of the governor. To become governor, an individual must be a U.S. citizen and a resident of the state for at least five years. In addition, he or she also must be at least 30 years of age. The governor serves a four-year term and may seek one additional term.

The governor is National Guard commander-in-chief and carries out the laws. The governor may also grant pardons and veto legislative bills or parts of appropriations bills. Yet the Constitution is vague on some crucial responsibilities. For example, "He . . . shall take care that the laws be faithfully executed" is extremely important. Although a short remark at the close of a long paragraph, this clause establishes the governor as the chief administrator/

manager of the state. Why does the Constitution devote more space to relatively minor responsibilities than to important ones? The answer is simple. In 1889, the tasks of state government were very different from today. None of the members of the Constitutional Convention probably imagined that at some point in the future the state would spend several million dollars a day and manage complicated state and federal programs. So, they hastily disposed of running the government in a sentence.

The Wyoming governor also derives authority from statutes approved over the years. One major role is chief budget officer. Every two years the governor develops a financial plan for state government with the assistance of the Budget Division of the Department of Administration and Information. Given annual state expenditures of about $2 billion, the governor cannot bother with pens and pencils, but instead sets broad priorities. Nevertheless, the governor's budget is only a proposal that must be approved by the legislature.

Each year the state receives hundreds of millions of dollars in federal grants, and therefore, another of the governor's roles is chief federal program officer. In this capacity, the governor is responsible for monitoring the state's compliance with federal programs. However, the governor's dealings with the federal government involve more than keeping tabs on federal funds.

Constantly seeking to insure that the state's interests are considered in the design and implementation of federal programs, the governor can be viewed as Wyoming's lobbyist to the federal government.

Governor Dave Freudenthal, elected in 2002.

The Wyoming governor also plays an important role in party politics. Sometimes the governor may be the official head of the party, but the governor is always chief spokesperson for his party. Equally important, as the chief executive, the governor, can more easily obtain media coverage than most other members of his political party. In addition, the governor can use past partisan loyalty as a criterion for some appointments to office. However, the current Democratic governor, Dave Freudenthal, has appointed a number of Republicans to key positions in his administration.

Nevertheless, we should not assume the governor is simply in charge of his or her political party. As in other states, party members' opinions differ about what government should do and how it should do it. Each party has some liberals and conservatives. Geographical loyalties can also be formidable. The Cheyenne-Casper rivalry is almost legendary. People from northern Wyoming may disagree with people from southern Wyoming. Despite these limitations, governors can play an important unifying role in their political party.

While governors have these various roles, their success often seems to depend more on personal skill and integrity than on formal powers. A student of American governors wrote:

> *The chief resource of the modern governor is that of persuasion—the use of charm, reason, solid arguments and the status of his/her office to make it difficult for those he/she must deal with to say no. (Berman, 1975: 104)*

This is a fair assessment of the use of gubernatorial power in Wyoming. Two expressions are particularly important: persuasion and influence. Effective governors use persuasion to gain influence over the executive branch.

There are many reasons why the office of governor is important and prestigious. For instance, governors sometimes go on to hold national public office. This is common both in Wyoming and the rest of the nation. Eight Wyoming governors have gone on to serve in the United States Senate. Five of these actually resigned the governorship in mid-term to take up their seats in the Congress.

Another reason why many people respect the governor may have to do with the language that candidates for the office use. Campaign rhetoric often implies that if the right candidate is not elected, the state will suffer. Campaign advertisements dramatize the importance of the office. Theme, image and style become important aspects of candidates' messages to voters. These media themes convey the impression that the candidates are "larger than life".

Also, there are several cultural and social factors which probably add to the prestige of the office. Americans often expect their public leaders to fill roles as both political and ceremonial leaders. Symbolism, patriotism and hero identification certainly do not lessen the public's perception of the importance of the office of governor.

The impression in the media of the governor as all-powerful can be overdone. American governors are often less powerful than their constituents realize. This is certainly true in Wyoming. While governors are obviously important, they are seldom as powerful as people think. At best, Wyoming governors are persuasive, influential leaders. They are not political "bosses."

Another way to assess the Wyoming governor is to consider five questions used by political science scholars to create a continuum that ranges from "strong governor" to "weak governor". In summary, these measures are:

1. Can the governor serve an unlimited number of terms in office?
2. Does the governor exercise leadership with the legislature?
3. Does the governor have substantial control over state finances?
4. Does the governor have to compete with other state-wide elected executive officials?
5. Does the governor have broad powers to appoint top administrative officials?

A "yes" answer to all five questions would indicate a strong governor, and a "no" answer to all five would indicate a weak governor. Let us now consider the Wyoming governor.

The Wyoming governor can only serve two four year terms. On this issue, Wyoming does not meet the strong governor test. In practice, however, of the 29 persons who have held the of-fice, only four have served two full terms or more. These were Stan Hathaway (1967-1975), Ed Herschler (1975-1987), Mike Sullivan (1987-1995), and Jim Geringer (1995-2003). (Prior to the 1990s, governors could serve an unlimited number of terms.)

The relationship between the governor and the legislature is less clear. The legislature does not dominate the governor, but it is also true that the governor does not control the legislature. This is especially true when the governor is of a different political party than the legislative majority. While the legislature has substantial power, its sessions are so short that its use of its power is often very limited. For example, the first legislative override of a gubernatorial veto occurred in 1991. Legislators generally do not have the time to research problems in order to initiate new programs or to investigate allegations of wrongdoing in the executive branch. Also, keep in mind that a governor's personality is often relevant. One Democratic governor may work well with the Republican leadership and majorities in the legislature, while another may be less effective. A Republican governor does not necessarily "have his way" with a Republican legislature, whose members may feel that they want to make independent contributions to Wyoming policy making. In sum, Wyoming's gubernatorial-legislative relations seem to be in balance.

Wyoming governors have executive budget authority. They submit their comprehensive proposals for state expenditures to the legislative budget session every two years. To assist them in the preparation of this proposal, they have the assistance of the Budget Division of DAI. Yet, Wyoming has much earmarked revenue; some programs are, in effect, excluded from the governor's review under the budget process. The Highway Department (now a unit of the Department of Transportation) budget is the largest example. The general fund (state finances most amenable to gubernatorial control) is only one quarter of the total state revenue. A few departments, notably Highway and Game and Fish, are almost completely outside the governor's financial purview. It is difficult to judge where these conditions place Wyoming governors on a strong-weak continuum. In some states, governors are weaker than in Wyoming. They may control only one-tenth of the finances. In other states, governors are clearly in charge. Wyoming's situation is probably close to the middle.

On the matter of the short ballot, where only a few of the executive officers are elected, Wyoming is once again in the middle, neither very strong nor very weak. Four is not a very large number of autonomous and competing officials, but is well above the ideal of having no independently elected officers besides the governor.

The Wyoming governor is in an increasingly strong position with regard to appointment power. Since the government reorganization effort of the late 1980s (see discussion below), the governor has gain the power to appoint most of the directors of state departments. This change has increased the governor's administrative and financial control of the state's bureaucracy.

SECRETARY OF STATE

Secretary of State Joseph B. Meyer, elected in 1998 and 2002

The secretary of state has several program responsibilities and serves as acting governor in the absence of the governor. Absence occurs when the governor leaves the state, resigns or dies. An important responsibility of the secretary of state is to supervise public elections to assure uniformity and legality in the application of the election laws. This task requires a continuing and cooperative relationship with the 23 county clerks who manage county elections.

Furthermore, the secretary of state's office, through its Corporations Division, charters Wyoming corporations and certifies out-of-state corporations that do business in Wyoming. The Securities Division of the Office of the Secretary of State investigates allegations of fraudulent activities in the securities industry, and the Publications Division publishes the annual <u>Wyoming Official Directory</u>, a listing of all the principal members of Wyoming state government.

Auditor Max Maxfield, elected in 1998 and 2002

the state does not want to rely entirely on figures developed and verified externally.

AUDITOR

The State Auditor's Office is responsible for insuring that the fiscal operations of the state are in compliance with all applicable statutes. It examines all claims against the state, records all expenditures of funds or receipts of revenue, and keeps the accounts for state government. The Auditing Division conducts post-audits of state agencies and also audits mineral production on state and federal lands in Wyoming. Mineral royalties are so important that

TREASURER

The treasurer receives and manages all state money. The State of Wyoming derives revenues from a variety of sources and spends money for many activities and purposes. The treasurer keeps accurate records of state monies. In addition, the treasurer invests state funds to secure interest. Wise and prudent management of state funds is an important skill. A skilled treasurer repays the state many times by securing high, yet safe, returns on the investment of state funds. As we will see below, interest on state investments is an important component of the State's overall revenue sources.

Treasurer Cynthia Lummis, elected in 1998 and 2002

SUPERINTENDENT OF PUBLIC INSTRUCTION

The superintendent of public instruction is responsible for the public school system of the state of Wyoming. He or she also administers the State Department of Education. While students attend locally-run public schools, the state supplies financial assistance and administers important standards of operation. The superintendent is at the center of a complex public policy system reaching from local schools to the federal Department of Education. Most Americans perceive that public education is a local function; therefore, independent school districts are common in much of the United States. At the same time, state governments have assumed extensive educational responsibilities. About two dozen states consider education so important and autonomous that they mandate a separate election for the chief state education official. A gubernatorially-appointed State Board of Education links the superintendent to the rest of state government. This is a confusing array of conflicting authority; both the superintendent and the

Superintendent of Public Instruction Trent Blankenship, elected in 2002

board share concerns for, and authority over, education. The absence of clear and simple lines of authority is common to many governments in the United States.

EXECUTIVE AGENCIES

In the minds of most US citizens, the words bureaucracy and government are synonymous. This is not really surprising. The basic function of the bureaucratic apparatus is to implement and enforce the programs, policies, and laws developed by elected officials. As a consequence, citizens have far more day-in/day-out interactions with bureaucratic officials than with their elected representatives. It then follows that most of the complaints people have about government are directed at the bureaucracy.

Although criticism of bureaucracy has always been a feature of politics in this country, the 1980s were a time of heightened complaints. The decade began with the election of President Ronald Reagan and his pledge to reduce the scope of the national bureaucracy. As the decade proceeded, reducing the size and cost of bureaucracy became a prominent feature of political discussions at all levels of government.

This general trend was clearly evident in Wyoming politics during the 1980s. In fact, the economic condition of the state made attention to greater efficiency in government an especially important issue in Wyoming. By the mid 1980s, the energy boom was waning, and, in consequence, state revenues were declining. Since revenue from energy development is a major component of the state budget (discussed below), the prognosis for the state was that state revenues would likely continue to decline in the future. Among the questions raised by this new economic reality was how to make state government more efficient. The answer to this question took shape during the late 1980s and early 1990s in the form of two major initiatives.

The first initiative addressed the issues of control and coordination of the executive branch. In 1988, a legislatively created Joint Legislative-Executive Government Efficiency Study Committee (JLEGESC) noted that the structure of the executive branch represented "a 'mish-mash' of agencies, departments, boards, commissions, institutions, divisions, programs, offices and activities that are difficult to coordinate and control by the State's Chief Executive. This lack of coordination and control translates into unnecessary spending, duplication of effort, ineffective program delivery, lack of continuum of services, and an absence of accountability" (JLEGESC, 1988: 3). To remedy this situation, the Committee proposed a major reorganization of the executive branch following the "cabinet form" of government similar to the structure of the national bureaucracy.

More specifically, the committee recommended: (1) that existing state agencies and departments be reorganized into 12 departments: (2) that the directors of these departments be appointed by the Governor with the advice and consent of the State Senate; and (3) that the Attorney General and directors of the new departments form a "Governor's Cabinet." The primary advantage of this new structure, according to the JLEGESC report, was that it would increase the ability of the governor to coordinate the various activities of the executive branch. It might also be noted that based on our above discussion about measuring the power of the governor, this new structure would also move the Wyoming governor closer to the strong governor model.

Although some aspects of the JLEGESC recommendations ran into political roadblocks—for instance, only 9 of the 12 proposed departments were created—most were implemented. Thus, by 1995, the executive branch had been reorganized into a cabinet form of government. While the new structure of the executive branch is certainly far less confusing than the old structure, it does not necessarily guarantee that the actual operation of government will be more efficient. The goal of greater efficiency was the subject of the second initiative.

Under the auspices of laws enacted in the early 1990s, The State of Wyoming adopted a strategic planning/performance review process. In essence, this process required all state agencies to undertake a thorough examination of their goals and the methods they used to achieve them. To guide the agencies in this project, the Legislature defined a relatively specific set of criteria. On the one hand, the agencies were to identify:

1. the "specific public benefit that does or should result" from their activities;
2. whether the public benefit was sufficient "to justify the necessary funding" for their activities; and,
3. the potential "consequences of discontinuing" their activities (WS 28-1-115).

On the other hand, agencies were also to consider whether or not:

1. there were "alternative courses of action" they could follow to carry out their activities in a "more efficient or effective manner;"
2. their activities "could be implemented more effectively by another level of government or by a private entity;" and,

3. the rules and policies they developed were cost-effective and imposed a "minimum of regulatory burden" (WS 28-1-115).

The end product of this exercise was a plan that outlined the agency's five year goals and the strategies it intended to use to accomplish them.

The strategic plans, in turn, provide the basis for an annual performance review of the executive branch agencies. On or before December 1 of each year, state agencies are required to submit a report to the Governor that identifies their overall progress in achieving their planned goals. This part of the process also gives agencies the opportunity to make adjustments and revisions in their initial plans. And finally, both the strategic plans and the annual performance reports were made part of the legislative budget process. The logic of doing so is that the strategic plans and performance reports give the members of the legislature better information in making decisions about budget requests from the executive branch.

Whether or not the reorganization, strategic planning, and annual performance reviews have actually made the executive branch more effective and efficient is a question not easily answered. Taken together, these initiatives have certainly changed the character of the executive branch. Indeed, it could be argued that the 1990s were the first time in state history since the adoption of the Constitution that so much energy and attention have been directed at the structure and function of the executive branch. At the same time, to fully understand the logic behind these initiatives, we need to view them in the context of the state's financial condition. It is to that subject that we now turn.

PUBLIC FINANCE

The underlying concepts of state finances are relatively easy to understand. Each year the state collects money from taxpayers and other sources (revenues) which it then uses to pay (expenditures) for the broad array of programs and services provided to the citizens of the state. A sound financial strategy, then, would be one in which the amount of revenues collected is equal to or exceeds the amount of expenditures paid out. While these concepts are the core of state finances, applying them to the actual financial transaction of Wyoming government (or any government for that matter) is not a project for the faint of heart.

Nevertheless, the state's overall financial condition is perhaps one of the most important topics regarding Wyoming government. We will provide a brief overview of several aspects of the state's financial management system. As we will see, it is possible to argue both that the state is in very good financial shape, and that the state faces serious financial problems, depending upon which aspects of the overall system are emphasized.

Let us begin with a brief overview of the basic structure of the state financial system. At the heart of the system is a complicated matrix of literally hundreds of funds and accounts that have been created either by provisions of the State Constitution or by state statute. Table 2 displays the major categories of the state fund system.

It is important to remember that this table is an extreme simplification of the fund system. For instance, the "Special Revenue" category under Governmental Funds contains 75 separate subcategories.

In many respects, the fund system functions much like bank accounts for the state. All revenue collected by the state is deposited into these funds and accounts, and the money to cover state expenditures is withdrawn from them. Some of these funds are like checking accounts in that they are simply a place to keep state money between the time revenues are collected and expenditures are made. The General Fund, which covers the operations of state agencies, is an example of this type of fund. Other state funds are more like savings accounts. The money deposited in them is used to earn interest which becomes a part of the state revenue mix, but the fund's principal is held permanently by the state. The Permanent Wyoming

---

Major Funds and Accounts

Governmental Funds

General Fund
Special Revenue
Capital Projects
Debt Service

Proprietary Funds

Enterprise
Internal Service

Fiduciary Funds

Expendable Trusts
Nonexpendable Trusts
Pension
Agency

Account Groups

University Funds

Table 2

Mineral Trust Fund (PWMTF) is an example of this type of fund. In 2002, the PWMTF had a balance of roughly $2 billion.

It is as we move from the structure of the state financial system to the management of state finances that we begin to appreciate the full complexity of the process. As noted above, the primary goal for state financial management is to balance revenues and expenditures. The first question to answer, then, is what are the sources of state revenue. Although the state collects revenue in a variety of ways, historically the three major sources are taxes, interest income, and intergovernmental transfers. The state levies taxes on a wide array of things (property, alcohol, tobacco, gasoline, etc.), however, the most important revenue sources are from sales and use taxes and the severance tax on mineral production. In 2002, for example, these two sources produced roughly $450 million, or about 71 percent of the state's general fund revenue. Interest income is revenue the state receives from investing the money in funds like the PWMTF. The fund typically generates about $120 million annually. Intergovernmental transfers are money the state receives from other levels of government. Most of these transfers come from the federal government in the form of grants, aid, and mineral royalties from mineral production on the federal lands within the state.

The next question to answer is how the revenue from these sources is distributed among the various funds and accounts. Viewed in one way, the distribution process is relatively straight forward. The legal mandates that created and/or modified the funds and accounts specify the source(s) and amount(s) of revenue that is to be deposited in them. Two examples help demonstrate how this process works. Table 3 displays the 2001-2002 distribution of the state severance tax; and Table 4 displays the 2002 revenue sources for the General Fund.

2001-2002 Distribution of Severance Tax Revenue ($000)	
General Fund	$117,185.4
Budget Reserve Account	39,270.6
PWMTF	72,869.1
Water Account I	19,319.8
Water Account II	3,435.8
Highway Fund	7,435.5
Cites and Towns	15,101.6
Counties	6,334.3
Capital Construction (Special Districts)	4,386.5
County Roads	4,495.0
Other Accounts	10,200.4
Total	$299,434.0

Source: Wyoming Consensus Revenue Estimating Group

Table 3

2002 General Fund Revenue Sources ($000)	
Severance Tax & Use	$117,185.4
Sales Tax	313,178.0
PWMTF Income	90,510.5
Pooled Income	29,114.8
Sales and Services	20,858.8
Franchise Tax	17,099.7
Revenues from Others	7,532.7
Penalties	6,360.0
Federal Aid & Grants	8,878.4
Other Sources	27,328.4
Total	$637,948.7

Source: Wyoming Consensus Revenue Estimating Group

Table 4

located among the various agencies, programs, and activities that constitute the day in/day out business of state government. As should be obvious, the discussions about allocating General Fund money precipitates numerous arguments and conflicts. Indeed, most of the discussion in the State Legislature about the "state budget" is actually about the allocation of the General Fund.

There is a sense in which the primary advantage of this distribution process is also its major disadvantage. The primary advantage is that the system reduces the number of decisions that have to be made about state finances in each budget cycle. Many of the funds and accounts are legally dedicated to rather specific purposes. For example, The State constitution (Article 15, Section 19) directs that money in the PWMTF "shall be invested . . .and all income from the fund investments shall be deposited . . .in the general fund on an annual basis."

Some of these revenues go into the General Fund. Once revenue is deposited in the General Fund, the legislature decides how this revenue should be al-

CHAPTER 6

THE WYOMING JUDICIARY

The courts are among the primary mechanisms for resolving conflicts in American society today. The relative decline in influence of social-control institutions such as the family, religion, and neighborhood, contrasts with the ever-increasing tendency of people to call upon legal rules and processes to manage disputes. Not only are the courts forums where the legal norms governing social conflict are enforced, they are the very symbols of the law itself. Most people think of courts and judges as the special repositories of our heritage of civil liberties, as the neutral referees between the fundamental rights of the individual and the expanding power of modern government. Judicial institutions benefit from the prestige this image accords to them. The status of courts as the third branch of government is not defined exclusively by their monopoly of power to apply settled legal rules; through judicial review, or their authority to translate the "majestic generalities" of the constitution into concrete law, they have implicitly staked out a claim to make the rules as well as to interpret them (Jacob, 1984: chs. 2-3).

These functions have enhanced the role of the state courts as well as the more-publicized federal courts. The state and local courts are the tribunals where the vast majority of civil and criminal cases are decided, notwithstanding the greater media attention paid to the activities of the United States Supreme Court. A person who is caught up in the machinery of the judicial process, whether as an aggrieved plaintiff or a reluctant defendant, is far more likely to find herself or himself in a state or local court than in a federal court. The intriguing notion that state constitutions, the final interpreters of which are the state supreme courts, might be made to yield a rich bounty of new individual liberties beyond those afforded by the federal constitution has achieved positive results in an expanding body of judicial rulings within the past thirty years.

Although the chapter deals with the state and local courts, readers are cautioned to remember that these are not the only tribunals of justice exercising jurisdiction over disputes which occur within the State's borders. These other courts—such as the United States District Court in Cheyenne and in Casper, and the newly established tribal courts of the Wind River Reservation — fall outside the scope of state government, and so they have been excluded from the discussion below.

THE STRUCTURE OF THE WYOMING COURT SYSTEM

Article 5 of the Wyoming Constitution, the judiciary article, goes into some detail about the structure and functions of the higher state courts, but leaves many of their other features, as well as the entire system of minor courts, up to the legislature or the courts themselves. The precise boundary lines separating the legislative, executive, and

star /Opinion

Sunday, October 15, 1989

'Picky, picky' Jack Sidi meets The Judge

CHEYENNE — After a long dull spell, we finally have a juicy fun spat between the Wyoming Supreme Court and the State Auditor's Office.

This neat little scrap isn't over a questionable million dollar purchase or even new tablecloths for the governor's mansion or a new state car for state Superintendent Public Instruction Lynn Simons who, for all we know, is still driving a junker beneath the dignity of her office.

The comedy-drama is over a measly $160 to pay Wyoming Supreme Court Chief Justice Joe Cardine's dues to the American Bar Association.

Such minor things spawn separation of powers' fights.

State Auditor Jack Sidi, who bounced vouchers for the mansion tablecloths and Simons' car, also rejected Cardine's voucher. Sidi said executive branch policy forbids the state from paying membership dues for an individual.

Cardine shot back the voucher with an explanation that the ABA won't accept dues in the name of a chief justice, only in the name of the individual.

Moreover, he said, Wyoming should be represented by a live body, not an empty chair, at ABA judicial meetings.

After conferring with the Attorney General's Office, Sidi wrote Cardine saying he would pay the $160 but only under certain conditions.

Those conditions, frankly, were picky.

Cardine must have erupted, or whatever supreme court justices do in the privacy of their chambers. Because Sidi received an order from the entire supreme court directing

him either to pay the $160 or show cause why he shouldn't be held in contempt of court.

It was a "frightening experience," a grim Sidi told the Joint Appropriations Committee.

The JAC members clucked sympathetically. After all, Sidi and his deputy, Tom Jones, who was there, too, are former JAC co-chairmen.

Sidi said if he went to jail, nobody would be around to sign the checks.

Sob.

My favorite comment came from Sen. Win Hickey, D-Laramie, who said drily that it was terrifying that JAC members might also face contempt charges if they cut the supreme court's budget.

"That almost frightens me more than you going to jail," Hickey said to Sidi.

Well, Sidi isn't going to jail. He paid the $160.

Cardine got his licks in the following day, however, referring to Sidi as an "emperor," and scolding him for asking the JAC for help like a "little kid."

The $160 fight could have been settled between them with a phone call, Cardine said.

The issue is one of separation of powers, however. Cardine said Sidi can't bounce supreme court vouchers unless they are clearly unlawful. Nor can he set conditions for payments of the bills.

Cardine also seemed disappointed the issue won't be settled in court.

It won't be, because Sidi cut short the fun by going on vacation after he dropped the bomb.

Phooey.

So who is the winner in this slice of theater?

Sidi, of course.

He and Jones emerge as righteous guardians of the state treasury, vigorous protectors of the taxpayers' dollars. A pair of Boy Scouts.

Cardine, who like most scholarly legal types isn't attuned to the political nuances, emerges as heavy-handed, too willing to unleash the power of the supreme court when thwarted.

Cardine said he won't be nervous when he goes before the JAC next year about the judiciary's budget.

Well, I would be.

I'll wager the first question out of the box will be whether the JAC members will get hit with a contempt citation if they cut the judicial budget.

Leave it to Sidi to stir up things.

Too bad he isn't going to run for governor.

From the Casper Star-Tribune of October 15, 1989.

Figure 1

judicial spheres of authority are hazy with respect to many aspects of the courts where the constitution is silent or ambiguous, a situation which has occasionally led to public clashes between members of these two branches of government. (See Figure 1)

The structure of Wyoming's court system can be visualized as a four-tier pyramid, with the numerous local courts at the base, and the number of each type of court declining the higher one goes up the organizational pyramid.

A vital feature of local government in Wyoming is the municipal court. The state legislature has authorized first class cities and incorporated towns to create municipal courts for the express and sole purpose of trying persons who are charged with violating city or town ordinances. In 2002, there were 67 such courts in Wyoming, staffed by a total of 64 judges. Municipal courts do not hear civil cases, and the maximum penalty which may be imposed upon a person convicted in these courts is a $750 fine and/or a jail term of six months. Appointed by the city or town mayor with the consent of the council, municipal judges are not legally required to be law-

OUTLINE OF THE WYOMING COURT SYSTEM

Court	Jurisdiction	Cases Disposed of in 2000 in All Courts of This Type	How Judges Chosen?	Judges Required to Be Lawyers?	Judges' Terms of Office	Salary of Judges (2003)	Appeals from this Court Go to
Supreme Court	Appellate: Unlimited Original: Limited	389	Merit Selection	Yes	8 Years	$105,000	No further appeal, except in cases involving questions of federal law, which may be appealed to the U.S. Supreme Court.
District Courts (9)	Civil: Unlimited (except for minor civil matters heard only by lower courts). Criminal: Unlimited. Hears appeals from lower courts.	16,008	Merit Selection	Yes	6 Years	$100,000	Supreme Court
Circuit Courts (15)	Civil: Where amount in dispute is no more than $7,000. Small claims. Criminal: All misdemeanors	100,701 Misdemeanor Counts	Merit Selection	Yes	4 Years	$82,000	District Court
Justice of the Peace Courts (8) (Replaced by Circuit Courts after 2002)	Civil: Where amount in dispute is no more than $3,000. Small claims. Criminal: Low misdemeanors.	20,632*	Popularly Elected	No	4 Years	As set by county Commissioners, but no higher than $45,000	District Court
Municipal Courts	Civil: None. Criminal: All violations of city or town ordinances.	61,043** (1997 figures)	By mayor, with consent of council	No	As set by municipality	As set by municipality	District Court

*Statistics for Weston County (including City of Newcastle) justice court not available for April – December 2000.
** Statistics for the municipal courts of Laramie, Granger, Worland, Greybull, Wheatland and Riverton not available for 1997.

Table 1

yers; in fact, only about half of them in the state are eligible to practice law. Indeed, the generally manageable case loads and uncomplicated nature of most of the matters coming before municipal judges require in nearly all Wyoming localities no more than part-time judges. As a consequence, these individuals rely on their legal practice or other employment to supplement the income they receive from the municipality for their work on the bench. Trials in municipal court are conducted according to procedures established by the Wyoming Supreme Court designed to insure fundamental fairness and protect the rights of the defendant (see Figure 2a and 2b). In cases where conviction may be punished by a jail term (as in drunk driving), the defendant may invoke his or her legally guaranteed right to trial by a six-member jury. Even in these cases, however, most defendants voluntarily give up the right to jury trial and opt for trial by judge alone. Persons who are convicted of offenses in municipal court may appeal their conviction to the district court, but such appeals are very few in number.

The formal jurisdiction conferred by statute and local ordinance upon municipal courts in Wyoming provides only the outer limits of the cases they hear. Within this framework, about one out of every two defendants in munici-

pal court are charged with committing traffic offenses, such as drunk or careless driving, speeding, or improper registration of a vehicle. Disorderly conduct and violations of local alcoholic beverage restrictions lead the list of non-traffic misdemeanors commonly handled in municipal court, although the variety of these kinds of offenses is as wide as the topics which are regulated by local ordinances around the state. As most offenses tried in municipal court are normally punishable by no more than a fine, the typical case is quickly disposed of through a guilty plea or "forfeiture of bond" (giving up the money one posted rather than appear for trial). Although the municipal courts and the matters they deal with are frequently classified in legal terminology as "minor," they—along with the circuit courts—are the tribunals in which most citizens experience at first hand the quality of judicial justice in Wyoming. The fairness, efficiency, and costs of the personnel and procedures which defendants encounter in these lower courts may shape most citizens' perceptions of the judicial system as a whole. In those municipalities where fines, forfeitures, and costs assessed as the result of conviction form a substantial portion of the municipal revenues, the tension between the municipal court's justice and fiscal responsibilities is no easy problem to solve.

INFORMATION SHEET DISTRIBUTED TO PERSONS CHARGED WITH DWUI OFFENSES IN LARAMIE MUNICIPAL COURT

STATE OF WYOMING)
COUNTY OF ALBANY) SS.
CITY OF LARAMIE   )

IN THE MUNICIPAL COURT
IN THE CITY OF LARAMIE

_____
JUDGE

STATEMENT OF RIGHTS
FOR
DRIVING WHILE UNDER THE INFLUENCE
FAILURE TO MAINTAIN LIBALITY INSURANCE
DRIVING WHILE LICENSE CANCELLED, SUSPENDED OR REVOKED

The matter that you are in Laramie Municipal Court for is a criminal misdemeanor charge. This first appearance is your arraignment, at which time you will be advised of the charge against you and asked if you understand and/or have any questions about the following rights and procedures.

If you enter a plea of "Not Guilty" to the charge the matter will be set down for a Jury Trial at a later date, unless you specifically waive your right to a jury trial. But this **must** be in writing. Trials are normally set for 10:00 A.M. on Monday, Thursday and Fridays and 8:30 A.M. on Wednesday. They also, will be set as soon as possible.

If you plead "Guilty" to the charge, you will be given an opportunity to explain the situation to the Judge, before any fine, jail sentence or other punishment is imposed.

Read the following rights thoroughly, if you completely understand them and have no questions, sign this form at the bottom, put the date on it and hand it to the Clerk when you are called.

1. You are presumed to be innocent (not guilty) until the City, at a trial, proves you guilty beyond a reasonable doubt or you enter a plea of guilty.

2. You have a right to a trial before a Judge or before a six (6) person jury. There is no penalty for asking for a trial, the fines and/or jail sentence will not be higher, simply because you ask for a trial, either to the Judge or Jury.

3. You have a right to remain silent at all times. If you are going to plead "Not Guilty" do not say anything now, anything you say now would be better for trial and may be used against you at trial. At trial you may, if you wish, waive your right to silence and testify on your own behalf.

4. You have a right to be represented by an attorney of your own choice, or if you are unable to afford an attorney and meet the financial guidelines set out by the court, an attorney will be appointed to represent you at no cost to you.

5. You have the right at trial to cross-examine (ask questions) anyone and everyone that the City calls to testify against you.

6. You have the right at trial to present evidence and call witnesses on your behalf. The Court clerk will help you in issuing subpoenas at no cost to you.

If, after a Jury trial or Bench trial you are found "Guilty" or you plead "Guilty"

To Driving While Under the Influence
A first offense "Driving While Under the Influence", a fine of up to $750.00 or jail sentence of up to six (6) months may be imposed or both.

If this is a second offense for "Driving While Under the Influence", a minimum fine of $200.00 up to $750.00 and a mandatory jail sentence of seven (7) days to six (6) months will be imposed.

If this is a third or subsequent offense for "Driving While Under the Influence", a minimum fine of $750.00 and a mandatory jail sentence of thirty (30) days to six (6) months will be imposed.

1

Figure 2a

Driving While Under the Influence (continued)

On Driving While Under the Influence offense a $50.00 victim compensation surcharge is added on top of any fine; in accordance with state law.

Notice of your plea will be sent to the State Department of Motor Vehicles. 1st offense suspension is up to 90 days: 2nd offenses suspension is up to 1 year and subsequent offenses may result in three (3) years revocation. This action will also affect your ability to keep your insurance or the cost of that insurance.

To Failure to Maintain Liability Coverage

A first offense "Failure to Maintain Liability Coverage", a minimum fine of $250.00 up to $750.00 will be imposed, a jail sentence of up to six (6) months may be imposed or both.

On a second or subsequent violation of 1307 A or upon conviction under this subsection after a conviction under W.S. 31-4-103, the person may be fined not less than $500.00 nor more than $750.00, a jail sentence of up to six (6) months may be imposed or both.

To Driving While License Cancelled, Suspended or Revoked

A first offense "Driving While License Cancelled, Suspended or Revoked ", a fine of up to $750.00 or jail sentence of up to six (6) months may be imposed or both.

If this is a subsequent offense (not first time) for "Driving While License canceled, suspended or Revoked", a minimum fine of $200.00 up to $750.00 will be imposed and a mandatory jail sentence of seven (7) days to six (6) months will be imposed.

If you enter a plea of "Guilty", you are waiving (giving up) your rights as stated above, including your right to appeal this matter to a higher court.

I hereby certify that I have read and fully understand the above rights that I have in this Court.

_____   _____
Signature   Date

_____
Social Security Number

Figure 2B

Circuit Courts: An Offer They Couldn't Refuse

The movement for court reform which has affected the Wyoming judiciary during the past thirty years has been especially noticeable in the realm of court organization. A felt need for genuine modernization and uniformity in the minor court system and decades of lobbying by the leaders of the Wyoming bench and bar convinced the legislature in 1971 to enact a law providing for the creation of a county court system to replace the existing justice of the peace (JP) courts. Only partially successful in achieving this goal, advocates of court reform doggedly kept up the momentum for change, finally convincing the legislature to adopt the Court Consolidation Act of 2000.

This law created the system of circuit courts, circuit judges, and magistrates, which presently exists in all of the counties of Wyoming. The principal features of this new system reflect a sustained effort on the part of the legislature to upgrade the older JP courts by a number of steps, including expansion of their limited jurisdiction. Minor cases involving state laws (as opposed to municipal ordinances) are now heard in the new circuit courts as they previously were in the county and JP courts. Unlike a JP court, a circuit court's criminal jurisdiction extends to the trial of all misdemeanors. While a judge of the circuit court may not try felonies[1], he or she can issue warrants, set bail, and conduct preliminary examinations of persons accused of committing felonies.[2] In civil cases, the circuit courts have exclusive jurisdiction to resolve disputes (except those which involve title to land) in which the amount of money or value of property claimed is not more than $7,000. Circuit judges can handle even more serious civil and criminal cases if requested to do so by a district judge. A significant number of civil cases are handled under small claims procedures, which seek to minimize litigational costs, delay, and formality. However, these procedures can be invoked only where the amount of money in dispute is not more than $3,000. (see Figure 3) With the permission of the state supreme court, a circuit judge can serve in a dual capacity as a municipal judge in his or her county.

The legislature has geographically divided the state into nine judicial districts (see Figure 5 on page 98), each possessing its own district court and its own circuit courts. The boundaries of each circuit are the same as those of each district. Circuit judges are able to hear cases in any county within their circuit. However—and this is a crucial element of the system—they can also be assigned to hear cases in other circuits if the need to relieve the workloads of other circuit judges calls for it.

The number of circuit judges assigned to any particular circuit/district is set by the legislature. Some circuits/districts, such as the third (which includes the cities of Rock Springs and Evanston), have as many as four judges. At present, there is a total of 24 circuit judges apportioned among the nine circuits/districts. The judges serve four-year terms, and are chosen according to the Missouri-type plan used to select

CLAIM FORM FOR PERSONS FILING A SMALL CLAIMS SUIT IN CIRCUIT COURT FOR ALBANY COUNTY (LARAMIE)

IN THE CIRCUIT COURT, 2ND JUDICIAL DISTRICT, ALBANY COUNTY, WYOMING

525 GRAND, ROOM 105, LARAMIE, WYOMING

DOCKET NO. _____

PLAINTIFF,

VS.

DEFENDANT.

SMALL CLAIMS AFFIDAVIT

1. I, _____ (name of person signing this Affidavit), being duly sworn on oath, state the Defendant is justly indebted to Plaintiff in the Principal sum of $ _____, plus the filing fee of $10.00, Sheriff's fees and for such other costs as Plaintiff is entitled. Plaintiff's claim is based upon the following:

_____

_____

_____

_____

_____

_____

_____.

2. Demand for payment has been made and refused.

3. Following are the Defendant's:

    a. Business Address: _____.
    b. Home Address: _____.
    c. Mailing address: _____.
    d. Phone number: Business: _____. Home: _____.

4. I request judgment in the amount stated above.

STATE OF WYOMING)   Signed: _____
) ss   (Plaintiff's/Agent's Signature)
COUNTY OF ALBANY)

Subscribed and sworn to before me this ____ day of _____, 200__.

(SEAL)   Judge/Clerk of Court/ Notary Public

Plaintiff's:

    a. Business Address: _____.
    b. Home Address: _____.
    c. Mailing address: _____.
    d. Phone number: Business: _____. Home: _____.

****

NOTICE TO PLAINTIFF AND DEFENDANT

TO THE PLAINTIFF AND DEFENDANT: You are hereby notified that this case has been set for trial. If you choose to appear, you MUST bring with you the witnesses, papers and evidence which will prove your case or defend your position. **IF YOU DON'T, YOU MAY LOSE YOUR CASE.**

Figure 3

district and supreme court judges (see below under Choosing the Judges). Only lawyers are eligible to serve as circuit judges; as it is full-time work they are prohibited from practicing law as long as they hold office. The current annual salary (also legislatively fixed) for a circuit judge is $82,000. The rules of procedure according to which these as well as other courts in the state operate are formulated by the state supreme court. Appeals from judgments of the circuit courts go to the district courts.

Another important feature of the new circuit court arrangement is the creation of full-time, state-funded "magistrates" for each county in which there is no resident circuit judge. These judicial officers are limited to dealing with cases in the county in which they live. If they are eligible to practice law their authority is roughly equivalent to that of a circuit judge. Non-lawyers can also be magistrates, but their jurisdiction is limited to criminal cases where conviction could result in no more than a $750 fine and/or six months in jail, as well as civil cases involving no more than $3,000. The circuit judges appoint the magistrates for their own circuit, subject to approval by the relevant board of county commissioners. Full-time magistrates have four-year terms of office, subject to retention by the voters of their county after they have served at least a year in office. Circuit judges can also appoint part-time magistrates, but the latter serve solely at the pleasure of the appointing judge. In certain circumstances part-time magistrates can exercise basically the same authority as their full-time colleagues, depending on whether they are legally-trained. If part-time but legally trained, they can also practice law, as long as this does not conflict with their judicial duties. All full-time and part-time magistrates are paid by the state. Some part-time magistrates double as municipal court judges, situations in which part of their pay comes from the municipality.

Wyoming's circuit courts, along with the district courts, have been aptly described as the workhorses of the state's judicial system. In 2000, the circuit courts disposed of 17,507 civil cases, a large portion of which involved small claims actions, suits brought by creditors, landlord-tenant disputes, and auto accident claims. They dealt with over 100,000 misdemeanor counts, primarily consisting of traffic-related offenses, but also including an array of other minor criminal charges such as shoplifting, assault and battery, and infractions of game and fish regulations. An overwhelming percentage of these cases ended in guilty pleas or forfeitures of bond. These numbers undoubtedly will swell as a result of the recent addition of new circuit courts in counties which formerly used justice of the peace courts. The circuit courts altogether turned over to the public school funds of their counties a total of $6.8 million they had collected in the form of fines and forfeitures imposed upon defendants. In addition to carrying on their judicial functions then, the circuit courts are an important revenue collection agency for local educational authorities.

District Courts: The Big Leagues

The next-to-highest tier on the organizational pyramid of courts in Wyoming is occupied by the state district courts. These tribunals exercise original jurisdiction in the most serious civil and criminal cases which enter the state court system. Formally, district courts may try cases which have not been assigned exclusively to one of the lower courts. What this means in practice is that district judges can and do decide lawsuits where large sums of money are at stake, as well as all cases of probate, divorce, paternity, adoption, and guardianship. On the criminal side, authority to try all felonies as well as capital crimes is vested exclusively in the district courts. Juvenile proceedings and the admission of aliens to United States citizenship (the process known as naturalization) are conducted in district court. Finally, these courts also have appellate jurisdiction to review the legal correctness of decisions appealed from the municipal, and circuit courts within their district.

The gravity of the issues adjudicated by the district courts indicates that it is in these tribunals where the full panoply of activities associated with a trial in the public imagination is most likely to be displayed: the crowded courtroom, cross-examination of unfriendly witnesses, the eloquent closing arguments, the figure of the stern, experienced judge, and the long-awaited moment when the jury (the 12 member jury of the common law tradition, if it is a felony case) delivers its verdict. Whether the opportunities for high melodrama latent in the adversary method of conducting a trial actually materialize or not, is often unpredictable, sometimes even alarming (see Figure 4), but it is significant that if they do occur, it is most likely to be in the courtroom of one of the district judges.

Figure 5 shows how district court boundaries are currently drawn in Wyoming. As mentioned previously, the legislature has geographically divided the state into nine judicial districts, each having its own district court and circuit courts. A district may be no larger than a single county (for example, the 7th Judicial District is made up of only Natrona County), while others, such as the 5th Judicial District, contain as many as four counties. The number of judges assigned to each district - also a legislative determination - was recently increased to three each in the case-heavy 1st, 3rd, and 7th Districts. The remaining districts have two each, except for the 4th, which has only one district judge.

Innocent verdict sparks commotion

SHERIDAN (UPI) — A Sheridan County District Court jury's innocent verdict for a man charged in a stabbing was so unpopular officers had to sneak jurors from the courthouse and the defense attorney spent the night in a motel.

The innocent verdict the jury returned late Thursday in the trial of Iftikar Khan sparked a commotion in the courtroom and harsh comments from presiding Judge Leonard McEwan.

Khan was charged with stabbing Rajab Kahn, a distant relative, last September in the middle of Sheridan's Main Street. It was believed the stabbing was the result of a long-standing financial dispute between two Pakistani families.

McEwan told the jurors he could not understand how they had reached the innocent verdict and said, "I hope none of you ever have to worry about someone trying to stab you."

The judge then turned to the acquitted defendant and said, "You got awfully lucky, I hope you know that."

After court was adjourned, Sheridan County sheriff's deputies sneaked the seven women and five men on the jury out a side entrance to the courthouse.

Defense attorney James Wolfe and his family did not return home and spent the night in a Sheridan motel as a security precaution.

One juror said the jury took three votes before settling on the innocent verdict.

The trial had been marred by communication problems and a Pakistani interpreter had been brought in from Denver. But represetatives of both families complained the interpreter was not interpreting the testimony word for word so the precise statement were not being conveyed.

It was unclear from the testimony who had started the altercation that resulted in the stabbing.

A member of the stabbing victim's family said a civil suit against Iftikar Khan is being considered.

From the Casper Star-Tribune, February 7, 1983, Page B1

Figure 4

District judges in multi-county districts have to spend part of their time travelling to each county seat in their districts in order to conduct court business. They can hold court for each other and, on rare occasions, a district judge may even be called upon to fill in for a supreme court justice in particular cases being heard by the state's highest court. District judges, who are chosen in the same manner as supreme court justices, serve for six year terms. The Wyoming Constitution requires them to be at least 28 years old, resident in the state for at

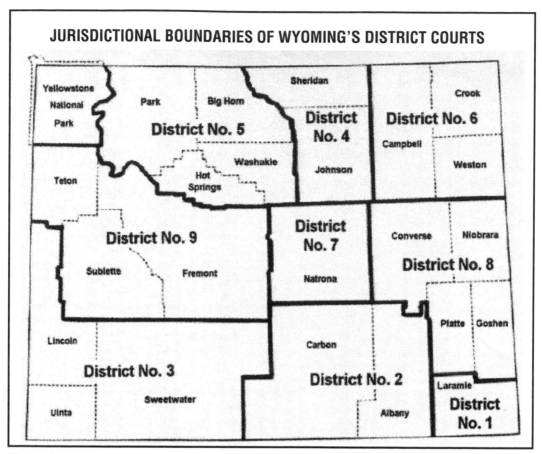

JURISDICTIONAL BOUNDARIES OF WYOMING'S DISTRICT COURTS

Yellowstone National Park

Park

District No. 5

Big Horn

Sheridan

District No. 4

Crook

District No. 6

Campbell

Weston

Teton

Washakie

Hot Springs

Johnson

District No. 9

District No. 7

Converse

Niobrara

Sublette

Fremont

Natrona

District No. 8

Platte | Goshen

Lincoln

Carbon

District No. 3

District No. 2

Laramie

District No. 1

Uinta

Sweetwater

Albany

Figure 5

least two years, and "learned in the law" (Wyoming Constitution, art. 5, sec.12). The last requirement, in reality, means that they must be lawyers. Neither they nor supreme court justices are allowed to practice law while serving as judges, however, and for this reason the legislature has sought to make the salaries attached to these offices high enough to attract well qualified attorneys who might otherwise be unwilling to sacrifice a lucrative private practice for a

career on the bench. Whether that aim has been realized is questionable, although the legislature has made strides in this direction lately. The current annual salary of a Wyoming district judge is $100,000, based on a 19.5 percent pay raise recently granted them. District judges may appoint commissioners (who also must be "learned in the law") to assist them in the "chamber business" of the court, that is, tasks ordinarily performed outside the courtroom, such as deciding petitions for a finding of mental incompetency and taking depositions (written testimony of witnesses taken down prior to trial in civil cases). Each district court is also staffed by an elected clerk responsible for keeping the court's records and maintaining the files of each case. A court reporter for keeping a verbatim record of court proceedings, and a probation counsellor who conducts pre-sentence investigations and supervises offenders placed on probation are also employed by a district court. Some of the judges employ staff attorneys (law clerks) to aid them in doing legal research.

While district courts have appellate jurisdiction over cases appealed from the lower courts, it is clear that they function overwhelmingly as trial courts. In 2000, the nine district courts as a whole received a total of 106 cases on appeal from the lower courts; during the same year, well over 15 thousand cases were filed in the district courts under their original jurisdiction. At the beginning of 2000, there were still 13,369 cases "pending" in the district courts, meaning cases from previous years which had not been disposed of yet.

Supreme Court: The End of the Line (Most of the Time)

At the pinnacle of the state court system is the Supreme Court of Wyoming. Located in Cheyenne not far from the Capitol Building, this court is the final interpreter of the laws and the constitution of the state. The only possible route of appeal after this is to the United States Supreme Court, and such efforts (in which the appealing party must convince the federal supreme court that his or her case hinges on an important question of federal law which demands judicial resolution) are typically unsuccessful. The state supreme court is the last resort for most people. (See Figure 6).

The primary significance of the Supreme Court of Wyoming is found in the exercise of its *general appellate* jurisdiction, that is, in hearing cases presented to it for review which were originally decided by some other court in the state, mainly - though not exclusively - the district courts. The supreme court has a limited amount of *original* jurisdiction granted to it by the state constitution, but this authority to function like a trial court extends only to petitions for issuance by the court of the prerogative writs of the common law, such as *habeas corpus*. Even here, however, a litigant who invokes the court's original jurisdiction must present the court with a convincing reason why it should take the case instead of directing the petitioner to one of the district courts. The supreme court conserves its time and energy for handling appeals, as the small fraction of petitions for original writs granted every year bears witness. The

Shall never see a law as lovely as a tree

CHEYENNE — Terry Rogers' five-year legal battle over his cottonless cottonwood tree is nearly at an end.

The U.S. Supreme Court last week for the second time refused to hear the case and let stand a Wyoming Supreme Court ruling

Joan Barron

Star-Tribune

that the City of Cheyenne was within the law to fine Rogers for refusing to trim the 48-foot tree. The city said the tree obstructed an approach zone at Cheyenne's Municipal Airport contrary to city ordinance.

Rogers' last hope is that the U.S. Tenth Circuit Court of Appeals will review the case. On appeal is a ruling by U.S. District Judge C. A. Brimmer that upheld the Cheyenne ordinance limiting the heighth of structures near the local airport.

But Rogers' attorney, Bernard Phelan of Cheyenne, says the

Tenth Circuit appeal is a "tough situation" because the federal courts are loath to interfere in state court decisions.

Meanwhile, Rogers last week receive a notice to appear before Cheyenne Municipal Judge Paul Galeotos May 12 to show cause why he shouldn't be fined $20,000 for refusing to trim the tree.

Galeotos fined Rogers $200 per day beginning Nov. 20, 1986 when he refused to trim the tree but stayed the fine during the appeal process.

Rogers, however, had the tree trimmed back to 25 feet a year ago on Phelan's advice.

The Wyoming Supreme Court, in effect, said the city's easement over Rogers' house was created when Congress passed the civil aviation act, giving the government the authority to regulate air space.

But Rogers's position is that the easement is a property right and he should have been compensated for it.

"A tree instigated it, but it was my property," the 33-year-old state government employee says in disgust. "I quit."

Faced with a $20,000 fine on top of thousands of dollars in legal fees, he says he may have to file for bankruptcy.

Rogers, who bought his home in 1976, said he let city crews trim the cottonwood tree as long as they didn't ruin it. The last time the city trimmed the tree was in either 1978 or 1979.

Then the tree grew unfettered. When the city asked Rogers to cut the tree by at least 13 feet in June 1983, he applied to the planning commission for a variance on grounds the cottonwood was

> Galeotos fined Rogers $200 per day beginning Nov. 20, 1986 when he refused to trim the tree but stayed the fine during the appeal process.

grandfathered because it was already too tall when the city ordinance was adopted. He didn't get the variance and the fight was on.

Rogers claimed that cutting the tree, which he valued at $2,064, would kill it.

Rogers warns that if the city can take an easement on his property without compensation, any unit of government can do the same to other property owners.

As an extreme example, he said the county could build a road through your house or land without paying for it.

People, he said, don't care and won't care until it happens to them.

And Phelan says he wishes the case didn't involve a tree.

"I wish it involved something else," Phelan said. "People laugh when they hear the case is about a tree."

Meanwhile, the cottonwood tree still is alive, although Rogers says it doesn't look well.

But Rogers also has three large pine trees in his yard, which he values at $5,000. Although the trees are capable of growing to 80 feet, they cannot grow above 25 feet because of the ordinance, he says.

The pine trees are growing, too.

From the Casper Star-Tribune of May 1, 1988, Page A12

Figure 6

Wyoming Supreme Court also has a vital influence upon state law through its administrative superintendence over the other courts in the state, and its power to prescribe the code of ethics governing the practice of law in Wyoming. The structural features of the state's highest judicial body, and the legal qualifications and method of appointment of its members are regulated, for the most part, by the Wyoming Constitution and statutes, with most of its internal decision-making process left to determination by the court itself.

The membership of the supreme court is fixed by law at five, consisting of a chief justice and four justices. Appointments to the court follow the plan used for selecting district and county court judges, but each justice serves for a term of eight years. The five members of the supreme court choose one from among themselves to be chief justice for a four-year term, and the practice of the court is to rotate the office of chief among all of the members. The chief justice is responsible for supervising the always heavy administrative work of the court, and presides when the court is in session and during conferences of the justices. In addition to these duties, the chief has the prerogative of designating who among the justices (including himself) is to write the opinion of the court in each case it decides. Finally, the chief is the principal spokesperson for the court in its relations with the legislature and the governor, as well as with the lower courts, the bar, the press, and the public. To be eligible for appointment to the Wyoming Supreme Court, one must be a lawyer with at least nine years of legal experience, 30 years of age, and a resident of the state for at least three years. With the pay raise voted by the legislature in 2002, a supreme court justice now earns an annual salary of $105,000.

To what extent is the state supreme court a force for social change in Wyoming? Historically, the court has played an essentially passive role in the state's policy-making process. Regardless of service on the court on the part of many excellent legal scholars and people of long, distinguished careers in public office, the justices over the years have by and large viewed policy-making as the prerogative of the legislative and executive branches of government. This has been true of Democratic as well as Republican members of the court. The role the supreme court has adopted should come as no surprise in a politically conservative state not easily susceptible to the winds of social change. The political role of the courts in Wyoming is distinctly unlike that enjoyed by the federal courts, especially the United States Supreme Court. Even here, however, the contrast is relative, not absolute. Even Wyoming's Supreme Court has been responsive to the pressures which have drawn federal and many other state courts into the making of social policy may be seen in such recent decisions of the court as its 1995 ruling that the state's system of financing the public school system of K through 12 was unconstitutional, and its 2001 decision ordering the legislature to raise and spend $563 million to correct the deficiencies in the school repair and new construction program, a decision provoking angry criticism from a number of legislators.

In addition, the state supreme court was the pivotal figure in settling sharp disputes between the legislature and the governor over the scope of the latter's veto power under the state constitution. Viewed from a different perspective, the state's highest judicial body has been a markedly progressive institution. The justices have made notable efforts in recent years to dispel their "ivory tower" image in peoples' minds by speaking more in public, lecturing to students about how the court works, granting interviews to the press and, in general, presenting their "human" side. Their decisions have been the objects of vitriolic humor. (See Figure 7) In conjunction with its efforts to make people more knowledgeable about its work, the court allows limited television coverage of its proceedings, and has held sessions outside Cheyenne in different communities around the state. In 1990, Chief Justice Walter Urbigkit amended the rules governing procedures in the lower courts to permit trial judges to decide individually whether they will allow still photography or television cameras in their courtrooms.

The Wyoming Supreme Court has strengthened the research and administrative aspects of its work by providing two *staff attorneys* (law clerks) to each justice to assist in identifying and researching the main issues in the cases which are appealed to the court. A

From the Casper Star-Tribune, January 29, 1992, Page A 10

Figure 7

single computer system for all Wyoming courts is in the process of development. Much of the supreme court's constitutional responsibility for administering the entire court system is carried on through the *Board of Judicial Policy and Administration*, which issues rules of practice and procedure for all courts, and is composed of three judges each from the supreme court, the district courts, and the circuit courts. The justices also employ a *court administrator* and staff to handle many of their non-judicial tasks, such as monitoring the operations of the lower courts, budget preparation, statistical analysis of case loads, and purchase of court property. These steps have helped free the court to devote more of its time to deciding cases. The assistance rendered to the court by the policy and administration board, the court administrator and the staff attorneys is a reflection of the increasing dependence of public officials throughout state government in Wyoming and other states upon adequate support staff to carry out the tasks practice of public administration.

The foregoing review of the Wyoming court structure should make it clear that the long-term stability of the higher courts has in fact been accompanied by a good deal of experimentation with the minor state courts. Tinkering with the statutory and constitutional details of jurisdiction, procedure, and judicial pay and qualifications occurs in most sessions of the legislature, and is one dimension of the more or less constant quest to fine-tune the agencies of government to serve better the requirements of the people who use them. Even the broader characteristics of the four-tier structure described above manifest this dynamic quality, as is shown by the growth of the minor state courts during the 1980s, as well as the legislature's funding of "drug court" programs for substance abusers and authorization for the creation of "teen" courts in recent sessions. Meanwhile, for the moment at least, the long struggle between the opponents and advocates of a more unified and centralized court system in Wyoming seems to have shifted decisively in favor of the latter. Gone are the locally-funded and locally-oriented justice of the peace courts, to be replaced by circuit courts, the salaries and operating expenses of which now are fully picked up by the state, and which may retain some link to the past in the form of non-lawyer "magistrates." Administrative control, including budgets for all courts except those on the municipal level, and rules of procedure for every court in the state, is now exercised by an agency which exists at the pleasure of the five justices on the state supreme court. The enticements of court modernization have proven irresistible.

THE HIRING, FIRING, AND RETIRING OF JUDGES

Choosing the Judges

How to select the men and women who staff the courts is one of the most baffling problems confronting our system of constitutional government. The issue essentially boils down to the tension between judicial independence and judicial accountability. We want judges who are not only competent and hard-working, but who will decide questions submitted to them according to the *law*, nothing else. Even though we may be ambiguous about how much influence factors such as money, popularity, lobbying, or other pressures should affect the legislative and executive branches of government, they are regarded as intolerable, possibly even illegal, when calculated to influence the outcome of specific court cases. Judges take an oath vowing to resolve conflicts according to the Constitution and other laws of the land. For this reason, great care must be taken to insure that the judicial branch of government is designed in such a way as to facilitate the freedom of the judges to pursue their tasks without being threatened by external attempts to manipulate the judicial process for political ends. For example, one of the devices inserted in the federal constitution to help secure judicial *in-dependence* is the unique protection judges enjoy from having their salaries cut while they are in office—a tactic which might otherwise be resorted to by politicians who want to strike back at the judges because of disagreements with their interpretations of law. Plainly, the same sensitivity to the dangers of political interference must be maintained when the question is how to pick the judges. What selection method would maximize the probability that those chosen for the bench will really be able to act free from improper influence by outside forces?

The trouble is, that independence is not the only value we cherish in judges. In addition to the virtues of competence and diligence, surely the quality which really complicates matters is that of *accountability*. In our democratic system of government, public policy is supposed to rest upon the consent of the governed. All public officials—judges are no exception—are accountable for what they do and fail to do, to the *people* who have the ultimate authority to remove them from office when they no longer enjoy popular support. Responsiveness of government officials to the public will is thus a means for gauging how democratic a society really is. It also follows that a political system based upon popular consent needs to have within it the procedural mechanisms to assure that leaders who do not respond to the people's wishes can be removed from power in favor of leaders who do respond. Popular elections and limited terms of office are two common examples of devices widely used to help insure accountability of government officials, and for much of American history an incredible variety of state and local officials, including judges, have been regularly held accountable through these mechanisms.

At this point, the dilemma begins to take shape. Independence and accountability are values to be realized in designing a method of choosing judges. But how to facilitate both, when they potentially contradict one another? By designing a selection method which stresses independence (e.g. a system in which judges, once appointed, serve in office for life), accountability may be endangered. By underscoring accountability to the people (e.g. through providing that judges must be elected by vote of the people every two years), a judge's fear of loss of popular support at the polls may seriously undermine his or her sense of independence. It becomes evident that neither value can be fully realized without sacrificing the integrity of the other. If both are truly wanted in deciding upon a judicial selection system, the question of *how much weight* is to be given to each of these (as well as other) values must first be settled, and then the plan which best incorporates the terms of the settlement will have to be mapped out. As it hap-

pens, these matters are far from easy get people to agree upon, and if there are such agreements, they may not endure for very long.

The methods which the people of Wyoming have employed to choose their judges have differed according to the evolving popular understanding of where the balance among these qualities expected of the judicial branch should be struck at any particular time, and depending upon what level of the courts was being looked at. Until 1972, the dominant mode of selection was through direct popular election, with judges at all but the lowest level running on a nonpartisan ballot. The non-partisan feature of judicial elections was adopted in 1915 as a reform of the previous system in which candidates for judicial office ran as Republicans, Democrats, Populists, etc. Reformers then had argued that this mixed the courts with party politics and threatened their role of being above politics. In 1972, a refurbished version of this criticism became the central theme of a well-organized campaign to convince Wyomingites to move even further away from popular election of judges. This campaign, led by the state bar and supported by most of the state's political leadership, contended that the method pioneered by Missouri in 1940 and adopted by several states since then, should be introduced in Wyoming in order to take the courts "out of politics" completely (Horan, 1972: 9). A constitutional amendment incorporating a slightly modified version of the "Missouri Plan" (also known as the "Merit Selection and Retention" Plan) was adopted by the voters of the state in 1972. The Plan governs how judges of the supreme court, the district courts, and circuit courts are to be chosen. Judicial selection for other courts was not affected by the change. In operation for 30 years now, this new process of picking judges is set in motion whenever a vacancy occurs—no matter what the reason—on any of the courts covered by the Plan. The selection process consists of four stages:

1. Nomination: Exclusive power to nominate persons to fill a vacancy belongs to the *Wyoming Judicial Nominating Commission*. This body, created in 1972, is made up of seven members: the *chief justice* of the Wyoming Supreme Court (who is chairperson, but who may vote only in the case of a tie among the other members); three practicing *attorneys* elected by the membership of the Wyoming State Bar; and three *non-lawyers* appointed by the governor of Wyoming. With the exception of the chief justice, no holders of public office or political party officers are eligible to serve on the commission. Their terms are for four years, again excepting the chief justice. The state compensates them for expenses incurred in the course of their duties, but otherwise

there is no salary attached to the position. The ultimate task of the Judicial Nominating Commission is to draw up a list of three names who are to be recommended to fill the vacancy. How the commission arrives at these three names is up to the members; in practice, they have fulfilled this function of judicial recruitment by inviting applications from interested and qualified persons, as well as encouraging others to recommend names of persons to the commission, which in turn contacts these individuals to ascertain whether they are interested in applying for the vacant judicial post. The commission looks into the background, qualifications, experience, and references of promising applicants and, as mentioned above, draws up a list of the three best qualified candidates. If the commission is split in its deliberations, decisions are made by majority rule. This list of three (which prior to 1995 was not made public) is then transmitted to the governor.

2. Appointment: The governor's role in the selection process is to appoint one of the persons named on the list to fill the vacant judicial post for a *minimum* of one year in office. Who the governor picks from among the three names is solely up to him, but his choice is confined to the three persons recommended by the Judicial Nominating Commission. Delay for more than 30 days, or outright refusal by the governor to select any name, simply transfers the right to fill the vacancy (again, from the list of three) to the chief justice. In fact, no governor has ever let the appointment be made by the chief justice. On July 25, 1995, Governor Jim Geringer became the first Wyoming chief executive to release to the press the names of all three persons on a list recommended to him by the judicial nominating commission for an expected vacancy on the 7th District Court.

3. Retention: The governor's appointee serves in office for at least one full year, after which, at the next November general election, the new judge or justice must be "retained" in office by a majority vote of the people of his or her jurisdiction—circuit, judicial district, or (in the case of supreme court justices) the entire state. The voters are simply asked to mark "Yes" or "No" on the question, "Shall Justice (Judge)____ of the _____ Court be retained in office for the term as prescribed by law?" There are no competing candidates or political party labels on the ballot; the incumbent simply runs on the record she or he has established during her or his time in office up to that point (i.e. her or his "merit"). If a majority of the electorate of her or his jurisdiction voting on the question vote "Yes," then the incumbent stays on the bench for a full term (four years, six years, or eight years, depending on which court is involved). If a majority of those answering the question mark "No," the incum-

bent must relinquish office the following January, and a vacancy is created on the court which triggers the selection process all over again.

4. Further Retention: As a judge nears completion of a full term in office, he or she must decide whether he or she wants to serve another term. If yes, he or she must be retained again by the voters of her or his jurisdiction in the kind of election described above in Stage 3. If the voters retain him or her, the incumbent stays in office for another full term. If the incumbent opts not to stand for another term of office, or is rejected by the voters, a vacancy is created in the post which is filled like any other vacancy, i.e. by proceeding through Stages 1 - 3 described above.

How has this system worked in practice? In Wyoming, the results thus far seem to be favorable. Judicial appointees under the system have been of high calibre, and were generally applauded by the legal community from which they were drawn. Pre-retention polls of attorneys who have appeared in these judges' courtrooms reveal, for the most part, very positive attitudes toward the judges' abilities, work habits, and temperaments.

The four Wyoming governors who served between 1972 and 2002 also praised this judicial selection method. An analysis of the partisan affiliations (which, in theory at least, are not supposed to play a role in the selection process) of Governor Hathaway's, Governor Herschler's, Governor Sullivan's and Governor's Geringer's appointees to the Wyoming Supreme Court and to the district courts reveals no obvious attempts to subvert the merit selection process in a partisan fashion. (See Table 2.) As for experience under the retention election phase of the system, a total of 112 retention elections have been conducted for district and supreme court judges since 1972, and in nearly all of them the incumbents were retained with heavy majority "Yes" votes. Four of the five noteworthy exceptions were district court judges John P. Ilsley of Sheridan in 1974, Paul A. Liamos of Newcastle in 1984, James N. Wolfe of Sheridan in 1992, and D. Terry Rogers of Jackson in 2002, each of whom was rejected by the voters of his district. The fifth exception was the unprecedented defeat of supreme court justice Walter C. Urbigkit, Jr. in 1992. Justice Urbigkit was seeking a second full term in office, but was rejected by a 51.5 percent "no" vote of the statewide electorate after a "campaign" marked by charges that he favored the rights of criminals over the rights of their victims.

Partisan Affiliation of Appointees to Wyoming District Courts and Supreme Court, 1973-2003, by Governor

	District Courts		Supreme Court	
	Democrats	Republicans	Democrats	Republicans
Governor Stan Hathaway (1973-75)(Republican)	1	4	1	2
Governor Ed Herschler (1975-87)(Democrat)	7	10	5	1
Governor Mike Sullivan* (1987-1995)(Democrat)	4	5	1	1
Governor Jim Geringer** (1995-2003) (Republican)	1	4	0	3

*Governor Sullivan's district court appointees also included two independents, for a total of 11 appointments by him to the district bench.

**Governor Geringer's district court appointees also included 3 judges whose party affiliations are unknown, for a total of 8 appointments by him to the district bench.

Table 2

There is a problematic side to all this, however. Experience with judicial retention elections wherever they are used (21 states currently hold these kinds of elections for at least some of their judges) demonstrates that incumbents almost inevitably roll up landslide "Yes" votes. Seldom is a judge defeated, even if a bar poll shows serious lack of support by the lawyers who practiced before him or her (Jenkins, 1973). Retention elections, by their very nature, confer such tremendous advantages upon an incumbent judge ("I haven't heard anything bad about him, so he must be o.k." is a familiar explanation for voting "Yes") (Griffin and Horan, 1983), that only very well-organized opposition in the right set of circumstances can succeed in convincing the electorate to actually turn a judge out of office (Horan and Griffin, 1989). Moreover, survey and voting data from past judicial retention elections in Wyoming and other states show that sizable numbers of voters simply skip over the portion of the ballot listing the retention questions ("My vote won't make any difference anyhow" is frequently heard); of those who do vote, up to half know nothing at all about the record and qualifications of the judges whose fate they are deciding (Griffin and Horan, 1979). Thus, while "merit retention" has succeeded in sheltering judicial independence from the fickleness of the electorate, it is an open question how

effectively retention elections provide for the accountability of judges to the people.

The other issue concerns whether the four-stage process described above really takes judicial selection "out of politics," as its supporters contend, and bases it upon merit alone. Leaving aside the question of how "merit" is to be defined, there is some justification that "politics" has been reduced or eliminated in many situations where the Missouri Plan is in use. Certainly in Wyoming very little money has been reported spent by judges in the course of seeking retention in office, unless they encountered public opposition, which is also rare (Griffin and Horan, 1983). On the other hand, the absence of election politics does not automatically mean that other kinds of politics have been excluded. Studies of the functioning of the Missouri Plan in other states indicate there is still plenty of room for partisan politics to creep in, such as by cueing governors in their choice of candidates from the list of nominees he or she receives (Alfini, 1974). Bar politics may enter into the process as well, particularly when lawyers who vote for the lawyer-members of the nominating commission have to decide between competing candidates for a vacancy on the commission (Jacob, 1984: 65-66, 126). Finally, retention-type elections do not guarantee no-need-to-campaign or spend large sums of money on behalf of judicial incumbents. The retention elections of three justices of the California Supreme Court in 1986 were accompanied by the expenditure of enormous amounts of money by groups which effectively used the media to persuade the voters to unseat those justices because of their participation in anti-death penalty decisions of the court (Wold and Culver, 1987).

Judicial Retirement, Discipline, and Removal

How the law deals with the thorny issues arising out of the problem of unfitness for judicial office provides another dimension to the quest of how to reconcile judicial independence with accountability. Certainly those on the bench who persist in behavior which is incompatible with or violative of the duties of their office must be called into account. The black robe cannot be permitted to shield the corrupt or incompetent judge any more than a uniform can excuse the unfitness of a ranking military officer for command. Society needs to set expected standards of judicial conduct and the mechanism through which those accused of violating those standards can either be subjected to the appropriate disciplinary action, including removal from office, or else have their names and reputations cleared. Simultaneously, however, the grounds for taking disciplinary measures against

judges have to be defined clearly enough so that they do not become a convenient way of penalizing them for making unpopular decisions; in addition, the procedures for enforcing judicial conduct standards should assure fair treatment, and not be susceptible to merely railroading members of the bench out of office.

How are these critical issues in the administration of justice handled in this state? One way of approaching the problem is through the process of *impeachment*. The Wyoming Constitution subjects judges of the supreme court, district courts, and circuit courts to the legislative power of impeachment and removal from office for "high crimes and misdemeanors, or malfeasance in office" (Wyoming Constitution, art. 3, secs. 17-18; art. 5, sec. 1). In this process, which is similar to that provided in the federal and most states' constitutions, the lower house of the state legislature may, by majority vote, "impeach" judicial and executive officers for committing the listed offenses. Accused officials are then tried by the state senate, with all 30 senators sitting as a "court of impeachment." If two-thirds of the whole Senate vote to convict on any of the impeachment charges, the judge or other officer is removed from office, and may be prohibited from ever holding state office again.

The most significant comment that can be made about the impeachment process is that it has never been used in the state's history, and for good reasons. The process is slow, typically commencing with a lengthy legislative committee investigation, hearings, witnesses' testimony, floor vote, etc., which is then repeated in the other house. When the Senate conducts a trial, other legislative business has to be put off. Politicians tend to be uncomfortable acting as judges, and prefer to see the matter handled in some other way. Perhaps the most serious defect of impeachment as a method for dealing with unfit judges, however, is that the grounds for impeachment seem to be limited to behavior defined by law as criminally punishable, such as taking a bribe or illegally evading income taxes. In reality, criminal behavior is only the tip of the iceberg of judicial unfitness, which is more likely to show up in the form of unethical behavior (such as conducting a trial in a partisan fashion), intemperate actions (e.g. rudeness, bullying, etc.) toward people in court, neglect of duty, chemical addiction, incompetence, or disability. These can be serious problems for the administration of justice, but solving them by impeachment may not only be grossly excessive, but plainly unfair in some instances.

Another approach to the issue of how to deal with the problem of unfit judges is to forestall it by making judges retire when they reach a certain age. On the presumption that advancing age and the onset of senility are the root causes of much of the behavior associated with unfitness in office, more than half the states, including Wyoming, have enacted compulsory retirement age laws for their judges. In this state, judges must step down when they reach the age of 70 (Wyoming Constitution, art. 5, sec. 5).[3] Mandatory retirement at a certain age is a familiar requirement of numerous jobs in America, private as well as public. Although many people think there are good justifications for it, blanket enforcement of such a policy without regard for the individual abilities or wishes of those subject to it is arguably unfair discrimination against older persons; nonetheless, court decisions in most states have upheld the principle of compulsory retirement age policies, at least as applied to judges.

Concurrent with the adoption of the Missouri Plan for choosing judges, Wyoming also supplemented its constitutional arrangements for disciplining them. During the past 30 years nearly all the states have set up special judicial conduct organizations with the responsibility for dealing with "problem" judges. In Wyoming, between 1972 and 1996, this organization was known as the Judicial Supervisory Commission. A constitutional amendment in 1996 renamed it the *Commission on Judicial Conduct and Ethics* and revamped its membership and procedures. It consists of three resident *attorneys* (chosen by the governing body of the Wyoming State Bar); six resident *non-lawyers* (selected by the governor, with the consent of the state senate); and three active *judges* (not on the supreme court)(elected by all the active, full-time judges in the state). These twelve members serve for three-year terms. All complaints or allegations of misconduct or unfitness on the part of any Wyoming judge or justice are submitted to the Commission on Judicial Conduct and Ethics, which has the initial task of screening out those complaints which have no substance. Matters which warrant further commission investigation may become the subject of hearings and, if appropriate, a recommendation to the supreme court by the commission for specific disciplinary actions against the judicial officer concerned. The disciplinary measures available include forced retirement (in instances where a judge is afflicted with a permanent, seriously incapacitating disability, e.g. Alzheimer's disease), censure, and suspension or removal from office. While it is up to the supreme court to actually invoke the more serious sanctions, the commission itself may impose lesser forms of discipline, such as "private" censure. The grounds for which disciplinary action can be imposed go far beyond conduct which is criminally punishable. In addition to disability, they include: willful misconduct in office, willful and persistent failure to perform one's official duties, habitual intemperance, and a catchall category labeled "conduct prejudicial to the administration of justice that brings the judicial office into disrepute" (Wyoming Constitution, art. 5, sec. 6 (f)).

How satisfactorily has the Commission on Judicial Conduct and Ethics performed its role of overseeing the conduct of judges in the state? Although the commission device is a vast improvement over the antiquated impeachment process, an overall evaluation of the agency is difficult to arrive at because so little is known about its substantive work. Its predecessor, the Judicial Supervisory Commission, handled complaints behind a veil of secrecy until the point at which it filed a disciplinary recommendation with the supreme court. If the complaint was dismissed at some earlier stage, it was never made public. From 1989 to the present, the commission and its successor have compiled annual statistical reports of its activities showing numbers of verified complaints filed and their disposition (most are dismissed without further action), but little else. Knowledgeable sources indicate that the commission tried to resolve complaints which had some basis in fact by informal negotiation, such as "talking to" the judge concerned and getting him or her to see there was a problem that needed correction; that was often enough to "take care of" the situation. The explanation for the confidentiality of the supervisory commission's work rested upon the need to protect the reputations of those judges who became the targets of baseless complaints; the result, however, was that the public was kept "in the dark" about how well in other respects the commission was doing its job (Griffin and Horan, 1980; Horan and Griffin, 1989). No judge has ever been permanently removed or forced to retire as a result of a formal recommendation by the Judicial Supervisory Commission. Lesser sanctions were imposed upon a district court judge (censure) and a county court judge (suspended removal). In both instances, alcoholism played a prominent role in the charges brought against the judges. Although this agency was reborn with a new name and expanded membership as well as more elaborate procedures in 1996, the newer version labors behind the same veil of secrecy that characterized its predecessor's work.[4]

JUDICIAL PROCEDURE - THE COURTS IN ACTION [5]

The sections you have just read outline the court system in Wyoming. The question which comes to mind now, is "how does it all work?" The process by which the courts resolve particular cases brought before them varies according to whether the case is either a criminal or a civil case.

Development of a Criminal Case to Trial

Investigation and Arrest.

For the most part a court begins its work on a criminal case after the police or the prosecuting attorney have filed a *complaint* or *information.* The only significant exception occurs when a *search warrant* is requested in the course of an investigation. A circuit court judge or magistrate may issue a warrant to permit law enforcement officers to search for particular property if the judge is satisfied that there is *probable cause* to believe that the property to be searched constitutes evidence that a crime has been committed or that a particular person has committed a crime. As the criminal investigation proceeds, the prosecuting attorney files a complaint or information with the circuit court judge or magistrate, or the city attorney files a complaint in municipal court. If the complaint or information establishes probable cause to believe that a particular person has committed a crime, the judge or magistrate issues an *arrest warrant* authorizing that person to be taken into custody.

Initial Appearance

Upon arrest, the accused is brought before the circuit court judge or magistrate as soon as possible. The judge informs the accused of the complaint against him or her and one's rights under the law. In all cases where conviction could result in a jail or prison term, or death, the accused has the right to be represented by a lawyer (one's own lawyer, or - if unable to pay for this - then a lawyer provided by the state). One may waive one's right to a lawyer and prefer to act as one's own attorney, but to do so is generally an exceedingly dubious course of action, and is best left for those infractions (such as an overtime parking ticket) where the impact of losing would have insignificant consequences for the individual. The accused also have the right to remain silent, to be warned that anything they say may be used against them, and that in serious criminal cases, they have the right to trial by jury. The judge also sets bail at the initial appearance. Release pending trial is often granted simply on the accused's "personal recognizance," but if the judge believes that under the circumstances of the case such a release would not reasonably insure the appearance of the accused when required, he may insist that the accused post a certain sum of money in order to guarantee appearance. Bail may be denied altogether (as in death penalty cases) or set at so high a figure that it is practically denied, if the judge believes this is necessary to insure appearance.

Preliminary Hearing

All felonies normally are tried in the district court. In these cases, the defendant is entitled to a *preliminary hearing* before a circuit court judge or a magistrate. The function of the preliminary hearing is to determine if there is probable cause to believe that a crime has been committed, and that the accused committed it. This stage of the process is designed to prevent the possibility of an unfounded prosecution, and has largely taken over the role played by a grand jury indictment, a procedure now used very rarely in Wyoming. If the circuit court judge or magistrate is satisfied that probable cause has been established, he or she orders the defendant bound over to the district court for arraignment and trial. If the evidence submitted does not establish probable cause, the judge dismisses the complaint and orders the defendant released, although the prosecutor may later charge the defendant again with the same offense if he or she has sufficient evidence to support the charge.

Arraignment

The next step in the process is arraignment. The arraignment occurs in the court in which the trial itself will take place, generally district court for a felony, circuit court or magistrate for a misdemeanor. At the arraignment, the defendant enters a formal *plea*, a critical step which should be taken only after considering the advice of one's lawyer. If the defendant pleads guilty, the judge must be satisfied that the guilty plea is voluntary, that the defendant understands the consequences of such a plea (including loss of the right to a trial), and that there is a factual basis for the guilty plea. If the court accepts the guilty plea, the judge either imposes *sentence* then and there, or else schedules sentencing for a later date, possibly following a pre-sentence investigation by a probation officer. If the judge refuses to accept the guilty plea, a plea of not guilty is entered for the defendant. In the case of a plea of not guilty, the judge will schedule the case for trial at a future date.

Most criminal cases never reach the stage of a full-fledged trial. If they did, the court system would quickly break down under the weight of the sheer numbers of cases which enter the criminal justice system. Many of these cases are dismissed during their early stages, either informally by the prosecutor, or by the court. Those that are not dismissed are typically settled through *plea-bargaining,* a behind-the-scenes process of negotiation between prosecutor and the defendant's lawyer, the upshot of which is an agreement by the prosecutor to reduce the number or gravity of the charges against the defendant, and/or to recommend leniency in the sentence to be imposed, in exchange for a plea of guilty by the defendant. Each side (except possibly the victim) gets something out of the deal, and the court is spared the time and expense of a trial. Only the cases which survive this filtering-out process go on to trial, and they are relatively few in number.

Development of a Civil Case to Trial

Pleadings

The initial papers in a civil case are called *pleadings*. A lawsuit begins when a *plaintiff* files a *complaint* in court against another person, known as the *defendant*, alleging that the plaintiff's rights have been infringed by some wrongful act of the defendant, and requesting the court to order the defendant to pay the plaintiff appropriate compensation for the infringement. The complaint must be accompanied by payment of a filing fee to the clerk of the court; this is a sum of money fixed by law equivalent to a "user fee" payable by those who wish to employ the machinery of the court to pursue their private claims. Acting upon the complaint, the judge issues a *summons* to the defendant describing the complaint and requiring that it be answered within a certain number of days. Failure to answer the complaint within the time allotted may result in the court's awarding a *summary judgement* to the plaintiff; thus, ignoring the court summons can cause the defendant to forfeit the lawsuit without a fight. The defendant's answer essentially argues why the complaint is factually and/or legally without merit. It may be accompanied by a *counterclaim* (suing the plaintiff in return) or a *cross-claim* (alleging responsibility for the matter belongs to someone else), to which the plaintiff may in turn file his or her own *answer*.

Discovery

The fact-finding done by both sides before the trial includes the important process of *discovery*. Discovery usually involves securing information relevant to the case from the other party in the lawsuit. This process can be carried out by an *oral deposition* (a sworn statement or testimony, recorded verbatim and signed); by written questions (called *interrogatories*), by physical or mental examination, or by requests to produce documents or other tangible evidence. Discovery may proceed on any relevant item except "privileged" material (such as information transmitted in husband-wife, doctor-patient, priest-penitent, or lawyer-client relationships).

Pre-Trial Conference

In complex civil cases, the court or either party may call for a *pre-trial conference* in order to discuss matters which may save time in the actual trial. In this conference both parties may agree, for example, to simplify the issues in dispute, to agree on particular facts, or to limit the number of witnesses. Following this, the court will issue an order summing up the actions and agreements of the conference. As with criminal cases, the vast majority of civil cases do not actually go to trial. They are settled "out of court" through a slow process of negotiation and bargaining between the parties and their lawyers (sometimes with the informal assistance of the trial judge) during the preparatory stages of the lawsuit described above, a frequently drawn-out period where exhaustion, uncertainty, and mounting legal costs may induce even the most righteous of litigants to call it a day and compromise their claims without resort to a full-fledged trial and the appeals which may follow after that.

Trial

The trial itself is largely the same in both criminal and civil cases, and in both district courts and the local courts. In a formal process refereed by a judge, each side presents its argument, evidence, and testimony, and then the judge and jury (or the judge alone, if sitting without a jury) must decide the case. Wyoming law strongly protects the right to trial by jury in both criminal and civil cases; most trials could involve a jury if either of the parties demanded it. In practice, however, the majority of both criminal and civil trials do not include juries because of the additional time and expense involved. Juries in felony trials in district court consist of 12 persons; those in other courts and in civil trials contain six persons. The jury is selected from a larger *panel* chosen at the start of a jury *term* lasting six months. Ideally, this larger panel contains a representative cross-section of the people living in that county. Panel members are called to court when a jury trial has been scheduled. In the crucial process known as *voir dire*, the judge and the attorneys in the case examine the panel members in order to select the required number of qualified, impartial and disinterested jurors for that particular case.

The jury is then sworn in and the trial itself commences. After opening statements by both sides, the presentation of evidence begins by the plaintiff, who may call witnesses and introduce exhibits. (In criminal cases, the state is the plaintiff, acting on behalf of the people, and the prosecutor presents the evidence.) The defendant may cross-examine the plaintiff's witnesses. Af-

ter the plaintiff completes his or her presentation, the defendant presents evidence, again with witnesses and exhibits and the opportunity for cross-examination. Following both presentations and closing arguments, the court retires to consider a decision. If the trial is by jury, the judge first explains to the jurors the *legal rules* governing the case, and then sends the jury out to decide the facts of the case, to apply the legal rules to these facts, and to announce their decision in the form of a *verdict*. In criminal cases in Wyoming, jury verdicts must be unanimous. In civil cases, jury verdicts may be less than unanimous if the parties have agreed to a particular percentage. If the trial is by judge alone, the judge decides the facts as well as the legal rules in order to arrive at her or his decision. In accordance with one of the cardinal principles of the Anglo-American legal tradition, conviction in a criminal case must be based upon proof of guilt "beyond a reasonable doubt." This is in contrast to verdicts in civil cases, which need be based only upon which side has been able to show that its claims are supported by "a preponderance of the evidence" in the case.

Sentencing is the next stage in the judicial process if the defendant is found guilty (a not-guilty verdict results in the defendant's release from custody as far as that offense is concerned). Punishments for particular offenses are prescribed generally by statute, but within the minimum and maximum limits set by the legislature, judges frequently have much discretion in sentencing in individual cases. The judge often requests a "pre-sentence investigation" in order to learn more about the defendant and determine a sentence appropriate both to the offense and to the offender. The sentence may include a fine and/or incarceration, or it may include probation or work release if the judge considers it appropriate. In a civil case, the court enters a *judgement* which contains the verdict or decision. Once the judgement is entered, the case may be reopened only by motions for a new trial, to amend the judgement, or by appeal.

Appeal

Wyoming law guarantees the right to appeal in any criminal case, and the trial judge must notify the defendant of this right at the time of sentencing. In civil cases, the right of appeal is qualified by statute, but it still extends broadly. District court decisions are appealed to the supreme court; the decision of a local court is appealed to the district court, and from there to the supreme court—if the supreme court is willing to hear it. In both instances the procedure is similar. An appeal must show that the trial judge wrongly interpreted or applied the legal rules governing the case, and that this prejudiced (significantly affected) the outcome of

the trial. Thus an appeal will not be successful merely by proving that legal errors were made at trial—they must also have been prejudicial errors. Moreover the *facts*, as found by the trial court, are usually of no concern to the appellate court, which is interested in the *law* governing the case.

Except in death penalty cases, where an appeal is automatic, the losing party must file a notice of appeal with the trial court within a set period of time. The party filing the appeal is called the *appellant*; the other party is the *appellee.*. The appellant must file (with the appropriate fee, of course) a "docketing statement" which outlines the issues presented by the appeal and the facts of the case. The appellate court and the appellee are thus made aware of the matters to be considered. Usually the trial court's sentence or civil judgement is "stayed" (delayed) while the appeal is being pursued, and indeed a convicted person may be released on bail during this period. The record of the case is transferred from the trial court to the appellate court. The record includes the case file (pleadings, motions, orders, judgment, etc.) and the transcript of the relevant portions of the trial proceedings. Each party prepares a *brief* containing a statement of the legal issues being presented to the appellate court, and the contentions and arguments (amply supported by citations to case precedents and other legal authorities) which it is hoped will persuade the justices of the higher court. The appellant's brief is filed first, followed by the appellee's. This may lead the appellant to submit a *reply* brief rebutting the points and arguments stated by the appellee, who in turn may come back with a reply brief of his or her own. After reading the briefs, the appellate court may schedule a time for hearing *oral argument* in the case. At oral argument the attorneys summarize their contentions to the court, and the justices have the opportunity to question them on doubtful or unclear aspects of their arguments.

An appeal hearing is thus quite unlike a trial. All five justices are normally present[6] when the Wyoming Supreme Court is in session. The court does not hear cases in "panels" (committees), as is the practice in some appellate courts. (See Fig. 8).

There is no testimony, because there are no witnesses. There is no jury, because the facts are not at issue. The justices alone decide the outcome of the case. The parties to the appeal may or may not be in the courtroom; it is only their attorneys who appear for them at this stage of the case. Although oral argument is publicly the most visible part of the appellate process, the absence of the dramatic features of the trial court usually dampens the interest of the general public in observing appellate court proceedings. Except for the few

The Wyoming Supreme Court as of February, 2003. The members of the Court, from left to right, are: Justice Marilyn S. Kite, Justice Michael Golden, Chief Justice William U. Hill, Justice Larry L. Lehman, and Justice Barton R. Voight

Figure 8

appeals which attract widespread public interest (e.g. the appeal in the famous *Jahnke* homicide case (Jahnke v. State, 1984), the courtroom may be nearly empty of spectators. In fact, since 1987, the supreme court has sought to speed up the appellate process by deciding some appeals on the basis of the written briefs alone, dispensing with oral argument altogether in those cases. In recent years, cases assigned to this "expedited docket" (no oral arguments) have accounted for between 50 and 60 percent of the supreme court's annual opinion production.

Immediately after arguments are heard in a case, the justices adjourn to their conference room on the top floor of the court building where, amidst strict confidentiality (and occasionally heated argument), they discuss the case and vote on how the court should decide it. If the court is split, the majority rules. After the vote, the chief justice assigns one of the justices in the majority the task of preparing the court's written *opinion* in the case. That opinion is then reviewed in draft form by the other justices, who comment on it and may suggest changes. This *draft majority opinion* may then be rewritten to accommodate recommended changes. A justice who feels the majority's decision is wrong may write her or his own *dissenting opinion*, while one who agrees with the majority decision, but for his or her own reasons, may write a *concurring opinion*. Once the majority opinion has

been approved in final form, and any concurring or dissenting opinions are ready, the decision is announced to the public, sent to the parties, and made available to the media. That decision may be to *affirm* the trial court's decision, to *reverse* it, or to *remand* (send the case back to the trial court) with instructions on how to proceed in the case (for example, to hold a new trial). The supreme court's opinions are officially published in the Wyoming Reporter, available in lawyers' offices and many libraries. Unless the supreme court takes the rare step of agreeing to *rehear* its own decision, or the losing party manages to convince the United States Supreme Court to review the case (an uncommon event, and possible only if there is a question of federal law in the case), the decision is final. It thus becomes a precedent binding upon all other agencies and courts in the state. Normally, the appeals process in Wyoming takes a full year to complete, and serious cases may require even longer.

The Wyoming Bench: A Collective Portrait

Inside our courthouses and municipal buildings, the body of rules which make up the substance of Wyoming law are applied and interpreted by identifiable human beings. Despite our tendency to idealize judges as remote, unfeeling people affected by nothing but clear legal principles in carrying out their official duties, they have their own individual characteristics and life experiences which, like other people, impact in varying degrees upon the way they do their work. Who are the 111 men and women who occupy the Wyoming bench at this point in time? Are they representative of Wyomingites generally? Even though judges do not "represent" us in the same way our legislators do, most people would be uneasy at the prospect of having judges who, because of differing backgrounds and experiences, were completely out of touch with the cultural environment of the state. If the judges are different, in what ways are they atypical? Can any changes be detected taking place in the characteristics of the judiciary? Some generalizations are possible.

For one thing, the bench in this state is overwhelmingly male. There are only 18 female judges, and most of them are found at the municipal court level. Marilyn Kite, the first and only woman to serve on the Equality State's supreme court, attained that post in 2000. Only four females have ever held a district court judgeship. In a state where the population is 49.9 percent female, the exceedingly small number of women judges seems anomalous until two facts are taken into account: (1) the ratio of male to female judges is hardly unique to Wyoming; and (2) it has only been in the past 25 years that legal and social discrimination against women in America pursuing legal careers has

eased to the point that female attorneys have been able to realistically aspire to appointment to the bench. The first woman to be admitted to the practice of law in Wyoming was Grace R. Hebard in 1914, only a few decades after the first woman was allowed to practice law anywhere in the United States (1870). Currently, of the female active members of the in-state section of the Wyoming state bar organization (women now make up about 25 percent of the state bar), a substantial number were admitted during the past 15 years, and a large segment of this group have been in practice for less than ten years. If, as seems reasonable, an attorney should have a distinguished record of trial experience before going on the bench, it is not entirely surprising that Wyoming's "Merit Selection" system of choosing judges has yielded only five female higher court appointees in 30 years. Change is surely in the wind, however. The first woman (Sandra Day O'Connor) took her seat on the United States Supreme Court only 22 years ago, and the second (Ruth Bader Ginsburg) was appointed 12 years after that. Today, females constitute about 17 percent of the number of judges on all levels in the United States. Nearly half the students in American law schools are women. Female attorneys have begun to achieve partner status in prestigious law firms. For example, a woman (Janet Reno) headed the U.S. Department of Justice. In this state, they have served in the legislature as well as the Attorney-General of Wyoming (Gay Woodhouse). As the number of women in the legal profession in Wyoming and the nation continues to grow, their numbers in the higher ranks of the judiciary will also increase.

As for the representation of racial and ethnic minorities on the Wyoming bench, the prognosis here is not so optimistic. Racially, Caucasians make up 94 percent of the state's population, there being only very small proportions of Blacks, Hispanics, American Indians, and people of Asian ancestry. There are no members of any of these groups in the state judiciary, and even their num-

bers in the legal profession in Wyoming are minuscule.[7] The problem of under-representation of these groups in the law is nationwide and, despite aggressive efforts on the part of American law schools to recruit more minority students, is very resistant to change. Discriminatory attitudes and socioeconomic conditions which are at the root of the problem have taken shape over centuries, and are not likely to be overcome by a few years of affirmative action alone. (See Figure 9).

In terms of age and experience, the judges of Wyoming's supreme court and district courts are not a very old group.

Sex bias in the court, on the bench

CHEYENNE — Women lawyers undoubtedly encounter sex discrimination in Wyoming courts.

Sexism in legal circles is euphemistically called "gender bias."

Whatever the name, Wyoming is the first state to adopt the American Bar Association's revision of its code interdiction against bias and prejudice.

Wyoming Supreme Court Justice Richard V. Thomas says that lawyers, male or female, don't complain much about anything to judges. But he feels gender bias does exist against women lawyers.

"If you sit down and talk with them, they will tell you that, yes, they do encounter gender bias in Wyoming," Thomas says.

Of course they do. I recall when Sharon Kinnison showed up in U.S. District Court in Cheyenne as the first woman female prosecutor in this district.

A couple of federal marshals were watching from the doorway of the courtroom.

One, whom I will not embarrass by identifying by name, was upset. "Look at her," the marshal said. "She doesn't belong in there."

"Why not?" I demanded.

"It just isn't right," the marshal answered, characteristically inarticulate.

Kinnison went on to become a county judge and did well from all reports. Judge Elizabeth Kail, the first women district judge in Wyoming, has collected anecdotes about the experiences of women attorneys in the state.

One woman lawyer, who joined an older attorney's office after being admitted to practice in Wyoming, found herself the object of his affections.

Joan Barron
Star-Tribune

Whenever the old coot [my description, not Kail's] was leaving on a trip, he would give her a big hug and a kiss on the lips.

It became constant. The young woman lawyer finally realized she had to stay away from him which made it impossible for her to stay in that office.

This same young woman lawyer, who must have been cursed, later hired a researcher who was older and who also taught in a paralegal school.

Whenever they were together in a meeting with a client, this researcher would try to seize control. The young woman lawyer, understandably, found this embarrassing.

In other moments, she also had to tell the guy to quit fondling her.

At least, Kail says, the woman lawyer was in a position to fire the obnoxious researcher.

Another woman lawyer found that a prosecuting attorney who freely turns over all information in criminal trials to men defense lawyers forced her to file motions with the court to get the same information.

The woman lawyer also complained that that two men lawyers once approached her in a courtroom [not in Lander] and pinched her cheeks. Facial cheeks, thank goodness.

Kail's file contains other gender bias incidents that are more subtle.

In these the young women were assumed to be a secretary or a paralegal rather than an attorney or they were referred to as "sweetheart," "honey," or "dear" by other lawyers.

All, Kail says, felt they were excluded by their peers only because they are women.

What about Kail, the role model? She acknowledges that she, too, sometimes feels left out in conversations with men. Her reaction is to assert herself, possibly more than she would normally.

While some women are intensely sensitive to hints of sexism, others are not.

Kail says one woman lawyer who comes from a large family maintains that sexism doesn't bother her; she treats it with humor.

I think Kail handled "the problem" with humor herself and didn't take it all that seriously.

She says that after only about six months on the bench, she bought lunch for all the women lawyers in Lander because she was getting rumors that she was harder on women lawyers than on men.

"It was shocking to me. Shocking. I immediately resented it and then I got to thinking about it and thought maybe it was true," Kail says. "Because I was so used to being alone both when I practiced and on the bench and there weren't women practicing in the old days when I was practicing."

There you go. Even women judges can be accused of gender bias toward women lawyers.

Everybody should lighten up.

Kail says a much larger problem is gender bias against women litigants.

Lynn Hecht Schafran, an attorney and director of the National Judicial Education Program to Promote Equality for Women and Men in the Courts, found wholesale evidence of women being denied equal justice and treatment in the courts.

This inequity is most prevalent in divorce cases and particularly in enforcement of child support awards. Schafran wrote in an article published in Trial magazine.

A judicial decision that affects a woman's economic status and that of her children is far more serious than being patted and called honey.

From the Casper Star-Tribune of January 19, 1992, Page A6

Figure 9

District court judges have served an average of 9 years on the bench, while their median age is 55. The justices of the supreme court have been on the bench for an average of eight years, and their median age is 55. The median age of the entire population of the state is about 32, so in that sense the general middle age of the judiciary, allowing for their earlier years in law school and legal practice, corresponds to the relatively young age of Wyomingites as a whole.

A further connection in this respect occurs in the area of higher education. Nearly 90 percent of the judges on the circuit, district, and supreme courts combined received their law degrees from the University of Wyoming College of Law. All five current members of the supreme court and all 19 district court judges studied law at the university. Three-fourths of all the judges of the courts mentioned above also received their bachelor's degrees from UW. That most judicial personnel received their undergraduate and professional degrees from their state's university may not seem remarkable until one considers that for most of the state's history, those who served on the state's highest court were born and legally trained outside Wyoming; the first Wyoming-educated justice was Glenn Parker, who was appointed to the supreme court in 1955. Until the 1970s, most of the justices had been educated in the East or Midwest (Whynott, 1971: 25-54).

Like all courts in the Anglo-American legal world, the courts of Wyoming are immersed in tradition. The black robes and Latin phrases, the precedents which are cited in deciding cases, and the procedural rights guaranteed to accused persons—all of these manifest the courts' heavy reliance upon the experience of the past in applying the techniques of the law to settle present disputes. But institutions of government, including the courts, have to face forward too, lest in their reverence for tradition, they lose touch with the very society they are designed to serve. The reforms in court organization, judicial selection, judicial discipline, and court administration which have been put into effect since the early 1970s are significant steps in the process of enabling the Wyoming judiciary to better grasp the legal issues of a changing society. How deeply the state courts become involved in the solutions to those problems is apt to be influenced not only by Wyoming's legal tradition, but also by the extent to which these problems are successfully managed by the legislative and executive branches of the state government. The astute observation of de Tocqueville (1956: 126) over a century and a half ago that in America sooner or later every political question turns into a judicial question, has enormous significance for all the courts, state as well as federal.

ENDNOTES

1. In Wyoming, a "felony" is defined as a criminal offense for which the penalty authorized by law includes imprisonment in a state penal institution for more than a year. Wyo. Stat. sec. 5-5-101 (a) (1997).

2. At the request of the town governing authority, and with the permission of the Wyoming Supreme Court, a circuit court judge may also try persons charged with violating town ordinances. Wyo. Stat. sec. 5-5-106 (2000). Under this law, for example, cases of persons accused of exceeding the posted speed limits within the limits of the town of Rock River (which has no municipal court of its own) are tried in the Circuit Court for Albany County, located in Laramie.

3. However, a retired judge may be reassigned to active duty when needed (with his or her consent). The legislature has enacted a law providing for voluntary retirement for judges also.

4. On February 6, 2001, by action of the Judicial Conduct and Ethics Commission and a special supreme court composed of five district court judges, Supreme Court Justice Richard V. Thomas was forced to resign "immediately" for judicial misconduct i.e. consistently failing to circulate on time opinions in cases which had been assigned to him.

5. The material in this section relies heavily upon the booklet "Wyoming's Judicial System," prepared under the supervision of the Supreme Court of Wyoming (Cheyenne, 2002).

6. If for any reason a justice does not participate in deciding a case, the chief justice may assign a retired justice or a district judge to sit in for the absent member.

7. For example, in 2002, approximately twelve Spanish-surnamed persons were listed as resident members of the Wyoming State Bar, an organization which includes all lawyers who practice in the state. Officials of the bar organization knew of only three black lawyers and one American Indian lawyer in the entire state.

CHAPTER 7

NON-STATE GOVERNMENT IN WYOMING

Like parents and their children, states and cities have a love-hate relationship. Local public officials exercise very few powers, implement very few programs, and provide very few services that are not in some way linked to their state or to the national government in Washington, DC. In an effort to better understand these complex relationships and, more specifically, Wyoming local government, Part One of this chapter explores the different units of local government that are sanctioned by the state to manage a variety of public needs. Part Two will look briefly at the government of the Eastern Shoshone and Northern Arapaho Indian tribes of the Wind River Reservation (WRR) in Wyoming.

PART ONE: LOCAL GOVERNMENT IN WYOMING

In 1997 there were more than 87,500 different governments in the United States.[1] This number includes federal (1), state (50), county (3,043), municipal (19,372), township (16,629), special (34,683), and school district (13,726) governments (U.S. Department of Commerce, 1998: 305). These numbers, despite their size, fail to include the more than 500 tribal governments and U.S. territories. Ninety-nine percent of all governments are considered "local," and 654 of these are located in Wyoming.

Often overlooked, local governments play an important role in the American federal system by providing significant administrative capacity for states and by providing important public services to citizens. Many of our most immediate governmental services are provided by local governments including police and fire protection, jails, utilities (water, sewer, gas, electricity), public education, hospitals, trash collection, and weed and pest control - to name only a few.

There are five types of local government in the United States. Three of these are characterized as general-purpose (counties, municipalities, and townships) while two are considered special-purpose (school districts and special purpose districts). Whether general- or special-purpose, all local governments are tightly linked to the states in which they are established. Through a state's constitutional provisions and statutory mandates, each state outlines local government powers and functions, which typically include zoning authority, finance capabilities, electoral processes, and many hiring practices. Legally speaking, units of local government are "creatures of the state" and have only those powers granted to them by the state.[2]

One of the most interesting qualities of local government is how power is organized and arranged. For instance, the formal organizational arrangements used to disperse power in local governments often appears unconventional compared to those arrangements used by states and the national government. Where separation of power and checks and balances are the norm in our states and in Washington, DC, there are several different ways power is arranged at the local level. Examples of these local government structures include those that consolidate the legislative and executive powers into one body (commission form) and others that more closely resemble the parliamentary structures that characterize many European democracies and private cor-

porations where a board of directors hires a professional manager to oversee the administrative affairs of a community (council-manager form).

There are reasons why Wyomingites might find the intricacies of local government alien. In part, the media pays scant attention to this level of government. Despite their large numbers and the necessary services they provide, local governments labor in relative obscurity. The media tends to concentrate on national issues while generally ignoring local events. The result of this media vacuum is that very few Wyomingites know the names of their county commissioners, or members of their city council, school board, or water and sewer district, let alone do they understand the powers associated with these organizations. Despite this fact, many Americans believe that local government is more democratic, more responsive to their needs, and more efficient and less corrupt than national government in Washington, D.C. (Dye and Ziegler, 1993: 358).

In general, local governments are created not only in response to changes in population (e.g., citizens move outside city boundaries but, later, realize that they miss the services that an incorporated city can provide and decide to incorporate themselves into a city once again) but for political reasons as well. For instance, the boundaries of local governments, particularly special districts, are often drawn to gain political power. Some of the most important political powers include the ability to tax and charge fees, to issue debt, and to acquire private land through the use of eminent domain. Counties and municipalities can, through zoning processes, define citizenship requirements for their locale by determining what types of structures can be built within a particular jurisdiction (Burns, 1994: 7-9; 117). Thus, the drawing of local government boundaries has much more to do than simply providing services to a needy population. These decisions can have implications for political power as well.

These multiple jurisdictional boundaries often create confusing patterns of accountability for citizens. For example, neighbors who live in the same county and who vote for the same county commissioners may, simultaneously, live in different school or irrigation districts. Thus, close neighbors may contend with separate government regulations, tax rates, political issues, and personalities (Burns, 1994: 9-12). It is not uncommon in Wyoming that different communities, often divided by nothing more than an alley, have access to different services, attend different schools, pay different taxes and fees, play by different electoral rules, and deal with different elected officials.

Local politics, too, can be very different from national politics in both positive and negative respects. Given the immediacy of issues and the easy access to elected officials, local politics can be very personal. It is not uncommon in Wyoming for a mayor or city manager to be approached by an angry constituent in a video rental store who has the urgent demand that a pothole be repaired or that something be done about a neighbor's barking dog.

Some Wyomingites are concerned about the lack of accountability that can occur and the needless duplication of effort that a system of multiple governments can create. An even greater potential problem is the way that multiple governments can be manipulated to serve the needs of the local elites. Though local governments are subject to open meeting requirements, they suffer from a nation-wide problem in that private interests are often portrayed as public concerns (for example, a law that gets proposed by a member of city council that requires all public parking lots be paved in order to keep dust to a minimum may really be a ploy to get a neighbor's business to pave their lot because it detracts from the aesthetics of their own business). Furthermore, because only a small number of individuals are involved in decision-making processes a large number of decisions affecting the community can be made in private with little public input (Dye, 1994: 109-117).

On a more positive note, the dispersion of political power throughout a system of multiple governments can protect citizens from arbitrary government action. Here, one benefit of a pluralistic system is that by creating many opportunities for citizens to participate, the system is made more democratic and accountable. These multiple governments coupled with numerous opportunities for participation allow for many "eyes" to keep watch over important community interests. In the end, whether viewed in a positive or negative light, these multiple local governments generally perform specific and often necessary functions that the state or federal government cannot or will not provide.

Financing Local Government

Funding is critical to all units of local government. We, therefore, begin our discussion of county, municipal, special and school district governments with a short introduction to the different mechanisms that are used to finance Wyoming's local governments. Some of the most important funding sources include a variety of taxes (property, sales, excise, and severance) and intergovernmental transfers (grants, PILT, and mineral royalties).

There have been property taxes in the United States since colonial times when levies were made on distinct types of property. Toward the end of the 19th Century a general property tax emerged and was applied to three specific classes of property: real (property such as land and buildings), tangible (property that has some intrinsic value - cars, boats, jewelry - and that is also moveable), and intangible (stocks and bonds).

Revenue generated by property taxes is very important to local governments in Wyoming where, on average, it accounts for approximately 50 percent of the income that local governments collect. This amount can be much higher for the mineral-rich counties of the state. All property in Wyoming is taxable, except as prohibited by the U.S. and Wyoming Constitutions, or that which is specifically exempted by state statute.

A property tax is an ad valorem tax, which means it is based on the value of the property. Wyoming has a three tier system of ad valorem property taxes: Tier I - minerals are assessed at their full market value; Tier II - industrial property is assessed at 11.5 percent of its fair market value; and Tier III - home and commercial property (including agricultural) that is assessed at 9.5 percent of its fair market value. A person's tax bill is based on a "mill levy." A mill is 1/10th of one cent, which means that a taxpayer owning property with an assessed value of $1,000.00 will owe $1.00 in taxes (.001 x 1,000 = 1.00). Maximum mill levies for counties, municipalities, special districts, and school districts are set by the Wyoming legislature. The average property tax levy in 2002 statewide (excluding municipalities) was 63.752 mills, while the average tax levy for municipalities was 72.855 mills (Wyoming State Dept. of Revenue, October 2002). In Wyoming, counties are the units of government that are required to collect property taxes and then, where required by law, redistribute funds to other units of government located within its jurisdiction. (More on counties later in this chapter.)

Another important source of revenue for local governments is the sales tax. A sales tax is a tax levied on the sale and use of goods and services. Sales taxes are a relatively recent phenomenon that developed in response to the decline of property tax revenues and the budget deficits that occurred during the Great Depression. Mississippi imposed the nation's first state sales tax in 1932. Since then the sales tax has increasingly become one of the most important sources of revenue for state and local governments (as of 2002 only five states - Alaska, Delaware, Montana, New Hampshire and Oregon - do not have some form of sales tax). The state of Wyoming has a four percent state sales tax that it uses to help fund state government.

Many states (37 in 2001) allow local governments to levy their own sales tax. In Wyoming, counties can levy an additional one percent sales tax for general operations and another one percent for facilities construction. The voters of a county must approve the operations tax, called a "fifth penny." The fifth penny can be renewed every four years either by voters, which is more common, or by the county commissioners. The facilities tax, or "sixth penny," must also be approved by the voters of a county and can only be used to fund special projects like roads, jails, or libraries. Once the special project is completed the sixth penny tax is automatically dropped.

In addition to the two percent in sales taxes that a county can levy, municipalities can also charge up to four percent in lodging taxes. A lodging tax is a tax levied on services often associated with tourism and travel (for example, an additional tax added to the cost of a hotel room). Revenue generated by a lodging tax is often earmarked so that it can only be used to advertise and promote the local tourist industry, which is the case in Wyoming. Despite its narrow use, the lodging tax is an important source of revenue in areas that have major tourist attractions.

Excise taxes are also used to fund state and local expenditures. Excise taxes are imposed on the sale of particular goods and commodities. The structure of excise taxes closely resembles that of sales taxes, though with more specific exemptions. There are two kinds of excise taxes - sumptuary and benefits-based. A sumptuary or "sin" tax seeks to discourage consumption of products considered to be unhealthy or unsafe both for the consumer and for the public as a whole. For example, Wyoming imposes a tax of sixty cents on the sale of each pack of cigarettes sold in the state (in addition to the regular state and local sales tax). On the other hand, benefits-based excise taxes operate as a quasi-price for a public good and are intended to finance some government endeavor by charging those who benefit from the activity. Gasoline taxes, which often finances road construction and maintenance, are excellent examples of this type of tax. In 2002, Wyoming levies fourteen cents on every gallon of gas sold in the state. A significant part of the revenue generated by cigarette and gasoline taxes is returned to local governments.

A severance tax, on the other hand, is a charge that is levied by the state on natural resources, such as oil, gas, and coal at the time they are extracted - or "severed" - from the earth. Wyoming has one of the nation's highest severance taxes, and is a very significant source of income for the state. It is also an important, albeit indirect, source of funding for local governments. A portion of the revenue generated by Wyoming's severance tax is deposited in the Permanent Wyoming Mineral Trust Fund (PWMTF). Local governments can apply to the state for loans from the PWMTF. A variety of other state accounts, such as those managed by the Wyoming Water Development Commission (WWDC), receive money from the severance tax. The WWDC oversees development of major water transmission projects. State funding of these projects allows local governments in Wyoming to provide much needed basic services without requiring imposition of additional taxes to pay for them.

Local governments also earn significant revenues by issuing different licenses and by imposing user charges. Types of licenses include franchise licenses to providers of local telephone, cable television, and gas and electricity services, liquor licenses, business licenses, and automobile and bicycle licenses. Local governments also generate money by charging fees for the services they provide. Common fees include those made for sewers, trash pickup, mosquito control, operation of sanitary landfills, and use of recreation facilities such as swimming pools, golf courses, and recreation centers.

The federal government also transfers significant sums of money to local governments, primarily in the form of grants-in-aid. Federal appropriations tend to be transmitted to local governments in two ways, either by categorical or block grants. A categorical grant is a competitive form of federal financial aid that is designed to fund a specific project or program. Since Congress has more control over their use, categorical grants have been a popular way for the federal government to transfer aid to local governments. Block grants, on the other hand, are funds given to local governments for more general purposes, such as education and transportation, with fewer strings attached. Block grants are popular with local governments because this funding mechanism provides them with more spending discretion.

In addition to grants, counties also receive federal funds in the form of Payment in Lieu of Taxes (PILT) monies. The PILT program was created by Congress to compensate those counties, particularly in the American West, where the federal government owns land but does not pay taxes for that property. The amount of money a county receives is based on the county population and the total acreage the federal government owns in that county. The minimum an eligible county may receive under this program is $100.00 and the maximum a county may receive is $2,200,000. Two formulae are used to determine how much a county's PILT reimbursement will be. The first formula pays the counties $1.99 (in fiscal year 2002) an acre for federal public land held in a county, reduced by the amount of funds received in the prior fiscal year under certain other federal land programs. A second formula gives the counties $0.27 an acre (fiscal year 2002) with no deduction for prior-year payments. The total amount of PILT money Wyoming received in 2002 was $12,908,750.

Finally, the federal government also gives the state and its counties mineral royalty payments. A mineral royalty is a share of the profit made by an individual or corporation from natural resource production on federal land. Mineral royalty payments are a large source of income for governments in Wyoming. In 2001, Wyoming received $448,774,537 in mineral royalty payments.

County Government

Counties are the basic administrative subdivision of state government, and are created by a state to provide services of a general nature at the local level. Although a basic county system is created by the U.S. Congress when an area becomes a territory, the states determine the number of counties, their boundaries, county seats, and their powers and responsibilities. The authority and structure of county government can be found in a state's constitution and statutes.

In 1997, there were 3,043 counties in the United States. Counties can be found in almost all fifty states. However, in Alaska they are called 'boroughs," and in Louisiana they are called "parishes," and in Rhode Island they are only judicial subdivisions of the state and not counted for census purposes. Wyoming has 23 counties. Article 12 of the Wyoming constitution provides for the organization of counties in the state and requires that the legislature establish county officers and procedures for their election. Wyoming's counties are each governed by a board of commissioners. County boards are unusual in that they combine legislative and executive powers into one governing body. A board of county commissioners consists of either three or five members who are elected to either full- or part-time positions and serve four-year terms.

The authority of county commissioners is extensive. Commissioners have the power to create ordinances, levy taxes and issue bonds, determine how county revenues will be spent, grant licenses and franchises, and provide for the construction and maintenance of a county's infrastructure and facilities.

In addition to the board of commissioners, Wyoming statutes also mandate the creation of several other offices of county government. Elected positions include:

- Assessor - responsible for maintaining records related to the ownership and valuation of property in the county.
- Attorney - represents the county in court, and acts as prosecutor for the state in all cases dealing with felonies and misdemeanors committed in the county.
- Clerk - keeps the seal, records, and papers for the board of commissioners; supervises elections, maintains

voter records, and registers voters; records all licenses.
- Clerk of Court - maintains records relating to child support, and for civil, criminal, juvenile, workers compensation, and probate matters.
- Coroner - investigates the circumstances surrounding mysterious and/ or violent deaths.
- Sheriff - responsible for various law enforcement duties and for the collection of fines and fees.
- Treasurer - responsible for collection of taxes and for the issuance of automobile license plates.
- County Judges or Justices of the Peace - preside over county courts (see Chapter 6 for a discussion of Wyoming courts).

Many elected county officials occupy full-time positions within county government and are paid salaries that are, like that of the commissioners, dependent on the wealth of the county. In theory, elected county officers are all independent of the power of the county commissioners. In reality, however, the commissioners exercise a significant degree of oversight over all agencies of county government because of the need for the other officers to submit budget requests and periodic financial reports to the commissioners.

County governments perform a variety of roles. First, counties function as the primary agent of state government. In this capacity the counties take care of auto licensing, maintain official documents such as wills and deeds to property, determine property values, collect taxes, and handle many law enforcement duties. Second, counties provide a variety of important local services. These include building and maintaining roads and bridges, providing land use planning, and operating libraries and hospitals.

As we observed in our introduction to this chapter, financing is the major issue facing all units of local government. Financing the operations of county government is complicated by constitutional limits on the amount of debt a county can accumulate. The Wyoming constitution establishes an absolute debt ceiling that is two percent of the assessed property value for each county in the state. Although the state constitution allows voters to approve debt that exceeds current tax revenues, the total debt limit cannot be surpassed even with voter approval (Article 16, section 3). This provision, and similar ones for municipalities in the state, were "designed to ensure local fiscal responsibility and provide a popular check against excessive governmental spending" (Keiter and Newcomb, 1993: 236).

Municipal Government

Municipal government is one of two types of subcounty government in the United States, the other being town-ships. In 1997 there were 19,372 municipal and 16,629 township governments in the United States (Statistical Abstract of the United States, 1998: 305). As indicated above, there are no townships in Wyoming but, as of 1997, there were 97 municipalities in the state (see Table 1).

State constitutions and statutes authorize the creation of municipalities. They are brought to life to provide general purpose government for a defined area which is usually a dense population cluster. A basic framework for municipal government in Wyoming can be found in Article 13 of the State constitution. This article requires that the legislature create statutes to deal with the incorporation of municipalities, the methods for altering municipal boundaries, and the procedures by which municipalities may merge, consolidate or be dissolved.

Article 13 also outlines municipal authority for local self-government, known as "home rule." Before 1972, Wyoming's cities and towns had only those powers delegated to them by the state. That changed in 1972 when Wyoming's electors approved an amendment to the State constitution providing for home rule. This amendment allows electors of a city or town to make changes to their municipal charter, thus freeing the state legislature from the need to micromanage Wyoming's municipalities. Home rule

POPULATION OF WYOMING MUNICIPALITIES
BASED ON 2000 U.S. CENSUS

MUNICIPALITY	POP.	MUNICIPALITY	POP.
Lost Springs	1		
Van Tassell	18	Dayton	678
Kirby	57	Ranchester	701
Riverside	59	Diamondville	716
Hartville	76	Marbleton	720
Dixon	79	Moorcroft	807
Bairoil	97	Upton	872
Manville	101	Hanna	873
Opal	102	Bar Nunn	936
Manderson	104	Dubois	962
Clearmont	115	Guernsey	1147
Albin	120	Mountain View	1153
Granger	146	Pine Bluffs	1153
Pavillion	165	Sundance	1161
Edgerton	169	Basin	1238
Yoder	169	Wright	1347
Deaver	177	Pinedale	1412
Elk Mountain	192	Lusk	1447
Frannie	209	Saratoga	1726
Pine Haven	222	Greybull	1815
Glendo	229	Afton	1818
Rock River	235	Lyman	1938
Fort Laramie	243	Glenrock	2231
Chugwater	244	Evansville	2255
Superior	244	Lovell	2281
Kaycee	249	Mills	2591
Burlington	250	Kemmerer	2651
Wamsutter	261	Newcastle	3065
East Thermopolis	274	Thermopolis	3172
Medicine Bow	274	Wheatland	3548
Burns	285	Buffalo	3900
Tensleep	304	Worland	5250
LaGrange	332	Douglas	5288
Thayne	341	Powell	5373
Baggs	348	Torrington	5776
Meeteetse	351	Lander	6867
Hudson	407	Rawlins	8538
Big Piney	408	Jackson	8647
Hulett	408	Cody	8835
Midwest	408	Riverton	9310
Sinclair	423	Evanston	11507
LaBarge	431	Green River	11808
Rolling Hills	449	Sheridan	15804
Cokeville	506	Rock Springs	18708
Lingle	510	Gillette	19646
Alpine	550	Laramie	27204
Byron	557	Casper	49644
Cowley	560	Cheyenne	53011
Shoshoni	635		

(SOURCE: U.S. Census Bureau, Census 2000)

Table 1

is significant because it injects a measure of power sharing into the state-municipal relationship, which is otherwise state-centered. A feature of Wyoming's home rule provision allows municipalities, through the creation of charter ordinances, to exempt themselves from those state statutes that are not uniformly applicable to all cities and towns in the state. A charter ordinance can be used in a variety of instances to negate any general law passed by the Wyoming legislature. As we will see, charter ordinances have been used by municipalities to create city administrator forms of government. However, cities and towns are not allowed to resort to charter ordinances to circumvent those statutes that place limits on municipal indebtedness (Article 13, Section 1(c)).

A municipality is given legal status as a corporate body by a state through the issuance of a municipal charter of incorporation. Wyoming statutes define two kinds of municipalities: first class cities and towns. The governor of the state can designate an incorporated municipality a "first class city" if it has a population of more than 4,000 residents (Article 15, Chapter 3). Wyoming has 17 first class cities: Casper, Cheyenne, Cody, Douglas, Evanston, Gillette, Green River, Kemmerer, Lander, Laramie, Newcastle, Powell, Rawlins, Riverton, Rock Springs, Sheridan, and Worland. There are several practical consequences that arise

from the differentiation between first-class cities and the rest. Among the most important are those that affect the size of a municipality's governing body, the terms of its members, and their duties and responsibilities.

In addition to this distinction, four different types of municipal government can be found in Wyoming: mayor-council, council-manager, commission, and administrator systems. Wyoming law provides for the first three, while the last occurs when a municipality passes a charter ordinance. In all four instances, a town or city council exercises a municipality's legislative powers. However, the structure of executive authority in a municipality differs in all four models.

By far the most prevalent form of municipal governing body in the state is the mayor-council, or "strong mayor," system. Mayor-council systems are characterized by a fairly conventional separation of powers between executive and legislative authorities. In Wyoming "towns," the mayor is elected to serve a two-year term, while in "first class cities" mayors are elected for four year terms. The mayor serves as a municipality's chief executive officer, which makes him or her responsible for the overall management of municipal government. It is this authority that makes the mayor in mayor-council systems a "strong" mayor. Among the mayor's tasks are the duties to oversee the operation of all municipal departments, to appoint and remove all city officers, and to direct the budget process.

The mayor also performs certain legislative functions. These include presiding over all meetings of the municipality's governing body, casting votes on propositions before the governing body, and, in the case of first class cities, presenting information and recommendations regarding financial issues. Perhaps the most important legislative power a mayor has (in this system of government) is the veto. A mayor can veto any action of the city council or exercise a power that is analogous to the line-item veto in that she or he can veto specific portions of an appropriations ordinance, while approving the remainder. Mayoral vetoes can be overridden by a two-thirds vote of the municipal council (Hunt, 1994: 40). The final set of mayoral responsibilities are primarily ceremonial. These include a variety of activities that range from greeting visiting dignitaries to opening a new municipal swimming pool (Hunt, 1994: 40-41).

A second type of municipal government found in Wyoming is the "council-manager" plan. In this model, the municipality's executive (the city manager) is not independent of a city or town council. The city manager is,

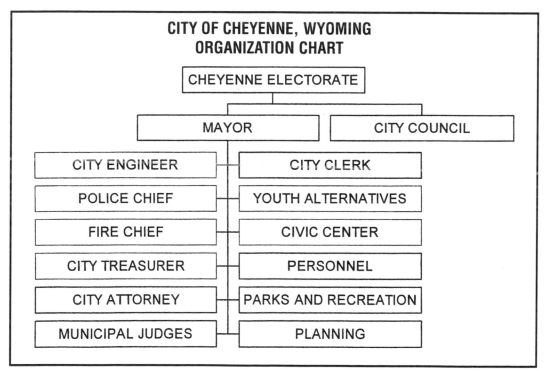

Table 2

instead, directly responsible to the legislative authority for everything he or she does. In this regard, council-manager governments resemble parliamentary systems of Western Europe.

In council-manager systems the voters elect a city council that is responsible for the overall direction of municipal policy. The number of city council members depends on the population of a municipality, i.e., municipalities with 4,000 have three, those 4,000 to 20,000 have seven, and those above 20,000 have nine members. Members of the municipal council are elected to staggered, four-year terms in all cases (Hunt, 1994: 13-14).

The council from among its members then elects a mayor to a two-year term. The mayor in a council-manager system does not possess many of the administrative or executive powers normally associated with this position. Instead, the mayor typically presides over council meetings, acts as a signatory for the city, and is the recognized head of municipal government for ceremonial and legal proceedings (Hunt, 1994: 14, 83-84).

In a council-manager government, the council is responsible for appointing an individual who possesses the special training and skills necessary for running a modern municipality. This person, called the city manager, functions as the municipality's chief executive officer and serves at the pleasure of a majority of the municipal council. The city manager is responsible for implementing the policies adopted by the council, for appointing all municipal officials (except those that are

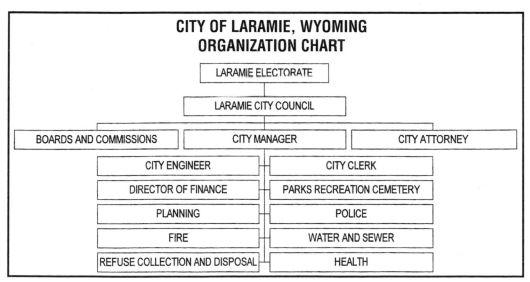

Table 3

elected), and for selecting and removing all subordinates, setting their salary, and establishing their duties and responsibilities (Hunt, 1994: 14, 84-85). (See Table 3 for an illustration of a city manager system.) Wyoming statutes also allow for a third type of municipal government, the commission form, although none currently exist in the State.

A fourth example of municipal government is the city administrator, or "weak" mayor system. City administrator systems are unique in that they are created by charter ordinances, not state statutes. In the city administrator system, the residents of a municipality elect a mayor and council. The mayor then appoints a professional city administrator, with the approval of city council, who is responsible for the day-to-day management of the municipality's affairs. The powers of the mayor in this kind of system are not extensive, which is why it is called a "weak" mayor system. The duties and responsibilities of a city administrator are similar to those of a city manager. (See Table 4 for a list of Wyoming municipalities and their systems of government.)

Special District Governments

Special districts make up the largest share of governmental units in the United States and in Wyoming as well. Special districts are defined as: "independent, special-purpose governmental

---

TYPES OF MUNICIPAL GOVERNMENT IN WYOMING AS OF 1995

MAYOR-COUNCIL SYSTEMS

MAYOR-COUNCIL SYSTEMS

All municipalities in Wyoming are governed by mayor-council systems, with part-time mayors, unless otherwise indicated.

Full-Time Mayors

Cheyenne	Sheridan	Cody

CITY MANAGER SYSTEMS

Casper	Laramie	Rawlins

CITY ADMINSTRATOR SYSTEMS

Douglas	Kemmerer
Gillette	Lovell
Green River	Lyman
Jackson	Powell

(Source: Wyoming Association of Municipalities)

Table 4

---

units that exist as separate entities with substantial administrative and fiscal independence from general purpose local governments" (U.S. Department of Commerce, 1994: vii).

Special districts are known by a variety of names including districts, boards, commissions, and authorities. These governing units are usually created to perform one of three functions: 1) develop and maintain facilities such as bridges, tunnels, airports and parks;

SPECIAL DISTRICTS IN WYOMING

Boards of Cooperative Education Services (BOCES) BOCES are created to provide a mechanism whereby school and community college districts, in any combination, can cooperate to provide a variety of educational services including vocational-technical training, adult education, and service for exceptional children (WS 21-20-102).

Cemetery Districts Cemetery districts are created by residents in a county or counties to create, maintain, and/or acquire a cemetery or cemeteries (WS 35-8-314).

Conservation Districts Conservation districts are formed to provide for the conservation of the district's soil and water resources, to preserve natural resources, to control and prevent soil erosion and flooding, to prevent impairment of dams and reservoirs, to protect public lands, to preserve wildlife, and to promote the health, safety, and welfare of the people of the state (WS 11-16-103).

Drainage Districts Drainage districts provide landowners in the district with a cooperative mechanism for the construction and maintenance of drains, ditches, levees, or other works, that allow for drainage of land, and for the promotion of public health and welfare (WS 41-9-101).

Fire Districts Fire districts provide fire protection for the persons and property within its boundaries (WS 35-9-201).

Hospital Districts Hospital districts are created to allow an area to construct and maintain a hospital, a medical care facility, or a related institution (WS 35-2-403).

Improvement and Service Districts I&S districts allow an unincorporated territory to construct and maintain infrastructure improvements and provide services, including streets, sidewalks, curbs, gutters, alleys, water and water distribution systems, solid waste disposal systems, and parks (WS 18-12-102 and -103).

Irrigation Districts Irrigation districts create the means for landowners to provide irrigation to an area, or to improve the existing water supply, or to purchase, extend, or maintain existing water works (WS 41-7-201).

Joint Powers Boards A Joint Powers Board is created to allow counties, municipalities, special and community college districts, to cooperate in the management of a joint undertaking such as water, sewerage, and solid waste disposal systems; recreation, police and fire protection, transportation, public school, community college, medical and public health, courthouse, jail, and administrative facilities; and lodging tax activities (WS 9-1-131).

Museum Districts Special museum districts are formed for the creation, acquisition, maintenance, and enlargement of a historical, archaeological, and geologic museum (WS 18-10-203)

Predatory Animal Districts Predatory animal districts are created for the control of those animals which prey on livestock, pigs, poultry, and other domestic animals, and on wildlife (WS 11-6-205). These include coyotes, jackrabbits, porcupines, raccoons, the red fox, wolves, skunks, and stray cats (WS 23-1-101).

Recreation Districts Recreation districts are formed by counties, municipalities, or school districts, either singly or in some combination as a joint powers board, to acquire, construct, maintain, and regulate public recreation facilities and playgrounds (WS 18-9-201 and -202).

Rural Health Care Districts RHC Districts are developed to construct, acquire, maintain, and supply a health care facility, or to provide health care services (WS 35-2-701).

Sanitary and Improvement Districts S&I districts facilitate the establishment, maintenance, and construction of water mains, sewers and disposal systems, and the disposal of drainage, waste and sewage (WS 35-3-106).

Solid Waste Disposal Districts Solid waste disposal districts provide a mechanism for the creation of rules and regulations relevant to the management of solid waste in an area (WS 18-11-102). Solid waste is defined as garbage and other discarded solid materials, including those resulting from industrial, commercial, and agricultural operations, and from community activities. Solid waste does not include domestic sewerage or other forms of water pollution (WS 35-11-103).

Water and Sewer Districts W&S districts are formed to allow the planning, design, construction, and maintenance of sewers and sewage treatment and disposal systems, and of water treatment and distribution systems (WS 41-10-113).

Water Conservancy Districts WC districts are intended to provide for the conservation of the state's water resources, and to contribute to the beneficial use of water within the state (WS 41-3-701).

Watershed Improvement Districts WI districts are designed to allow for the preservation and protection of the state's land and water resources, and for the promotion of the health, safety, and general welfare of the people of the state, through the prevention and control of erosion, flood and sediment damages, and storage and disposal of water (WS 41-8-102).

Weed and Pest Districts W&P districts are created to provide a mechanism for the control of those plants, animals, and insects which have been determined to be harmful to the general welfare of persons residing within a district, either by virtue of some direct effect, or as carriers of disease or parasites (WS 11-5-105 and -102).

Table 5

WYOMING SPECIAL DISTRICTS

District Name	Method of Formation	Governing Body	No.	Elected	Terms	Provision For Tax Authority	Amount[g]	Statute	Provision for Authority to Issue Bonds
Boces									
Cemetery		Board of Trustees	6	Y	4 yrs.	Y	3 Mills (+)	WS 35-8-314,316	Y
Conservation	Referendum	Board of Supervisors	5	Y	3 yrs.	Y	1 Mill	WS 11-16-133, 134	N
Drainage	Court Order	Board of Commissioners	3	Y	2 yrs.	N			N
Fire Protection	Election	Board of Directors	3-5	Y	4 yrs.	Y	3 Mills (+)	WS 35-9-203, 204	Y
Hospital		Board of Trustees	6	Y	4 yrs.	Y	6 Mills (+)	WS 35-2-414, 415	Y
Improvement and Service	Resolution	Board of Directors	3	Y[b]	5 yrs.	N			Y
Irrigation (and Public Power)	Court Order	Board of Commissioners	3-5	Y	3 yrs.	N			Y
Joint Powers Boards									
Museum	Election	Board of Trustees	6	Y	4 yrs.	Y	1 Mill (+)	WS 18-10-213, 214	Y
Predatory Animal		Board of Directors	6 (7)[f]	Y(N)[d]	3yrs.	N			N
Recreation									
Rural Health Care	Election	Board of Truestees	5	Y	4 yrs.	Y	2 Mills	WS 35-2-708	Y
Sanitary and Improvement	Election	Board of Trustees	5	Y	4 yrs.	Y	1 Mill (+)	WS 35-3-109, 115	Y
School[e]	State	Board of Trustees	5-9	Y	4 yrs.	Y		WS 39-2-402(e)	Y
Solid Waste Disposal	Resolution	?	3-9	N[g]	3 yrs.	Y	3 Mills	WS 18-11-103	N
Water and Sewer	Election	Board of Directors	5	Y	6 yrs.	Y	8 Mills (+)	WS 41-10-114, 127, 119	Y
Water Conservancy	Court Order	Board of Directors	5-9	Y	5 yrs.	Y	1 Mill	WS 41-3-771, 775	Y
Watershed Improvement	Referendum	Board of Directors	5	Y	3 yrs.	N			Y
Weed and Pest Control		Board of Directors	5-7	N[f]	4 yrs.	Y	1 (+ 1) Mill	WS 11-5-111, 303	N

NOTE: [b] Can be Board of County Commissioners
[c] Three directors are required to be sheep owners, three required to be cattle owners. A seventh member can be appointed from electors in county who are not engaged in raising cattle or sheep.
[d] Seventh member appointed by Board of County Commissioners
[e] Included for comparative purposes
[f] Appointed by Board of County Commissioners
[g] Source: WS 39-2-402(e)

Table 4

2) provide a specific service such as waste collection, health care, weed and pest control, or fire protection; 3) engage in regulatory activities, particularly those related to flood control and soil and water conservation (Woll and Binstock, 1991: 550-552). Tables 5 and 6 describe the nineteen types of special districts that have been authorized by the Wyoming legislature.

To qualify as a discreet government unit a special district must be completely autonomous. Generally speaking, special districts are free to create a relatively independent body of administrators, exercise complete fiscal control over their operations, levy taxes, elect officers, employ staff, negotiate contracts, and construct and maintain infrastructure and facilities often with little or no oversight by any other governmental entity. Some districts are, however, governed by officers appointed by other governing entities, and they must often get electoral approval for their activities (Porter, Lin, and Peiser, 1987: v).

Special districts have been a feature of the American political system for a considerable period of time. Some of the first were formed in Rhode Island in the late 1700s. Since then there has been a steady growth in their numbers in response largely to limitations being placed on the amount of debt other units of local government can accrue. Since the end of World War II, the number of special districts in the United States has doubled every 20 years (Porter, Lin, and Peiser, 1987: 1). In 1992, there were 31,555 special districts in the United States and by 1997 that number had increased to 34,683. In 1997, Wyoming had 478 special districts, an increase from 399 in 1992 (Statistical Abstract of the United States, 1998; 1994).

The creation of a special district can also be useful as a means of shifting costs for a project or service from all taxpayers to only those who would benefit from that program (Porter, Lin, and Peiser, 1987: 10-11). Furthermore, special districts can provide a means of overcoming a variety of jurisdictional problems. Some governmental entities are prevented by law from providing services beyond their boundaries. In many cases, a particular problem may cross boundaries and, thus, cover multiple jurisdictions (Bowman and Kearney, 1990: 334). In these situations, Wyoming uses a Joint Powers Board that enables counties, municipalities, and special districts to enter into joint or cooperative agreements in the management of a common undertaking such as water, sewage, and solid waste disposal systems. Finally, special districts function, in theory, to insulate specific activities from local partisan politics (Porter, Lin, and Peiser, 1987: 11-12; Woll and Binstock, 1991: 550-552).

Wyoming statutes provide a variety of ways for special districts to be formed. Generally, the process begins when a group of individuals petition a governing body (usually the county commissioners or a county court) to create a special district. The petition will normally outline the reasons for, and purposes of, the district. Included will be the boundaries of the district and the powers and the authority the district will have. Hearings will be held regarding the desirability of the district, and comments, data, and information will be collected and analyzed. If need be, adjustments will be made to the provisions of the original petitions. After it is determined that the district is necessary, the issue will be handled in one of three ways: 1) it will be put to the affected electorate for a vote; 2) the district will be created by a county court order; 3) the district will be created by a resolution of the county commissioners. Guidelines for the formation of a particular kind of special district can be found in the statutes that govern the particular body. Provisions are also made in Wyoming statutes for dissolution of special districts.

Special districts are intended to possess significant administrative and fiscal autonomy from their general purpose local government counterparts. As a result, many of them possess the power to levy a tax to finance their operations. Many special districts are formed just to take advantage of this power, allowing them to then fund an existing operation. Once individuals fall under the jurisdiction of a special district, they must pay for its services regardless of whether they want the services or not. Additional funding for special districts comes in the form of bonds, which can be issued for a variety of improvements.

There are a variety of problems associated with special districts in Wyoming. A major problem is attempting to track them accurately. The number of special districts in Wyoming tends to be very fluid. New units periodically appear. Others, because they were never intended to be permanent, disappear (especially those created to deal with a particular project such as a road, sewer, or drainage ditch). Still others become inactive due to lack of funding, only to reappear when a bond issue is finally approved by affected voters. Record keeping is also hampered by a lack of consistent and accurate reporting regarding the activities of individual special districts. The existence of multiple governmental units makes it difficult for understaffed and overworked state agencies to monitor their activities.

Large numbers of special districts also confuse voters who are often unsure about the jurisdiction, responsibilities, and powers of the districts that affect them — often producing dismally low voter participation on special district issues. The pluralistic nature of special districts in Wyoming can also baffle the governing bodies of the special districts themselves. The large number of these governmental units tends to obscure the fact that they are governmental entities and, as such, are subject to a variety of legal requirements and restrictions and especially to a number of compliance issues relating to the handling of public tax monies, to election procedures, and to the bonding of treasurers.

School District Governments

The unit of government charged with public education in Wyoming is the school district. School districts are defined as: "organized local entities providing public elementary, secondary, and/or higher education which, under state law, have sufficient administrative and fiscal autonomy to qualify as separate governments" (U.S. Department of Commerce, 1994: B-1). School districts are, therefore, units of local government that provide a single, very specific kind of service, i.e., education. Although they technically meet the definition of a special district, the historical origins and characteristics of school districts are such that they are considered separate entities.

The Tenth Amendment to the U.S. Constitution leaves the responsibility for the regulation of education largely to the states. In general, school districts are created as autonomous units by the states to assure local control of education, guarantee accessible education to children in each community neighborhood, and keep education separate from politics (Woll and Binstock, 1991: 552). In practice, however, these ideals have often been difficult to achieve.

The basic governing body of school districts in the United States is the school board. Wyoming has 48 school districts, which are governed by boards of trustees. Each board has from five to nine members who are elected from the district to serve four-year terms. Officers, including a chairperson, are elected from the board's membership. In December of each year the board is reorganized, and new officers are elected. A school district's board of trustees functions as the district's legislative authority and has a variety of powers and responsibilities. Most of the board's influence comes from its ability to make district policy; thus, controlling the direction and general operation of a school district. The school board's most important policy tool is its control over the district's budget process.

School boards also have the authority to create the rules, regulations, and standards for the schools under their jurisdiction, consistent with state laws and regulations. School boards also determine the need and siting of facilities to meet efficiently the district's needs; authorize the construction, maintenance and staffing of district buildings; establish school district boundaries; provide transportation for students to and from schools; approve the selection of instructional materials, and the content of school library holdings; and provide for a safe and healthy environment. School boards also establish the times for, and hold, regular meetings, and keep an official record of them.

The boards of trustees are responsible for appointing the district's top administrative positions. These include the school superintendent, who acts as the chief administrative officer of the district, and who is responsible for its day-to-day operation. In addition to what are considered typical administrative duties the superintendent manages the district's property and physical plant, supervises the operation of the district's personnel system, helps create the district's budget, formulates strategies related to elections to pass tax levies and bond issues, and acts as advisor to the school board regarding education issues. In this last capacity, the superintendent has direct input into many of the policy decisions the trustees make.

Finally, the board of trustees oversees development of a district's curriculum. Although districts are free, in principle, to develop their own course of study, they are influenced by the Wyoming's State Superintendent of Public Instruction (SSPI), and by regional accreditation authorities. A poorly developed curriculum can not only threaten a district's accreditation, but also its funding.

School districts are funded from a number of different sources. Among the most important are federal grants and mineral royalty payments, state and local property taxes, and revenue generated by the lease or sale of the state's School Trust Lands.

PART TWO: GOVERNMENT OF THE WIND RIVER RESERVATION

In this section we change focus by examining the government of the two Indian tribes that reside in Wyoming: the Eastern Shoshone and the Northern Arapaho. Although tribal governments are local in the sense that they serve a specific geographic place, in this case the Wind River Reservation is fundamentally different from local governments we reviewed in the preceding section.

The major political distinction between tribal and local governments is that, throughout the history of their relationship with the United States government, tribes have been treated as sovereign powers, and have, at times, been dealt with much like self-governing foreign nations. This and other factors make the relationship between Native Americans and the United States very complex. In the analysis of tribal governments that follows, we will examine two factors: the Federal-Tribal relationship, and the nature of government on the Wind River Reservation.

The Federal-Tribal Relationship

Historically, the policy of the United States towards Native American peoples has been characterized by two very different tendencies. On the one hand, the United States has displayed great willingness to treat the tribes as sovereign nations, possessed of treaty-making powers and rights to their own lands. On the other hand, the United States has very often engaged in assimilationist activities designed to "civilize" Indians, to eradicate their unique tribal identities, and to give them more contact with the dominant white society (AILTP, 1988: 5).

During the early 19th Century, a broad judicial definition of tribal sovereignty was developed, in the U.S. Supreme Court decisions of Johnson v. McIntosh (1823), Cherokee Nation v. Georgia (1831), and Worcester v. Georgia (1832). In the three cases, known as the Marshall Trilogy, Chief Justice John Marshall developed a model of Indian sovereignty that "called for largely autonomous tribal governments subject to an overriding federal authority but essentially free of state control" (Wilkinson, 1987: 24).

Another important event of this formative period occurred in 1824. In that year, Secretary of War John C. Calhoun created an agency, which later became known as the Bureau of Indian Affairs (BIA), charged with actually overseeing the Federal-Tribal relationship.

In the 1830s, the federal government forcibly removed 19 eastern tribes, with a population of over 50,000 people, to areas west of the Mississippi River. Although the removal process was known to the Cherokee people as the "trail of tears," so far as many whites were concerned, the policy was completely legal.

In the 1850s, the U.S. Government began creating reservations for Native American peoples. This policy was intended to accomplish two objectives. The first was to remove Indians from areas where there was a potential for conflict with white settlers. The second was to "regenerate" the Native American tribes along lines advocated by Christian reformers. Reservation policy called for concentrating tribes on small, well-defined tracts of land, which would isolate them from a variety of negative white influences and preserve some measure of tribal cultural identity and political sovereignty. At the same time, Indians would become agriculturally self-sufficient and they would eventually enjoy the blessings of Christian civilization (Utley, 1984: 46).

In 1871, American policy toward the tribes changed focus and became more assimilationist. This attempt at absorbing large numbers of tribes into white society began when Congress stopped negotiating treaties with the Indian tribes. Advocates of this change argued that the treaty-making process, which recognized the sovereignty of the Indian tribes, hindered more humane treatment of native peoples. The policy was consequently terminated (Wunder, 1994: 29-31; O'Brien, 1989: 71). In 1885, Congress launched another attack on tribal sovereignty when it passed the Major Crimes Act (MCA), which was itself a response to the U.S. Supreme Court decision of Ex Parte Crow Dog (1883).

In Crow Dog, which dealt with the conviction of an Indian who had murdered another Indian, the Supreme Court ruled that Native Americans could not be tried in federal courts for what were essentially tribal matters. The Supreme Court argued that U.S.-Tribal relationships were governed entirely by treaty provisions. Since no treaty between the tribe in question and the United States allowed the United States to try a member of that tribe for murder, and because Congress had provided no additional or specific guidance, the conviction was ruled invalid (Wunder, 1994: 29-31; O'Brien, 1989: 71). The Congress responded by passing the MCA, which made it a federal crime for an Indian to commit seven specific crimes: murder, manslaughter, rape, assault with intent to kill, arson, burglary, or larceny (Wunder, 1994: 36-37; O'Brien, 1989: 71-72). The U.S. Congress continued its assault on tribal sovereignty two years later with the General Allotment, or Dawes, Act of 1887.

The Dawes Act had several important provisions. The BIA was given the authority to allot tribal land to individual Indians. Land that was not allotted to Indians was to be considered "excess," and could be sold to non-Indians. If allotted land was occupied continuously for 25 years, title would be transferred to resident Indians. In the interim, title was to be held in trust by the United States government. Finally, Indians who accepted allotments were made United States citizens (Wunder, 1994: 32-33; O'Brien, 1989: 77-79; AILTP, 1988: 8-9). The consequences of the Dawes Act were momentous. Sales of reservation lands to non-Indians resulted in a significant loss of territory for Native Americans. The Dawes Act also defined citizenship rights based on ownership of property and not traditional criteria for tribal members. Finally, the Act fundamentally changed the nature of tribal authority by emphasizing the rights of the individual over those of the tribe (Flynn, 1991: 21-24; Utley, 1984, 203-226). In the long run, the Dawes Act was a disaster for Native Americans. As a result of leasing, speculation, and outright theft, Indian lands in the United States decreased from 138 million acres in 1887, to 48 million in 1934, when the allotments ended.

The relentless federal attack on Indian sovereignty continued with the Indian Citizenship Act (ICA). Passed in 1924, the ICA made all Native Americans citizens of the United States. However, the ICA did not require that Indians give up their tribal affiliation. In fact, as a result of the ICA, Native Americans became citizens of three different sovereign entities: their tribe, the state in which they resided, and the United States, enjoying the rights and privileges of all three (Wunder, 1994: 48-49; O'Brien, 1989: 78-79). It was hoped that, as a result of the ICA, there would be a decrease in the allegiance of individual Indians to their tribes.

The assimilationist era which began in 1871, ended in 1934. In that year, the U.S. Congress enacted the Indian Reorganization Act (IRA), arguably the most controversial piece of Indian legislation ever passed by Congress. The goals of the IRA were simple: stop the allotment process, and thus the loss of tribal lands; lessen the influence of the BIA over tribal affairs; and strengthen the authority of tribal governments by allowing them to develop written constitutions. The process by which this last goal was to be realized was complicated. Tribes were first required to individually vote on whether they should accept or turn down the provisions of the IRA. A tribe that approved the IRA was then allowed to write its own constitution, and apply for a charter of incorporation from the Secretary of the Interior. Tribes that voted against accepting the IRA were not covered by its provisions, although segments of the IRA could be accepted on an ad hoc basis later. Tribes that rejected the IRA could not subsequently write a constitution that would receive any federal sanction (Flynn, 1991: 42-46; Wunder, 1994: 66-71; O'Brien, 1989: 66-71).

The IRA provided tribes that accepted it with several potential benefits. Most importantly, the IRA created a mechanism by which Native Americans could reassert their control over property and resources, establish a variety of means for economic development and business management, create legal codes for reservations, and promote projects designed to improve health, education and welfare on the reservations. Despite these very positive aspects, the IRA also had drawbacks. The IRA itself was written without any Indian input. In addition, the creation of new constitutions was a threat to political systems that had developed on the reservations. The creation of European-style written constitutions also imposed an alien form of government on those tribes which accepted the IRA. Furthermore, acceptance of the IRA was a threat to Indian sovereignty because those tribes that accepted its provisions lost important treaty rights. Finally,

there were irregularities in the ratification process, since an abstention counted as a positive vote for the IRA (Flynn, 1991: 42-46; Wunder, 1994: 66-71; O'Brien, 1989: 82-83).

A vote on the IRA was held on the Wind River Reservation in June, 1935. While the Shoshone voted in favor of accepting the IRA, albeit by one vote, the Arapaho voted overwhelmingly against it. The BIA subsequently ruled that both tribes had to approve the IRA for it to go into effect. Consequently, the Wind River Reservation is not governed by a written constitution. The lack of constitutions for the Shoshone and Arapaho means that the BIA exercises more influence over tribal affairs on the Wind River Reservation than it does on incorporated, self-governing reservations (Flynn, 1991: 46).

Another important development occurred in 1946, when the Congress created the Indian Claims Commission (ICC). The ICC provided Native Americans with a mechanism to sue the United States government for land that was taken from them illegally. However, restitution could come only in the form of money, not land. The amount of money a tribe received was, in turn, based on the value of the land at the time it was taken, and the amount of money the federal government had already spent on the tribe was to be deducted from the total judgement. Finally, it took a very long time to resolve individual cases (Wunder, 1994: 89-93; O'Brien, 1989: 84). Despite these problems, between 1947-1952, various Indian tribes initiated 850 claims against the federal government, and $800 million was awarded to them (Wunder, 1994: 90).

The primary purpose of the ICC was to resolve all outstanding claims against the U.S. government. Following conclusion of ICC activities, Congress began dismantling the system of laws and regulations that treated the tribes as discrete entities. These included ending prohibitions against selling liquor and firearms to Indians, transferring the obligation for providing health services from the BIA to the federal Department of Health, Education, and Welfare (now Health and Human Services), and directing the BIA to transfer responsibility for education of Native Americans to state agencies (O'Brien, 1989: 84-85; AILTP, 1988: 11-12).

During the 1960s, U.S. policy toward Native Americans swung once more toward encouraging self-government. The watershed event that marked the transition from the assimilationist era of the 1940s and 1950s, and the period of self-determination in the 1960s, '70s, and '80s, was the Indian Civil Rights Act (ICRA) of 1968. ICRA, which was actually a last minute amendment to the federal Civil Rights Act of 1968, extended many of the protections found in the U.S. Bill of Rights to Native Americans as far as their dealings with tribal governments were concerned. While recognizing tribal authority, ICRA, by significantly extending broad constitutional guarantees to individual Indians, served to further erode traditional tribal authority (Wunder, 1994: 124-146; Flynn, 1991: 73).

Government On The Wind River Reservation

The Wind River Reservation (WRR) was created by the Second Treaty of Fort Bridger in 1868 as the home for the Eastern Shoshone people. Although they had earlier been promised a much larger expanse of territory, which would have included land in what is now Colorado, Utah, Idaho, and Wyoming, the Shoshone Reservation was actually much smaller and was located in central Wyoming. In 1878, 1,000 Arapahoes arrived at the Shoshone Reservation under military escort. Although their stay was supposed to be temporary, they never left, despite protests by the Shoshone. In 1927, the Shoshone sued the federal government for settling the Arapahoes on their land without permission or restitution. In 1937, the U.S. Court of Claims in the decision of Shoshone Tribe of Indians v. U.S., awarded the Shoshone Tribe $4.4 million in damages, plus interest. In 1939, the name of the agency was changed from the Shoshone Reservation to the Wind River Reservation (Flynn, 1991: 32-36: Wunder, 1994: 90).

The structure of government on the Wind River Indian Reservation is a complex web of relationships. Government on the reservation consists primarily of two separate general councils (one for each tribe) made up of all tribal members of each tribe who are above the age of 18, two separate tribal Business Councils, a Joint Business Council (JBC) consisting of the six members of each business council of each individual tribe (which deals with matters affecting both tribes), and the Bureau of Indian Affairs (Flynn, 1991: 68; http://www.osec.doc.gov/eda/pdf/44Wyoming.pdf). The Business Councils prepare tribal budgets and administer tribal affairs. They also have the authority to contract with the federal government to manage any of the Indian programs that have been authorized by Congress. The Joint Business Council deals with questions related to reservation budgets, land and resource management, environmental quality, and health, education, and welfare. The BIA has a variety of duties that tend to focus on administration and budget.

In addition to their distinct responsibilities, some matters on the WRR are managed jointly by the tribes and the BIA. For instance, the BIA and the JBC work together on questions regarding leases of reservation lands. While the BIA accepts applications for leases on the WRR, and does most of the paperwork associated with leasing, the JBC actually approves the lease. The tribes and the BIA also work together to develop the budget for the WRR which is sent, first, to the Secretary of the Interior and, later, to the President for transmission to the Congress.

The State of Wyoming also has responsibility for managing certain affairs that are important to residents of the WRR. A major service that Wyoming provides is education. Although the BIA was once solely responsible for the education of Indian children, many now receive a public education in schools that are managed by the state's school districts. The State of Wyoming also manages some social service programs, such as Temporary Assistance to Needy Families (TANF) (formally AFDC) that are available to Native Americans.

The structure of the governing bodies of the tribes is relatively straightforward. Each tribe on the reservation is governed by a Business Council, consisting of six individuals who are enrolled members of the tribe. They are elected to serve two-year terms in a full-time, paid capacity. A chairperson is selected from the membership of each Business Council, which is required to hold regular meetings. The two Business Councils, meeting together, form the Joint Business Council of the Reservation, which is chaired alternately by the heads of the two Business Councils. Members of the JBC also serve on one or more sub-committees, which range from land and resource management to social welfare, and recommend possible actions to the entire JBC (Flynn, 1991: 64-65).

The actual authority of the two Business Councils flows from the General Councils of the two tribes. A tribe's General Council consists of the enrolled adult members of that tribe. Each tribe's General Council meets irregularly to discuss those matters not considered the jurisdiction of the Business Councils. A meeting of the General Council must be advertised prior to it being held. Any binding decision requires that a quorum of 75 Shoshone or 150 Arapaho (neither number representing a majority) be present at a meeting of their respective General Councils. Since tribal government on the Wind River Reservation operates without a constitution, which would stipulate the powers and responsibilities of tribal government, the Business Councils have only authority to deal with matters that are considered traditional. When other problems arise the Business Council of a tribe must approach its General Council for authority to deal with them, or let the General Council resolve them directly.

The power of the General Councils is potentially very great. The General Council of a tribe can remove a member of its Business Council at any time and without cause, as long as a quorum is present. Given the absence of a constitution on the WRR, there are no written rules that govern the actions of a General Council on the WRR, and there is very little consensus about what limitations, if any, should be placed on their power and authority. It is expected that the General Council of each tribe operate in a manner that is consistent with the accepted norms and values of their respective tribes. In general, the Wind River tribes place great stock in maintaining tribal health and harmony, in achieving consensus, and in conflict resolution. Winning is, however, often de-emphasized, reflecting the philosophy that lack of resolution of a problem is often preferable to a bad solution. A product of this belief is that no provision has been made for a tie-breaking mechanism for any deadlocked votes taken by the Business and Joint Business Councils. (See Table 7 for an illustration of tribal government on the WRR.)

Government on the WRR has been heavily influenced by the dominant white society of the United States. An indication of this is that tribal councils have become more focused on their political decision-making and administrative functions, and less so on their more traditional mediative and judicial roles. As a result, a system of tribal courts have emerged on the WRR which have

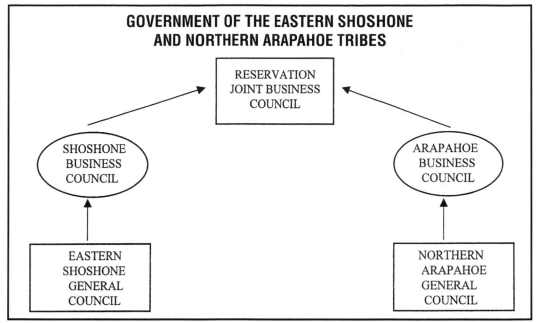

Table 4

become important factors in dealing with conflict resolution. In general, tribal law does not apply to non-Indians, the laws of the State of Wyoming do not apply to the Reservation, and tribal courts are more informal than those of white society. For instance, tribal courts are less attentive to legal technicalities than federal or state courts. The role of the courts in tribal society is also very different, with goals that are more focused on mediation, compromise, and settlement (Flynn, 1991: 69, 76).

On the Wind River Reservation, the tribal courts consist of three associate judges and one chief judge, all of whom are selected by the JBC. The as-

sociate judges are not required to have any legal training, and are appointed to four-year terms. The chief judge, who serves for life, must, however, be a lawyer. The JBC has the power to remove a judge at any time in cases of gross misconduct or major violations of the law. The actual jurisdiction of tribal courts is a matter of some controversy, because there is considerable disagreement over where the authority of tribal courts ends, and state and federal jurisdiction begins. In addition to tribal courts, there are three other types of courts on the WRR. These include probate court, children's court, and a court of appeals. The tribal courts offer two choices for defendant's representation: representation by an attorney or an advocate chosen at their discretion. Advocates are NOT lawyers - though they must pass the same legal exam administered to the tribal associate judges before representing a client (Flynn, 1991: 75-76). Other problems also exist regarding the ability of the tribal courts to enforce their decisions, inadequate funding and staffing, and comity with state courts (Flynn, 1991: 72-76).

In a variety of circumstances, the activities of the two Business Councils on the WRR, and of the JBC, must be sanctioned by, or coordinated with, the Bureau of Indian Affairs. This is a result of tribal rejection of the Indian Reorganization Act, which left the BIA with considerable influence on the Reservation.

On the WRR, the BIA is responsible for administrating those federal Indian programs that the tribes do not manage themselves. These include policies related to law enforcement, forestry, range management, social service, infrastructure improvement, and real estate activities. The administration of the BIA for the WRR is headquartered at the Fort Washakie Agency. At the top of the BIA administrative structure is the superintendent, who is a career civil servant. Below the superintendent are various departments staffed by more than 100 people, the majority of whom are Native Americans.

Although the BIA continues to be a provider of many basic services, the role of the BIA is moving subtly in other directions. Today, the BIA often functions in an oversight capacity, ensuring that the activities of the tribes conform to federal statutes. The BIA can also find itself acting as a referee between elements within tribes, between the tribes themselves, between the tribes and non-Indian residents of the WRR, and between the tribes and the BIA itself. On still other occasions, the BIA functions as a liaison and facilitator between the tribes and the state of Wyoming, and between the tribes and the federal government.

CONCLUSION

As this chapter has suggested, local governments exist within a complex web of state and federal authority. Given their important functions and large number, non-state governments play an important role in citizens' lives. The lack of media attention paid to this level requires citizens to make special efforts if they wish to keep track of local public policy issues. In the end, there are many opportunities for participation in local-level politics. A well-informed and interested citizen can be a powerful and important actor in influencing community affairs.

ENDNOTES

[1] All of these figures relating to governments - local, state, county — are the most recent according to the 1997 census. The government census is due out next year because the "census of governments" (unlike the population census) takes place in years ending in a "2" and "7".

[2] The United States Constitution sets forth the basic distribution of governmental powers in the American system. The Constitution mentions only two levels of government. It assigns powers to the national government and the states; nowhere is there a mention of local governments. The legal assumption that results from this constitutional admission is that cities and other local governments fall under the jurisdiction of the states. No city has an inherent right to exercise governmental powers. Instead, such powers must first be conferred on the local unit either by the state's constitution or by an act of the state legislature.

The legal posture of municipal corporations and other local jurisdictions was given its classic formulation in 1868 by Iowa Supreme Court Judge John Dillon. Dillon's Rule, the name by which this constitutional doctrine is usually identified, denotes a clear, hierarchical, superior-subordinate relationship between a state and its local governments. According to this rule, "municipalities are creatures of the states" and possess only those powers delegated to them by the states. Furthermore, as a state creates, it may destroy. The state's power is so great that "the Legislature might, by a single act, sweep from existence all municipal corporations in a state."

In 1903 and again in 1923, the United States Supreme Court upheld Dillon's rule. In brief, local governments are subunits of states. A state, at its pleasure, may modify or withdraw the powers it entrusts to its cities.

A set of contrary pressures exist, however, to give cities more self-government powers than those allowed by a strict interpretation of Dillon's Rule. That is, there is the notion of home rule or home rule charters. Generally, home rule is an attempt to give cities the widest possible latitude to handle their own affairs without first having to obtain expressed state permission. A home rule charter is drafted by the municipality (not the state as are standard charters) and grants the city a high degree of independence in making its own laws. Home rule cities are generally free to enact laws of their own, just so long as these local laws do not contradict or preempt state statures or states constitutions. Again, the idea is to give cities more control over their own affairs. Yet, as home rule charters are granted under the authority of a state's constitution or statutes, it is still the state that ultimately defines just which powers are a city's under home rule.

Home rule is fairly popular. Forty-eight states presently give their cities some measure of home rule authority (Alabama and Vermont are the exceptions). A few striking examples of the exercise of home rule are: Morton Grove, Illinois who used home rule authority to enact local handgun control and New York City and Seattle, Washington where they instituted the partial public funding of election campaigns, despite the fact that no expressed state authority had been given to either city to enact such a law. Dillon's rule, however, remains the prevailing legal doctrine regarding the law making powers of cities.

References

AILTP (American Indian Lawyer Training Program). 1988. Indian Tribes as Sovereign Governments: A Sourcebook on Federal-Tribal History, Law and Policy. Oakland, CA: AIRI Press.

Alfini, James. 1974. Partisan Pressures on the Nonpartisan Plan. Judicature, 58: 216-321.

Almond, Gabriel A., and Sidney Verba. 1965. The Civic Culture: Political Attitudes in Five Nations. Boston: Little, Brown.

Bakken, Gordon M. 1987. Rocky Mountain Constitution Making, 1850-1912. New York: Greenwood Press.

Berman, David R. 1975. State and Local Politics. Boston: Holbrook Press.

Bowman, Ann O. and Richard C. Kearney. 1990. State and Local Government. Boston: Houghton Mifflin.

Brown v. Thomson 462 U.S. 835 (1983).

Burns, Nancy. 1994. The Formation of American Local Government: Private Values in Public Institutions. New York: Oxford.

Carey, John M., Richard G. Niemi, and Lynda W. Powell. 2000. Incumbency and the Probability of Reelection in State Legislative Elections. Journal of Politics 62:671-7000.

Cawley, Gregg, Janet Clark, Michael Horan, Maggi Murdock, Alan Schenker, and Oliver Walter. 1991. The Equality State: Government and Politics in Wyoming 2d. Dubuque, Iowa: Eddie Bowers Publishing.

Chapman, Miriam Gantz, 1952. The Story of Womans' Suffrage in Wyoming, 1869-1896. M.A. Thesis, University of Wyoming.

Cherokee Nation v. Georgia 30 U.S. 1 (1831).

Clark, Janet, and Oliver Walter. 1987. Wyoming: Populists Versus Lobbyists. In Ronald J. Hrebenar and Clive S. Thomas, eds. Interest Group Politics in the American West. Salt Lake City: University of Utah Press.

Council of State Governments. The Book of the States. 2002 ed.

Darcy, R., Susan Welch, and Janet Clark. 1994. Women, Elections, and Representation 2d. Lincoln: University of Nebraska Press.

De Tocqueville, Alexis. 1956. Democracy in America. Richard Heffner, ed. New York: New American Library. (Original work published in 1835).

Drake, Kerry. 1995. Legislative Races - What It Costs to Win. Casper Star Tribune, January 15, p. A1.

Dye, Thomas R. 1994. Politics in States and Communities. Englewood Cliffs, New Jersey: Prentice Hall.

Dye, Thomas and Harmon Ziegler. 1993. The Irony of Democracy: An Uncommon Introduction to American Politics. Belmont, California: Wadsworth.

Engstrom, Richard N. 2002. "Wyoming: Money and Politics in a Citizen Legislature." In Money, Politics, and Campaign Finance Reform Law in the States, edited by David Schultz. Durham, N.C.: Carolina Academic Press.

Ex Parte Crow Dog 109 U.S. 556 (1883).

Flynn, Janet. 1991. Tribal Government: Wind River Reservation. Riverton, Wyoming: Big Bend Press.

<u>Geringer v. Bebout</u> WY 165, 10 P.3d 514 (2000).

<u>Gorin v. Karpan</u> 755 F. Supp. 1430 (D. Wyo. Oct. 15, 1991).

Grant, Daniel R. and Lloyd B. Omdahl. 1989. <u>State and Local Government in America</u>. Boston: Allyn and Bacon.

Griffin, Kenyon N. and Michael J. Horan. 1980. Judicial Merit Retention in Wyoming: An Analysis and Some Suggestions for Reform. <u>Land and Water Law Review</u>, 15: 567-691.

Griffin, Kenyon N. and Michael J. Horan. 1979. Merit Retention Elections: What Influences the Voters? <u>Judicature</u>, 63: 78-88.

Griffin, Kenyon N. and Michael J. Horan. 1983. Patterns of Voting Behavior in Judicial Retention Elections for Supreme Court Justices in Wyoming. <u>Judicature</u>, 67: 69-77.

Heritage Foundation Public Opinion Poll. 1987. Casper, Wyoming: Wyoming Heritage Foundation.

Horan, Michael J. 1991. The Wyoming Constitution: A Centennial Assessment. <u>Land and Water Law Review</u>, 26:13-31.

Horan, Michael J. 1972. Choosing Judges in Wyoming: Popular Election or Merit Selection? Laramie, Wyoming: University of Wyoming Government Research Bureau.

Horan, Michael J. and Kenyon N. Griffin. 1989. Ousting the Judge: Campaign Politics in the 1984 Wyoming Judicial Retention Elections. <u>Land and Water Law Review</u>, 24: 371-399.

Horan, Michael J., and James D. King. 1999. The 1992 Reapportionment Law: The Demise of the Multi-Member Districts System and Its Effect upon the Representation of Women in the Wyoming Legislature. <u>Land and Water Law Review</u> 34 (#2): 407-425.

Hunt, Kathleen. 1994. <u>Handbook for Wyoming Mayors and City Council Members</u>. Cheyenne, Wyoming: Wyoming Association of Municipalities.

Jacob, Herbert. 1984. <u>Justice in America: Courts, Lawyers and the Judicial Process</u>. Boston: Little Brown.

<u>Jahnke v. State</u> WY 114, 692 P.2d 911 (1984).

Jenkins, William, 1973. Retention Elections: Who Wins When No One Loses? <u>Judicature</u>, 61: 79-86.

<u>Johnson v. McIntosh</u> 21 U.S. 543 (1823).

Jordan, Roy. 1990. Wyoming: A Centennial Reflection. <u>Annals of Wyoming</u>, 62: 114.

Keiter, Robert B. and Tim Newcomb. 1993. <u>The Wyoming Constitution: A Reference Source</u>. Westport, Connecticut: Greenwood.

King, James D. 1993. Term Limits in Wyoming. <u>Comparative State Politics</u> 14 (#2): 1-18.

Larson, T.A. 1965. <u>History of Wyoming</u>. Lincoln: University of Nebraska Press.

Larson, T.A. 1977. <u>Wyoming: A Bicentennial History</u>. New York: W.W. Norton.

Luckett, Bill. 2002a. Few Complain About Districts. <u>Casper Star-Tribune</u>, January 5, A1.

Luckett, Bill. 2002b. Redistricting Bill on Governor's Desk. <u>Casper Star-Tribune</u>, March 2, A4.

Luckett, Bill. 2002c. Some Run, Some Stay. <u>Casper Star-Tribune</u>, February 26, A4.

Magleby, David B. 1984. <u>Direct Legislation: Voting on Ballot Propositions in the United States</u>. Baltimore: Johns Hopkins University Press.

Management Council of the Wyoming Legislature v. Geringer 953 P.2d. 839 (Wyo. 1998).

Miller, Warren E., and J. Merrill Shanks. 1996. The New American Voter. Boston: Harvard University Press.

Morton, Tom. 2002. Declaring Conflicts Personal Decision. Casper Star-Tribune, March 7, A1.

O'Brien, Sharon. 1989. American Indian Tribal Governments. Norman, Oklahoma: University of Oklahoma Press.

Pelkey, Charles. 1991a. PACs Fund Major Share of Successful House Campaigns. Casper Star-Tribune, February 9: A1.

Pelkey, Charles. 1991b. PACs Spent $50,000 in Senate Campaigns. Casper Star-Tribune, February 3: A1.

Pelkey, Charles. 1992. Sullivan Vetoes Redistrict Plan. Casper Star-Tribune, February 18, A1.

Peterson, Henry. 1940. The Constitutional Convention of Wyoming. University of Wyoming Publications, 7: 101-131.

Porter, Douglas R., Ben C. Lin and Richard Peiser. 1987. Special Districts: A Useful Technique for Financing Infrastructure. Washington, D.C.: Urban Land Institute.

Press, Charles and Kenneth VerBurg. 1983. State and Community Governments in the Federal System. New York: Wiley.

Ray, David. 1982 The Sources of Voting Cues in Three State Legislatures. Journal of Politics 44 (November):1074-1087.

Reynolds v. Sims 337 U.S. 533 (1964).

Richard, John B. 1974. Government and Politics of Wyoming. Dubuque, Iowa: Kendall/Hunt Publishing Company.

Sniffin, Bill. 2003. Are Legislators Snowed Under? Laramie Daily Boomerang, February 9, p. 4.

Songer, Donald R., James M. Underwood, Sonja G. Dillon, Patricia E. Jameson, and Darla W. Kite. 1985. Voting Cues in Two State Legislatures: A Further Application of the Kingdon Model. Social Science Quarterly 66 (December): 983-990.

Sturm, Albert L. 1982. The Development of American State Constitutions. Publius: The Journal of Federalism, 12: 57.

Thomas, Clive S., and Ronald J. Hrebenar. 1990. Interest Groups in the States. In Virginia Gray, Herbert Jacob, and Robert B. Albritton, eds. Politics in the American States: A Comparative Analysis. Glenview, Ill.: Scott, Foresman/Little, Brown.

Trenholm, Virginia Cole. 1974. Wyoming Historical Blue Book. Cheyenne, Wyoming: Wyoming State Archives and Historical Department.

Tucker, Harvey J., and Ronald E. Weber. 1992. Electoral Change in U.S. States: System versus Constituency Opinion. In Gary F. Moncrief and Joel A. Thompson, eds. Changing Patterns in State Legislative Careers. Ann Arbor: University of Michigan Press.

United States Government. Department of Commerce. Bureau of the Census. Statistical Abstract of the United States. 1998. Washington, D.C.: Government Printing Office.

United States Government. Department of Commerce. Bureau of the Census. Statistical Abstract of the United States. 1994. Washington, D.C.: Government Printing Office.

Utley, Robert M. 1984. The Indian Frontier of the American West. Albuquerque: University of New Mexico Press.

Walker, Jack. 1969. The Diffusion of Innovations Among the American States. The American Political Science Review, 63: 880-889.

Walter, B. Oliver, and Kendall L. Baker. 1973. The Wyoming Legislature: Lawmakers, the Public, and the Press. Laramie, Wyo.: Government Research Bureau, University of Wyoming.

Walter, Brett. 1987. Wyoming's Constitutional Convention Delegates. (An unpublished paper). Department of Political Science. University of Wyoming.

Whynott, Phillip. 1971. The Wyoming Supreme Court and Municipal Corporations: A Study in Judicial Policy Making. Unpublished M.A. Thesis, University of Wyoming.

Wilkinson, Charles F. 1987. American Indians, Time, and the Law: Native Societies in a Modern Constitutional Democracy. New Haven, Connecticut: Yale.

Wold, John T., and John H. Culver. 1987. The Defeat of the California Justices. Judicature, 41: 348-355.

Wolfinger, Raymond E., David P. Glass, and Peverill Squire. 1990. Predictors of Electoral Turnout: An International Comparison. Policy Studies Review 9: 551-574.

Woll, Peter and Robert H. Binstock. 1991. America's Political System: A Text with Cases. New York: McGraw Hill.

Worcester v. Georgia 31 U.S. 515 (1832).

Wunder, John R. 1994. Retained by the People: A History of American Indians and the Bill of Rights. New York: Oxford.

Wyoming. Constitution of the State of Wyoming. Cheyenne, Wyoming: Office of the Secretary of State.

Wyoming (Ter.) Constitutional Convention. 1893. Journal and Debates of the Constitutional Convention of the State of Wyoming. Cheyenne, Wyoming: The Daily Sun.

Wyoming County Courts. 2000 Caseload Statistics. Cheyenne, Wyoming: Supreme Court of Wyoming.

Wyoming Election Year Survey. Various years. Conducted by the Government Research Bureau, University of Wyoming.

Appendix

CONSTITUTION OF THE STATE OF WYOMING

Table of Contents

THE EQUALITY STATE Government and Politics in Wyoming

CONSTITUTION
of the
STATE OF WYOMING

PREAMBLE

We, the people of the State of Wyoming, grateful to God for our civil, political and religious liberties, and desiring to secure them to ourselves and perpetuate them to our posterity, do ordain and establish this Constitution.

ARTICLE 1

DECLARATION OF RIGHTS

Sec. 1. Power inherent in the people. All power is inherent in the people, and all free governments are founded on their authority, and instituted for their peace, safety and happiness; for the advancement of these ends they have at all times an inalienable and indefeasible right to alter, reform or abolish the government in such manner as they may think proper.

Sec. 2. Equality of all. In their inherent right to life, liberty and the pursuit of happiness, all members of the human race are equal.

Sec. 3. Equal political rights. Since equality in the enjoyment of natural and civil rights is only made sure through political equality, the laws of this state affecting the political rights and privileges of its citizens shall be without distinction of race, color, sex, or any circumstance or condition whatsoever other than individual incompetency, or unworthiness duly ascertained by a court of competent jurisdiction.

Sec. 4. Security against search and seizure. The right of the people to be secure in their persons, houses, papers and effects against unreasonable searches and seizures shall not be violated, and no warrant shall issue but upon probable cause, supported by affidavit, particularly describing the place to be searched or the person or thing to be seized.

Sec. 5. Imprisonment for debt. No person shall be imprisoned for debt, except in cases of fraud.

Sec. 6. Due process of law. No person shall be deprived of life, liberty or property without due process of law.

Sec. 7. No absolute, arbitrary power. Absolute, arbitrary power over the lives, liberty and property of freemen exists nowhere in a republic, not even in the largest majority.

Sec. 8. Courts open to all; suits against state. All courts shall be open and every person for an injury done to person, reputation or property shall have justice administered without sale, denial or delay. Suits may be brought against the state in such manner and in such courts as the legislature may by law direct.

Sec. 9. Trial by jury inviolate. The right of trial by jury shall remain inviolate in criminal cases. A jury in civil cases and in criminal cases where the charge is a misdemeanor may consist of less than twelve (12) persons but not less than six (6), as may be prescribed by law. A grand jury may consist of twelve (12) persons, any nine (9) of whom concurring may find an indictment. The legislature may change, regulate or abolish the grand jury system.

Sec. 10. Right of accused to defend. In all criminal prosecutions the accused shall have the right to defend in person and by counsel, to demand the nature and cause of the accusation, to have a copy thereof, to be confronted with the witnesses against him, to have compulsory process served for obtaining witnesses, and to a speedy trial by an impartial jury of the county or district in which the offense is alleged to have been committed. When the location of the offense cannot be established with certainty, venue may be placed in the county or district where the corpus delecti [delicti] is found, or in any county or district in which the victim was transported.

Sec. 11. Self-incrimination; jeopardy. No person shall be compelled to testify against himself in any criminal case, nor shall any person be twice put in jeopardy for the same offense. If a jury disagree, or if the judgment be arrested after a verdict, or if the judgment be reversed for error in law, the accused shall not be deemed to have been in jeopardy.

Sec. 12. Detaining witnesses. No person shall be detained as a witness in any criminal prosecution longer than may be necessary to take his testimony or deposition, nor be confined in any room where criminals are imprisoned.

Sec. 13. Indictment. Until otherwise provided by law, no person shall, for a felony, be proceeded against criminally, otherwise than by indictment, except in cases arising in the land or naval forces, or in the militia when in actual service in time of war or public danger.

Sec. 14. Bail; cruel and unusual punishment. All persons shall be bailable by sufficient sureties, except for capital offenses when the proof is evident or the presumption great. Excessive bail shall not be required, nor excessive fines imposed, nor shall cruel or unusual punishment be inflicted.

Sec. 15. Penal code to be humane. The penal code shall be framed on the humane principles of reformation and prevention.

Sec. 16. Conduct of jails. No person arrested and confined in jail shall be treated with unnecessary rigor. The erection of safe and comfortable prisons, and inspection of prisons, and the humane treatment of prisoners shall be provided for.

Sec. 17. Habeas corpus. The privilege of the writ of habeas corpus shall not be suspended unless, when in case of rebellion or invasion the public safety may require it.

Sec. 18. Religious liberty. The free exercise and enjoyment of religious profession and worship without discrimination or preference shall be forever guaranteed in this state, and no person shall be rendered incompetent to hold any office of trust or profit, or to serve as a witness or juror, because of his opinion on any matter of religious belief whatever; but the liberty of conscience hereby secured shall not be so construed as to excuse acts of licentiousness or justify practices inconsistent with the peace or safety of the state.

Sec. 19.   Appropriations for sectarian or religious societies or institutions prohibited. No money of the state shall ever be given or appropriated to any sectarian or religious society or institution.

Sec. 20.   Freedom of speech and press; libel; truth a defense. Every person may freely speak, write and publish on all subjects, being responsible for the abuse of that right; and in all trials for libel, both civil and criminal, the truth, when published with good intent and [for] justifiable ends, shall be a sufficient defense, the jury having the right to determine the facts and the law, under direction of the court.

Sec. 21.   Right of petition and peaceable assembly. The right of petition, and of the people peaceably to assemble to consult for the common good, and to make known their opinions, shall never be denied or abridged.

Sec. 22.   Protection of labor. The rights of labor shall have just protection through laws calculated to secure to the laborer proper rewards for his service and to promote the industrial welfare of the state.

Sec. 23.   Education. The right of the citizens to opportunities for education should have practical recognition. The legislature shall suitably encourage means and agencies calculated to advance the sciences and liberal arts.

Sec. 24.   Right to bear arms. The right of citizens to bear arms in defense of themselves and of the state shall not be denied.

Sec. 25.   Military subordinate to civil power; quartering soldiers. The military shall ever be in strict subordination to the civil power. No soldier in time of peace shall be quartered in any house without consent of the owner, nor in time of war except in the manner prescribed by law.

Sec. 26.   Treason. Treason against the state shall consist only in levying war against it, or in adhering to its enemies, or in giving them aid and comfort. No person shall be convicted of treason unless on the testimony of two witnesses to the same overt act, or on confession in open court; nor shall any person be attained of treason by the legislature.

Sec. 27.   Elections free and equal. Elections shall be open, free and equal, and no power, civil or military, shall at any time interfere to prevent an untrammeled exercise of the right of suffrage.

Sec. 28.   Taxation; consent of people; uniformity and equality. No tax shall be imposed without the consent of the people or their authorized representatives.

Sec. 29.   Rights of aliens. No distinction shall ever be made by law between resident aliens and citizens as to the possession, taxation, enjoyment and descent of property.

Sec. 30.   Monopolies and perpetuities prohibited. Perpetuities and monopolies are contrary to the genius of a free state, and shall not be allowed. Corporations being creatures of the state, endowed for the public good with a portion of its sovereign powers, must be subject to its control.

Sec. 31.   Control of water. Water being essential to industrial prosperity, of limited amount, and easy of diversion from its natural channels, its control must be in the state, which, in providing for its use, shall equally guard all the various interests involved.

Sec. 32.   Eminent domain. Private property shall not be taken for private use unless by consent of the owner, except for private ways of necessity, and for reservoirs, drains, flumes or ditches on or across the lands of others for agricultural, mining, milling, domestic or sanitary purposes, nor in any case without due compensation.

Sec. 33.   Compensation for property taken. Private property shall not be taken or damaged for public or private use without just compensation.

Sec. 34.   Uniform operation of general law. All laws of a general nature shall have a uniform operation.

Sec. 35.   Ex post facto laws; impairing obligation of contracts. No ex post facto law, nor any law impairing the obligation of contracts, shall ever be made.

Sec. 36.   Rights not enumerated reserved to people. The enumeration in this constitution, of certain rights shall not be construed to deny, impair, or disparage others retained by the people.

Sec. 37.   Constitution of United States supreme law of land. The State of Wyoming is an inseparable part of the federal union, and the constitution of the United States is the supreme law of the land.

ARTICLE 2

DISTRIBUTION OF POWERS

Sec. 1.   Powers of government divided into three departments. The powers of the government of this state are divided into three distinct departments: The legislative, executive and judicial, and no person or collection of persons charged with the exercise of powers properly belonging to one of these departments shall exercise any powers properly belonging to either of the others, except as in this constitution expressly directed or permitted.

ARTICLE 3

LEGISLATIVE DEPARTMENT

Sec. 1.   Composition and name of legislature. The legislative power shall be vested in a senate and house of representatives, which shall be designated "the legislature of the State of Wyoming."

Sec. 2.   Members' terms and qualifications. Senators shall be elected for the term of four (4) years and representatives for the term of two (2) years. The senators elected at the first election shall be divided by lot into two classes as nearly equal as may be. The seats of senators of the first class shall be vacated at the expiration of the first two years, and of the second class at the expiration of four years. No person shall be a senator who has not attained the age of twenty-five years, or a representative who has not attained the age of twenty-one years, and who is not a citizen of the United States and of this state and who has not, for at least twelve months next preceding his election resided within the county or district in which he was elected.

Sec. 3.   Legislative apportionment. Each county shall constitute a senatorial and representative district; the senate and house of representatives shall be composed of members elected by the legal voters of the counties respectively, every two (2) years. They shall be apportioned among the said counties as nearly as may be according to the number of their inhabitants. Each county shall have at least one senator and one representative; but at no time shall the number of members of the house of representatives be less than twice nor greater than three times the number of members of the senate. The senate and house of representatives first elected in pursuance of this constitution shall consist of sixteen and thirty-three members respectively.

Sec. 4.   Vacancies. [Repealed.]

Sec. 5.   When members elected and terms begin. Members of the senate and house of representatives shall be elected on the day provided by law for the general election of a member of congress, and their term of office shall begin on the first Monday of January thereafter.

Sec. 6.   Compensation of members; duration of sessions. The legislature shall not meet for more than sixty (60) legislative working days excluding Sundays during the term for which members of the house of representatives are elected, except when called into special session. The legislature shall determine by statute the number of days not to exceed sixty (60) legislative working days to be devoted to general and budget session, respectively. The legislature shall meet on odd-numbered years for a general and budget session. The legislature may meet on even-numbered years for budget session. During the budget session no bills except the budget bill may be introduced unless placed on call by a two-thirds vote of either house. The legislature shall meet for no more than forty (40) legislative working days excluding Sundays in any (1) calendar year, except when called into special session. The compensation of the members of the legislature shall be as provided by law; but no legislature shall fix its own compensation.

Sec. 7.   Time and place of sessions.

(a)   The legislature shall meet at the seat of government at twelve o'clock noon, on the second Tuesday of January of the odd-numbered years for general and budget session and may meet on the second Tuesday of January of the even-numbered years for budget session, and at other times when convened by the governor or upon call of the legislature as herein provided. The governor by proclamation may also, in times of war or grave emergency by law defined, temporarily convene the legislature at a place or places other than the seat of government. The legislature may convene a special session not to last longer than twenty (20) working days as follows:

(i)   Upon written request to the presiding officer of each house of the legislature by a majority of the elected members of each house, the legislature shall convene in special session; or

(ii)   The presiding officers of each house shall also jointly call a special session for the purpose of resolving a challenge or a dispute of any kind in the determination of the presidential electors.

Sec. 8.   Members disqualified for other office. No senator or representative shall, during the term for which he was elected, be appointed to any civil office under the state, and no member of congress or other person holding an office (except that of notary public or an office in the militia) under the United States or this state, shall be a member of either house during his continuance in office.

Sec. 9.   Compensation not to be increased during term. No member of either house shall, during the term for which he was elected, receive any increase of salary or mileage under any law passed during that term.

Sec. 10.   Presiding officers; other officers; each house to judge of election and qualifications of its members. The senate shall, at the beginning and close of each regular session and at such other times as may be necessary, elect one of its members president; the house of representatives shall elect one of its members speaker; each house shall choose its other officers, and shall judge of the election returns and qualifications of its members.

Sec. 11.   Quorum. A majority of each house shall constitute a quorum to do business, but a smaller number may adjourn from day to day, and compel the attendance of absent members in such manner and under such penalties as each house may prescribe.

Sec. 12.   Rules, punishment and protection. Each house shall have power to determine the rules of its proceedings, and [to] punish its members or other persons for contempt or disorderly behavior in its presence; to protect its members against violence or offers of bribes or private solicitation, and with the concurrence of two-thirds, to expel a member, and shall have all other powers necessary to the legislature of a free state. A member expelled for corruption shall not thereafter be eligible to either house of the legislature, and punishment for contempt or disorderly behavior shall not bar a criminal prosecution for the same offense.

Sec. 13.   Journals. Each house shall keep a journal of its proceedings and may, in its discretion, from time to time, publish the same, except such parts as require secrecy, and the yeas and nays on any question, shall, at the request of any two members, be entered on the journal.

Sec. 14.   Sessions to be open. The sessions of each house and of the committee of the whole shall be open unless the business is such as requires secrecy.

Sec. 15.   Adjournment. Neither house shall, without the consent of the other, adjourn for more than three days, nor to any other place than that in which the two houses shall be sitting.

Sec.16.   Privilege of members. The members of the legislature shall, in all cases, except treason, felony, violation of their oath of office and breach of the peace, be privileged from arrest during their attendance at the sessions of their respective houses, and in going to and returning from the same; and for any speech or debate in either house they shall not be questioned in any other place.

Sec. 17.   Power of impeachment; proceedings. The sole power of impeachment shall vest in the house of representatives; the concurrence of a majority of all the members being necessary to the exercise thereof. Impeachment shall be tried by the senate sitting for that purpose, and the senators shall be upon oath or affirmation to do justice according to law and evidence. When the governor is on trial, the chief justice of the supreme court shall preside. No person shall be convicted without a concurrence of two-thirds of the senators elected.

Sec. 18.   Who may be impeached. The governor and other state and judicial officers except justices of the peace, shall be liable to impeachment for high crimes and misdemeanors, or malfeasance in office, but judgment in such cases shall only extend to removal from office and disqualification to hold any office of honor, trust or profit under the laws of the state. The party, whether convicted or acquitted, shall, nevertheless, be liable to prosecution, trial, judgment and punishment according to law.

Sec. 19. Removal of officers not subject to impeachment. Except as hereafter provided, all officers not liable to impeachment shall be subject to removal for misconduct or malfeasance in office as provided by law. Any person appointed by the governor to serve as head of a state agency, or division thereof, or to serve as a member of a state board or commission, may be removed by the governor as provided by law.

Sec. 20. Laws to be passed by bill; alteration or amendment of bills. No law shall be passed except by bill, and no bill shall be so altered or amended on its passage through either house as to change its original purpose.

Sec. 21. Enacting clause of law. The enacting clause of every law shall be as follows: "Be it Enacted by the Legislature of the State of Wyoming."

Sec. 22. Limitation on time for introducing bill for appropriation. No bill for the appropriation of money, except for the expenses of the government, shall be introduced within five (5) days of the close of the session, except by unanimous consent of the house in which it is sought to be introduced.

Sec. 23. Bill must go to committee. No bill shall be considered or become a law unless referred to a committee, returned therefrom and printed for the use of the members.

Sec. 24. Bill to contain only one subject, which shall be expressed in title. No bill, except general appropriation bills and bills for the codification and general revision of the laws, shall be passed containing more than one subject, which shall be clearly expressed in its title; but if any subject is embraced in any act which is not expressed in the title, such act shall be void only as to so much thereof as shall not be so expressed.

Sec. 25. Vote required to pass bill. No bill shall become a law except by a vote of a majority of all the members elected to each house, nor unless on its final passage the vote taken by ayes and noes, and the names of those voting be entered on the journal.

Sec. 26. How laws revised, amended or extended. No law shall be revised or amended, or the provisions thereof extended by reference to its title only, but so much thereof as is revised, amended, or extended, shall be re-enacted and published at length.

Sec. 27. Special and local laws prohibited. The legislature shall not pass local or special laws in any of the following enumerated cases, that is to say: For granting divorces; laying out, opening, altering or working roads or highways; vacating roads, town plats, streets, alleys or public grounds; locating or changing county seats; regulating county or township affairs; incorporation of cities, towns or villages; or changing or amending the charters of any cities, towns or villages; regulating the practice in courts of justice; regulating the jurisdiction and duties of justices of the peace, police magistrates or constables; changing the rules of evidence in any trial or inquiry; providing for changes of venue in civil or criminal cases; declaring any person of age; for limitation of civil actions; giving effect to any informal or invalid deeds; summoning or impaneling grand or petit juries; providing for the management of common schools; regulating the rate of interest on money; the opening or conducting of any election or designating the place of voting; the sale or mortgage of real estate belonging to minors or others under disability; chartering or licensing ferries or bridges or toll roads; chartering banks, insurance companies and loan and trust companies; remitting fines, penalties or forfeitures; creating[,] increasing, or decreasing fees, percentages or allowances of public officers; changing the law of descent; granting to any corporation, association or individual, the right to lay down railroad tracks, or any special or exclusive privilege, immunity or franchise whatever, or amending existing charter for such purpose; for punishment of crimes; changing the names of persons or places; for the assessment or collection of taxes; affecting estates of deceased persons, minors or others under legal disabilities; extending the time for the collection of taxes; refunding money paid into the state treasury, relinquishing or extinguishing, in whole or part, the indebtedness, liabilities or obligation of any corporation or person to this state or to any municipal corporation therein; exempting property from taxation; restoring to citizenship persons convicted of infamous crimes; authorizing the creation, extension or impairing of liens; creating offices or prescribing the powers or duties of officers in counties, cities, townships or school districts; or authorizing the adoption or legitimation of children. In all other cases where a general law can be made applicable no special law shall be enacted.

Sec. 28. Signing of bills. The presiding officer of each house shall, in the presence of the house over which he presides, sign all bills and joint resolutions passed by the legislature immediately after their titles have been publicly read, and the fact of signing shall be at once entered upon the journal.

Sec. 29. Legislative employees. The legislature shall prescribe by law the number, duties and compensation of the officers and employes of each house, and no payment shall be made from the state treasury, or be in any way authorized to any such person except to an acting officer or employe elected or appointed in pursuance of law.

Sec. 30. Extra compensation to public officers prohibited. No bill shall be passed giving any extra compensation to any public officer, servant or employe, agent or contractor, after services are rendered or contract made.

Sec. 31. Supplies for legislature and departments. All stationery, printing, paper, fuel and lights used in the legislature and other departments of government shall be furnished, and the printing and binding of the laws, journals and department reports and other printing and binding, and the repairing and furnishing the halls and rooms used for the meeting of the legislature and its committees shall be performed under contract, to be given to the lowest responsible bidder, below such maximum price and under such regulations as may be prescribed by law. No member or officer of any department of the government shall be in any way interested in any such contract; and all such contracts shall be subject to the approval of the governor and state treasurer.

Sec. 32. Changing terms and salaries of public officers. Except as otherwise provided in this constitution, no law shall extend the term of any public officer or increase or diminish his salary or emolument after his election or appointment; but this shall not be construed to forbid the legislature from fixing salaries or emoluments of those officers first elected or appointed under this constitution, if such salaries or emoluments are not fixed by its provisions.

Sec. 33. Origin of revenue bills. All bills for raising revenue shall originate in the house of representatives; but the senate may propose amendments, as in case of other bills.

Sec. 34. General appropriation bills; other appropriations. The general appropriation bills shall embrace nothing but appropriations for the ordinary expenses of the legislative, executive and judicial departments of the state, interest on the public debt, and for public schools. All other appropriations shall be made by separate bills, each embracing but one subject.

Sec. 35. **Money expended only on appropriation.** Except for interest on public debt, money shall be paid out of the treasury only on appropriations made by the legislature, and in no case otherwise than upon warrant drawn by the proper officer in pursuance of law.

Sec. 36. **Prohibited appropriations.** No appropriation shall be made for charitable, industrial, educational or benevolent purposes to any person, corporation or community not under the absolute control of the state, nor to any denominational or sectarian institution or association.

Sec. 37. **Delegation of power to perform municipal functions prohibited.** The legislature shall not delegate to any special commissioner, private corporation or association, any power to make, supervise or interfere with any municipal improvements, moneys, property or effects, whether held in trust or otherwise, to levy taxes, or to perform any municipal functions whatever.

Sec. 38. **Investment of trust funds.** The legislature may authorize the investment of trust funds by executors, administrators, guardians or trustees, in the bonds or stocks of private corporations, and in such other securities as it may by law provide.

Sec. 39. **Aid to railroads prohibited.** The legislature shall have no power to pass any law authorizing the state or any county in the state to contract any debt or obligation in the construction of any railroad, or give or loan its credit to or in aid of the construction of the same.

Sec. 40. **Debts to state or municipal corporation cannot be released unless otherwise prescribed by legislature.** No obligation or liability of any person, association or corporation held or owned by the state or any municipal corporation therein shall ever be exchanged, transferred, remitted, released, postponed or in any way diminished except as may be prescribed by the legislature. The liability or obligation shall not be extinguished except by payment into the proper treasury or as may otherwise be prescribed by the legislature in cases where the obligation or liability is not collectible.

Sec. 41. **Resolutions; approval or veto.** Every order, resolution or vote, in which the concurrence of both houses may be necessary, except on the question of adjournment, or relating solely to the transaction of the business of the two houses, shall be presented to the governor, and before it shall take effect be approved by him, or, being disapproved, be repassed by two-thirds of both houses as prescribed in the case of a bill.

Sec. 42. **Bribery of legislators and solicitation of bribery defined; expulsion of legislator for bribery or solicitation.** If any person elected to either house of the legislature shall offer or promise to give his vote or influence in favor of or against any measure or proposition, pending or to be introduced into the legislature, in consideration or upon condition that any other person elected to the same legislature will give, or promise or assent to give his vote or influence in favor of or against any other measure or proposition pending or proposed to be introduced into such legislature, the person making such offer or promise shall be deemed guilty of solicitation of bribery. If any member of the legislature shall give his vote or influence for or against any measure or proposition pending or to be introduced in such legislature, or offer, promise or assent thereto, upon condition that any other member will give or will promise or assent to give his vote or influence in favor of or against any other measure or proposition pending or to be introduced in such legislature, or in consideration that any other member has given his vote or influence for or against any other measure or proposition in such legislature, he shall be deemed guilty of bribery, and any member of the legislature, or person elected thereto, who shall be guilty of either of such offenses, shall be expelled and shall not thereafter be eligible to the legislature, and on conviction thereof in the civil courts shall be liable to such further penalty as may be prescribed by law.

Sec. 43. **Offers to bribe.** Any person who shall directly or indirectly offer, give or promise any money or thing of value, testimonial, privilege or personal advantage, to any executive or judicial officer or member of the legislature, to influence him in the performance of any of his official duties shall be deemed guilty of bribery, and be punished in such manner as shall be provided by law.

Sec. 44. **Witnesses in bribery charges.** Any person may be compelled to testify in any lawful investigation or judicial proceeding against any person who may be charged with having committed the offense of bribery or corrupt solicitation, or practices of solicitation, and shall not be permitted to withhold his testimony upon the ground that it may criminate himself, or subject him to public infamy; but such testimony shall not afterwards be used against him in any judicial proceeding, except for perjury in giving such testimony, and any person convicted of either of the offenses aforesaid shall, as part of the punishment therefor, be disqualified from holding any office or position of honor, trust or profit in this state.

Sec. 45. **Legislature shall define corrupt solicitation.** The offense of corrupt solicitation of members of the legislature or of public officers of the state, or of any municipal division thereof, and the occupation or practice of solicitation of such members or officers to influence their official actions shall be defined by law and shall be punishable by fine and imprisonment.

Sec. 46. **Interested member shall not vote.** A member who has a personal or private interest in any measure or bill proposed or pending before the legislature shall disclose the fact to the house of which he is a member, and shall not vote thereon.

APPORTIONMENT

Sec. 47. **Congressional representation.** One representative in the congress of the United States shall be elected from the state at large, the Tuesday next after the first Monday in November, 1890, and thereafter at such times and places, and in such manner as may be prescribed by law. When a new apportionment shall be made by congress, the legislature shall divide the state into congressional districts accordingly.

Sec. 48. **State census.** At the first budget session of the legislature following the federal census, the legislature shall reapportion its membership based upon that census. Notwithstanding any other provision of this article, any bill to apportion the legislature may be introduced in a budget session in the same manner as in a general session.

Sec. 49. **District representation.** Congressional districts may be altered from time to time as public convenience may require. When a congressional district shall be composed of two or more counties they shall be contiguous, and the districts as compact as may be. No county shall be divided in the formation of congressional districts.

Sec. 50. Apportionment for first legislature.

Until an apportionment of senators and representatives as otherwise provided by law, they shall be divided among the several counties of the state in the following manner:

Albany County, two senators and five representatives.
Carbon County, two senators and five representatives.
Converse County, one senator and three representatives.
Crook County, one senator and two representatives.
Fremont County, one senator and two representatives.
Laramie County, three senators and six representatives.
Johnson County, one senator and two representatives.
Sheridan County, one senator and two representatives.
Sweetwater County, two senators and three representatives.
Uinta County, two senators and three representatives.

Sec. 51. Filling of vacancies.

When vacancies shall occur in the membership of either house of the legislature of the State of Wyoming through death, resignation or other cause, such vacancies shall be filled in such manner as may be prescribed by law, notwithstanding the provisions of section 4 of article III of the constitution which is by this section repealed.

This section was added by an amendment proposed by the 1947 legislature, ratified by a vote of the people at the general election held November 2, 1948, and proclaimed in effect December 1, 1948.

Sec. 52. Initiative and referendum.

(a) The people may propose and enact laws by the initiative, and approve or reject acts of the legislature by the referendum.

(b) An initiative or referendum is proposed by an application containing the bill to be initiated or the act to be referred. The application shall be signed by not less than one hundred (100) qualified voters as sponsors, and shall be filed with the secretary of state. If he finds it in proper form he shall so certify. Denial of certification shall be subject to judicial review.

(c) After certification of the application, a petition containing a summary of the subject matter shall be prepared by the secretary of state for circulation by the sponsors. The petition may be filed with the secretary of state if it meets both of the following requirements:

(i) It is signed by qualified voters, equal in number to fifteen percent (15%) of those who voted in the preceding general election; and

(ii) It is signed by qualified voters equal in number to fifteen percent (15%) of those resident in at least two-thirds (2/3) of the counties of the state, as determined by those who voted in the preceding general election in that county.

(d) An initiative petition may be filed at any time except that one may not be filed for a measure substantially the same as that defeated by an initiative election within the preceding (5) years. The secretary of state shall prepare a ballot title and proposition summarizing the proposed law, and shall place them on the ballot for the first statewide election held more than one hundred twenty (120) days after adjournment of the legislative session following the filing. If, before the election, substantially the same measure has been enacted, the petition is void.

(e) A referendum petition may be filed only within ninety (90) days after adjournment of the legislative session at which the act was passed, except that a referendum petition respecting any act previously passed by the legislature may be filed within six months after the power of referendum is adopted. The secretary of state shall prepare a ballot title and proposition summarizing the act and shall place them on the ballot for the first statewide election held more than one hundred eighty (180) days after adjournment of that session.

(f) If votes in an amount in excess of fifty percent (50%) of those voting in the general election are cast in favor of adoption of an initiated measure, the measure is enacted. If votes in an amount in excess of fifty percent (50%) of those voted in the general election are cast in favor of rejection of an act referred, it is rejected. The secretary of state shall certify the election returns. An initiated law becomes effective ninety (90) days after certification, is not subject to veto, and may not be repealed by the legislature within two (2) years of its effective date. It may be amended at any time. An act rejected by referendum is void thirty (30) days after certification. Additional procedures for the initiative and referendum may be prescribed by law.

(g) The initiative shall not be used to dedicate revenues, make or repeal appropriations, create courts, define the jurisdiction of courts or prescribe their rules, enact local or special legislation, or enact that prohibited by the constitution for enactment by the legislature. The referendum shall not be applied to dedications of revenue, to appropriations, to local or special legislation, or to law necessary for the immediate preservation of the public peace, health, or safety.

Sec. 53. Creation of criminal penalties not subject to governor's power to commute.

Notwithstanding Article 4, Section 5 of this Constitution, the legislature may by law create a penalty of life imprisonment without parole for specified crimes which sentence shall not be subject to commutation by the governor. The legislature may in addition limit commutation of a death sentence a sentence of life imprisonment without parole which sentence shall not be subject to further commutation. In no event shall the inherent power of the governor to grant a pardon be limited or curtailed.

This section was added by an amendment proposed by the 1967 legislature, ratified by a vote of the people at the general election held November 5, 1968, and proclaimed in effect December 9, 1968.

ARTICLE 4

EXECUTIVE DEPARTMENT

Sec. 1. Executive power vested in governor; term of governor. The executive power shall be vested in a governor, who shall hold his office for the term of four (4) years and until his successor is elected and duly qualified.

Sec. 2. Qualifications of governor. No person shall be eligible to the office of governor unless he be a citizen of the United States and a qualified elector of the state, who has attained the age of thirty years, and who has resided 5 years next preceding the election within the state or territory, nor shall he be eligible to any other office during the term for which he was elected.

Sec. 3. Election of governor. The governor shall be elected by the qualified electors of the state at the time and place of choosing members of the legislature. The person having the highest number of votes for governor shall be declared elected, but if two or more shall have an equal and highest number of votes for governor, the two houses of the legislature at its next regular session shall forthwith, by joint ballot, choose one of such persons for said office. The returns of the election for governor shall be made in such manner as shall be prescribed by law.

Sec. 4. Powers and duties of governor generally. The governor shall be commander-in-chief of the military forces of the state, except when they are called into the service of the United States, and may call out the same to execute the laws, suppress insurrection and repel invasion. He shall have power to convene the legislature on extraordinary occasions. He shall at the commencement of each session communicate to the legislature by message, information of the condition of the state, and recommend such measures as he shall deem expedient. He shall transact all necessary business with the officers of the government, civil and military. He shall expedite all such measures as may be resolved upon by the legislature and shall take care that the laws be faithfully executed.

Sec. 5. Pardoning power of governor. The governor shall have power to remit fines and forfeitures, to grant reprieves, commutations and pardons after conviction, for all offenses except treason and cases of impeachment; but the legislature may by law regulate the manner in which the remission of fines, pardons, commutations and reprieves may be applied for. Upon conviction for treason he shall have power to suspend the execution of sentence until the case is reported to the legislature at its next regular session, when the legislature shall either pardon, or commute the sentence, direct the execution of the sentence or grant further reprieve. He shall communicate to the legislature at each regular session each case of remission of fine, reprieve, commutation or pardon granted by him, stating the name of the convict, the crime for which he was convicted, the sentence and its date, and the date of the remission, commutation, pardon or reprieve with his reasons for granting the same.

Sec. 6. Acting governor. If the governor be impeached, displaced, resign or die, or from mental or physical disease or otherwise become incapable of performing the duties of his office or be absent from the state, the secretary of state shall act as governor until the vacancy is filled or the disability removed.

Sec. 7. When governor may fill vacancies in office. When any office from any cause becomes vacant, and no mode is provided by the constitution or law for filling such vacancy, the governor shall have the power to fill the same by appointment.

Sec. 8. Approval or veto of legislation by governor; passage over veto. Every bill which has passed the legislature shall, before it becomes a law, be presented to the governor. If he approve, he shall sign it; but if not, he shall return it with his objections to the house in which it originated, which shall enter the objections at large upon the journal and proceed to reconsider it. If, after such reconsideration, two-thirds of the members elected agree to pass the bill, it shall be sent, together with the objections, to the other house, by which it shall likewise be reconsidered, and if it be approved by two-thirds of the members elected, it shall become a law; but in all such cases the vote of both houses shall be determined by the yeas and nays, and the names of the members voting for and against the bill shall be entered upon the journal of each house respectively. If any bill is not returned by the governor within three days (Sundays excepted) after its presentation to him, the same shall be a law, unless the legislature by its adjournment, prevent its return, in which case it shall be a law, unless he shall file the same with his objections in the office of the secretary of state within fifteen days after such adjournment.

Sec. 9. Veto of items of appropriations. The governor shall have power to disapprove of any item or items or part or parts of any bill making appropriations of money or property embracing distinct items, and the part or parts of the bill approved shall be the law, and the item or items and part or parts disapproved shall be void unless enacted in the following manner: If the legislature be in session he shall transmit to the house in which the bill originated a copy of the item or items or part or parts thereof disapproved, together with his objections thereto, and the items or parts objected to shall be separately reconsidered, and each item or part shall then take the same course as is prescribed for the passage of bills over the executive veto.

Sec. 10. Bribery or coercion of or by governor. Any governor of this state who asks, receives or agrees to receive any bribe upon any understanding that his official opinion, judgment or action shall be influenced thereby, or who gives or offers, or promises his official influence in consideration that any member of the legislature shall give his official vote or influence on any particular side of any question or matter upon which he is required to act in his official capacity, or who menaces any member by the threatened use of his veto power, or who offers or promises any member that he, the governor, will appoint any particular person or persons to any office created or thereafter to be created, in consideration that any member shall give his official vote or influence on any matter pending or thereafter to be introduced into either house of said legislature; or who threatens any member that he, the governor, will remove any person or persons from office or position with intent in any manner to influence the action of said members, shall be punished in the manner now or that may hereafter be provided by law, and upon conviction thereof shall forfeit all right to hold or exercise any office of trust or honor in this state.

Sec. 11. State officers; election; qualifications; terms. There shall be chosen by the qualified electors of the state at the times and places of choosing members of the legislature, a secretary of state, auditor, treasurer, and superintendent of public instruction, who shall have attained the age of twenty-five (25) years respectively, shall be citizens of the United States, and shall have the qualifications of state electors. They shall severally hold their offices at the seat of government, for the term of four (4) years and until their successors are elected and duly qualified. The legislature may provide for such other state officers as are deemed necessary.

Sec. 12. State officers; powers and duties. The powers and duties of the secretary of state, of state auditor, treasurer and superintendent of public instruction shall be as prescribed by law.

Sec. 13.   Salaries of governor and other elective state officers. Until otherwise provided by law, the governor shall receive an annual salary of two thousand and five hundred dollars, the secretary of state, state auditor, state treasurer and superintendent of public instruction shall each receive an annual salary of two thousand dollars, and the salaries of any of the said officers shall not be increased or diminished during the period for which they were elected, and all fees and profits arising from any of the said offices shall be covered into the state treasury.

Sec. 14.   Examination of accounts. The legislature shall provide by law for examination of the accounts of state treasurer, supreme court clerks, district court clerks, and all county treasurers, and treasurers of such other public institutions as the legislature may prescribe.

Sec. 15.   Great seal of state. There shall be a seal of state which shall be called the "Great Seal of the State of Wyoming"; it shall be kept by the secretary of state and used by him officially as directed by law.

The seal of the Territory of Wyoming as now used shall be the seal of the state until otherwise provided by law.

ARTICLE 5

JUDICIAL DEPARTMENT

Sec. 1.   How judicial power vested. The judicial power of the state shall be vested in the senate, sitting as a court of impeachment, in a supreme court, district courts, and such subordinate courts as the legislature may, by general law, establish and ordain from time to time.

This section was amended by a resolution adopted by the 1965 legislature, ratified by a vote of the people at the general election held November 8, 1966, and proclaimed in effect on January 17, 1967.

Sec. 2.   Supreme court generally; appellate jurisdiction. The supreme court shall have general appellate jurisdiction, co-extensive with the state, in both civil and criminal causes, and shall have a general superintending control over all inferior courts, under such rules and regulations as may be prescribed by law.

Sec. 3.   Supreme court generally; original jurisdiction. The supreme court shall have original jurisdiction in quo warranto and mandamus as to all state officers, and in habeas corpus. The supreme court shall also have power to issue writs of mandamus, review, prohibition, habeas corpus, certiorari, and other writs necessary and proper to the complete exercise of its appellate and revisory jurisdiction. Each of the judges shall have power to issue writs of habeas corpus to any part of the state upon petition by or on behalf of a person held in actual custody, and may make such writs returnable before himself or before the supreme court, or before any district court of the state or any judge thereof.

Sec. 4.   Supreme court generally; number; election of chief justice; quorum; vacancies in supreme court or district court; judicial nominating commission; terms; standing for retention in office.

(a)   The supreme court of the state shall consist of not less than three nor more than five justices as may be determined by the legislature. The justices of the court shall elect one of their number to serve as chief justice for such term and with such authority as shall be prescribed by law. A majority of the justices shall constitute a quorum, and a concurrence of a majority of such quorum shall be sufficient to decide any matter. If a justice of the supreme court for any reason shall not participate in hearing any matter, the chief justice may designate one of the district judges to act for such nonparticipating justice.

(b)   A vacancy in the office of justice of the supreme court or judge of any district court or of such other courts that may be made subject to this provision by law, shall be filled by a qualified person appointed by the governor from a list of three nominees that shall be submitted by the judicial nominating commission. The commission shall submit such a list not later than 60 days after the death, retirement, tender of resignation, removal, failure of an incumbent to file a declaration of candidacy or certification of a negative majority vote on the question of retention in office under section [subsection] (g) hereof. If the governor shall fail to make any such appointment within 30 days from the day the list is submitted to him, such appointment shall be made by the chief justice from the list within 15 days.

(c)   There shall be a judicial nominating commission for the supreme court, district courts and any other courts to which these provisions may be extended by law. The commission shall consist of seven members, one of whom shall be the chief justice, or a justice of the supreme court designated by the chief justice to act for him, who shall be chairman thereof. In addition to the chief justice, or his designee, three resident members of the bar engaged in active practice shall be elected by the Wyoming state bar and three electors of the state not admitted to practice law shall be appointed by the governor to serve on said commission for such staggered terms as shall be prescribed by law. No more than two members of said commission who are residents of the same judicial district may qualify to serve any term or part of a term on the commission. In the case of courts having less than statewide authority, each judicial district not otherwise represented by a member on the commission, and each county, should the provisions hereof be extended by law to courts of lesser jurisdiction than district courts, shall be represented by two nonvoting advisors to the commission when an appointment to a court in such unrepresented district, or county, is pending; both of such advisors shall be residents of the district, or county, and one shall be a member of the bar appointed by the governing body of the Wyoming state bar and one shall be a nonattorney advisor appointed by the governor.

(d)   No member of the commission excepting the chairman shall hold any federal, state or county public office or any political party office, and after serving a full term he shall not be eligible for reelection or reappointment to succeed himself on the commission. No member of the judicial nominating commission shall be eligible for appointment to any judicial office while he is a member of the commission nor for a period of one year after the expiration of his term for which he was elected or appointed. Vacancies in the office of commissioner shall be filled for the unexpired terms in the same manner as the original appointments. Additional qualifications of members of the commission may be prescribed by law.

(e)   The chairman of the commission shall cast votes only in the event of ties. The commission shall operate under rules adopted by the supreme court. Members of the commission shall be entitled to no compensation other than expenses incurred for travel and subsistence while attending meetings of the commission.

(f)   The terms of supreme court justices shall be eight years and the terms of district court judges shall be six years.

(g)   Each justice or judge selected under these provisions shall serve for one year after his appointment and until the first Monday in January following the next general election after the expiration of such year. He shall, at such general election, stand for retention in office on a ballot which shall submit to the appropriate electorate the question whether such justice or judge shall be retained in office for another term or part of a term, and upon filing a declaration of candidacy in the form and at the times prescribed by law, he shall, at the general election next held before the expiration of each term, stand for retention on such ballots. The electorate of the whole state shall vote on the question of retention or rejection of justices of the supreme court, and any other statewide court; the electorate of the several judicial districts shall vote on the question of retention or rejection of judges of their respective districts, and the electorate of such other subdivisions of the state as shall be prescribed by law shall vote on the question of retention or rejection of any other judges to which these provisions may be extended.

(h)   A justice or judge selected hereunder, or one that is in office upon the effective date of this amendment, who shall desire to retain his judicial office a succeeding term, following the expiration of his existing term of office, shall file with the appropriate office not more than 6 months nor less than 3 months before the general election to be held before the expiration of his existing term of office a declaration of intent to stand for election for a succeeding term. When such a declaration of intent is filed, the appropriate electorate shall vote upon a nonpartisan judicial ballot on the question of retention in or rejection from office of such justice or judge, and if a majority of those voting on the question vote affirmatively, the justice or judge shall be elected to serve the succeeding term prescribed by law. If a justice or judge fails to file such a declaration within the time specified, or if a majority of those voting on the question vote negatively to any judicial candidacy, a vacancy will thereby be created in that office at the end of its existing term.

This section was amended by a resolution adopted by the 1957 legislature, ratified by a vote of the people on November 4, 1958, and proclaimed in effect on December 10, 1958. This section was amended again by a resolution adopted by the 1971 legislature, ratified by a vote of the people at the general election held November 7, 1972, and proclaimed in effect December 12, 1972. This section was amended again by a resolution adopted by the 1975 legislature, ratified by a vote of the people at the general election held November 2, 1976 and proclaimed in effect November 23, 1972.

Sec. 5.   Voluntary retirement and compensation of justices and judges. Subject to the further provisions of this section, the legislature shall provide for the voluntary retirement and compensation of justices and judges of the supreme court and district courts, and may do so for any other courts, on account of length of service, age and disability, and for their reassignment to active duty where and when needed. The office of every such justice and judge shall become vacant when the incumbent reaches the age of seventy (70) years, as the legislature may prescribe; but, in the case of an incumbent whose term of office includes the effective date of this amendment, this provision shall not prevent him from serving the remainder of said term nor be applicable to him before his period or periods of judicial service shall have reached a total of six (6) years. The legislature may also provide for benefits for dependents of justices and judges.

This section was amended by a resolution by the 1971 legislature, ratified by a vote of the people at the general election held November 7, 1972, and proclaimed in effect December 12, 1972.

Sec. 6.   Commission on judicial conduct and ethics.

(a)   There is hereby created the Commission on Judicial Conduct and Ethics. The commission shall have twelve (12) members who reside in Wyoming consisting of:

(i)   Three (3) active Wyoming judges, who are not members of the supreme court, elected by the full-time, active Wyoming judges;

(ii)   Three (3) members of the Wyoming state bar, appointed by its governing body; and

(iii)   Six (6) electors of the state, who are not active or retired judges or attorneys, appointed by the governor and confirmed by the senate.

(b)   All terms shall be for three (3) years duration. Members shall be eligible for reappointment to a second term.

(c)   The commission shall divide itself into investigatory and adjudicatory panels for each case considered. No commission member may serve on an adjudicatory panel in any case in which that member served in an investigatory capacity.

(d)   The commission, or a panel thereof, shall consider complaints of judicial misconduct made against judicial officers and, to the extent permitted and as provided for by the code of judicial conduct, may:

(i)   Discipline a judicial officer; or

(ii)   Recommend discipline of a judicial officer to the supreme court or a special supreme court.

(e)   The supreme court shall adopt a code of judicial conduct applicable to all judicial officers and adopt rules governing:

(i)   The election of judges to the commission;

(ii)   The staggering of terms, and the removal and filling of vacancies of commission members;

(iii)   The appointment of a special supreme court composed of five (5) district judges who are not members of the commission, to act in the place of the supreme court in any case involving the discipline or disability of a justice of the supreme court; and

(iv)   Procedures for the operation of the commission including exercise of the commission's disciplinary powers.

(f)   The supreme court or special supreme court, on recommendation of the commission or on its own motion may:

(i) Suspend a judicial officer without salary when the judicial officer is charged with or is convicted in the United States of a crime punishable as a felony or one involving moral turpitude under Wyoming or federal law, and remove that judicial officer in the event such conviction becomes final;

(ii) For any judicial officer removed from office, order a forfeiture of any pension or retirement benefits accrued after the offending conduct, except for those that have been vested under the Wyoming retirement act or any local plan;

(iii) Suspend the judicial officer from practicing law in this state; and

(iv) Remove a judicial officer from office or impose other discipline permitted by the rules for judicial discipline for conduct that constitutes willful misconduct in office, or for a willful and persistent failure to perform the duties of the office, or for habitual intemperance, or for conduct prejudicial to the administration of justice that brings the judicial office into disrepute, or for a violation of the code of judicial conduct.

(g) The code of judicial conduct shall provide for the mandatory retirement of a judicial officer for any disability that seriously interferes with the performance of the duties of the office and is, or is likely to become, permanent. A judicial officer retired by the supreme court or a special supreme court for a disability shall be considered to have retired voluntarily without loss of retirement benefits.

(h) A judicial officer removed from office is ineligible for any judicial office.

(j) This section applies to all judicial officers during their service on the bench and to former judicial officers regarding allegations of judicial misconduct occurring during service on the bench if a complaint is made within one (1) year following service. The term "judicial officer" includes all members of the judicial branch of government performing judicial functions.

Sec. 7.   Supreme court generally; terms of court. At least two terms of the supreme court shall be held annually at the seat of government at such times as may be provided by law.

Sec. 8.   Supreme court generally; qualifications of justices. No person shall be eligible to the office of justice of the supreme court unless he be learned in the law, have been in actual practice at least nine (9) years, or whose service on the bench of any court of record, when added to the time he may have practiced law, shall be equal to nine (9) years, be at least thirty years of age and a citizen of the United States, nor unless he shall have resided in this state or territory at least three years.

Sec. 9.   Supreme court generally; clerk. There shall be a clerk of the supreme court who shall be appointed by the justices of said court and shall hold his office during their pleasure, and whose duties and emoluments shall be as provided by law.

Sec. 10.   District courts generally; jurisdiction. The district court shall have original jurisdiction of all causes both at law and in equity and in all criminal cases, of all matters of probate and insolvency and of such special cases and proceedings as are not otherwise provided for. The district court shall also have original jurisdiction in all cases and of all proceedings in which jurisdiction shall not have been by law vested exclusively in some other court; and said court shall have the power of naturalization and to issue papers therefor. They shall have such appellate jurisdiction in cases arising in justices' and other inferior courts in their respective counties as may be prescribed by law. Said courts and their judges shall have power to issue writs of mandamus, quo warranto, review, certiorari, prohibition, injunction and writs of habeas corpus, on petition by or on behalf of any person in actual custody in their respective districts.

Sec. 11.   District courts generally; judges to hold court for each other. The judges of the district courts may hold courts for each other and shall do so when required by law.

Sec. 12.   District courts generally; qualifications of judges. No person shall be eligible to the office of judge of the district court unless he be learned in the law, be at least twenty-eight years of age, and a citizen of the United States, nor unless he shall have resided within the State or Territory of Wyoming at least two years next preceding his election.

Sec. 13.   District courts generally; clerks. There shall be a clerk of the district court in each organized county in which a court is holden who shall be elected, or, in case of vacancy, appointed in such manner and with such duties and compensation as may be prescribed by law.

Sec. 14.   District courts generally; commissioners. The legislature shall provide by law for the appointment by the several district courts of one or more district court commissioners (who shall be persons learned in the law) in each organized county in which a district court is holden, such commissioners shall have authority to perform such chamber business in the absence of the district judge from the county or upon his written statement filed with the papers, that it is improper for him to act, as may be prescribed by law, to take depositions and perform such other duties, and receive such compensation as shall be prescribed by law.

Sec. 15.   Style of process. The style of all process shall be "The State of Wyoming." All prosecutions shall be carried on in the name and by the authority of the State of Wyoming, and conclude "against the peace and dignity of the State of Wyoming."

Sec. 16.   Supreme court judges limited to judicial duties. No duties shall be imposed by law upon the supreme court or any of the judges thereof, except such as are judicial, nor shall any of the judges thereof exercise any power of appointment except as herein provided.

Sec. 17.   Salaries of judges of supreme and district courts. The judges of the supreme and district courts shall receive such compensation for their services as may be prescribed by law, which compensation shall not be increased or diminished during the term for which a judge shall have been elected, and the salary of a judge of the supreme or district court shall be as may be prescribed by law; provided, however, that when any legislative increase or decrease in the salary of the justices or judges of such courts whose respective terms of office do not expire at the same time, has heretofore or shall hereafter become effective as to any member of such court, it shall be effective from such date as to each of the members thereof.

This section was amended by a resolution proposed by the 1953 legislature, ratified by a vote of the people at the general election held November 2, 1954, and proclaimed in effect on December 7, 1954.

Sec. 18.   Appeals from district courts to supreme court. Writs of error and appeals may be allowed from the decisions of the district courts to the supreme court under such regulations as may be prescribed by law.

Sec. 19. State divided into districts; election and terms of district judges. Until otherwise provided by law, the state shall be divided into three judicial districts, in each of which there shall be elected at general elections, by the electors thereof, one judge of the district court therein, whose term shall be six (6) years from the first Monday in January succeeding his election and until his successor is duly qualified.

Sec. 20. Districts defined. Until otherwise provided by law, said judicial districts shall be constituted as follows: District number one shall consist of the counties of Laramie, Converse and Crook. District number two shall consist of the counties of Albany, Johnson and Sheridan. District number three shall consist of the counties of Carbon, Sweetwater, Uinta and Fremont.

Sec. 21. Increase in number of districts and judges. The legislature may from time to time increase the number of said judicial districts and the judges thereof, but such increase or change in the boundaries of the district shall not work the removal of any judge from his office during the term for which he may have been elected or appointed; provided the number of districts and district judges shall not exceed four (4) until the valuation of taxable property in the state shall be equal to one hundred million $100,000,000) dollars.

Sec. 22. Jurisdiction of justices of the peace. [Repealed.]

Sec. 23. Appeals from justices' courts. [Repealed.]

Sections 22 and 23 were repealed by a resolution adopted by the 1965 legislature, ratified by the people at the general election held November 8, 1966, and proclaimed in effect on January 17, 1967.

Sec. 24. Terms of district courts; attaching unorganized territory to organized counties. The time of holding courts in the several counties of a district shall be as prescribed by law, and the legislature shall make provisions for attaching unorganized counties or territory to organized counties for judicial purposes.

Sec. 25. Judges of supreme and district courts shall not practice. No judge of the supreme or district court shall act as attorney or counsellor at law.

Sec. 26. Power to fix terms of court. Until the legislature shall provide by law for fixing the terms of courts, the judges of the supreme court and district courts shall fix the terms thereof.

Sec. 27. Judges of supreme and district courts shall not hold other office. No judge of the supreme or district court shall be elected or appointed to any other than judicial offices or be eligible thereto during the term for which he was elected or appointed such judge.

Sec. 28. Appeals from boards of arbitration. Appeals from decisions of compulsory boards of arbitration shall be allowed to the supreme court of the state, and the manner of taking such appeals shall be prescribed by law.

Sec. 29. Juvenile delinquency and domestic relations courts. The legislature may by general law provide for such juvenile delinquency and domestic relations courts as may be needed, and for the number, qualifications and election of judges of such courts. Appeals shall lie in such cases and pursuant to such regulations as may be prescribed by law. Such courts shall have such jurisdiction as the legislature may by law provide.

ARTICLE 6

SUFFRAGE AND ELECTIONS

Sec. 1. Male and female citizens to enjoy equal rights. The rights of citizens of the State of Wyoming to vote and hold office shall not be denied or abridged on account of sex. Both male and female citizens of this state shall equally enjoy all civil, political and religious rights and privileges.

Wyoming was the first state in the Union to grant women equal suffrage with men.

Sec. 2. Qualifications of electors. Every citizen of the United States of the age of twenty-one years and upwards, who has resided in the state or territory one year and in the county wherein such residence is located sixty days next preceding any election, shall be entitled to vote at such election, except as herein otherwise provided.

There are no longer durational residency requirements for electors.
Since ratification of the 26th Amendment to the U.S. Constitution, twenty-one should read eighteen.

Sec. 3. Electors privileged from arrest. Electors shall in all cases except treason, felony or breach of the peace, be privileged from arrest on the days of election during their attendance at elections, and going to and returning therefrom.

Sec. 4. Exemption of electors from military duty. No elector shall be obliged to perform militia duty on the day of election, except in time of war or public danger.

Sec. 5. Electors must be citizens of United States. No person shall be deemed a qualified elector of this state, unless such person be a citizen of the United States.

Sec. 6. What persons excluded from franchise. All persons adjudicated to be mentally incompetent or persons convicted of felonies, unless restored to civil rights, are excluded from the elective franchise.

Sec. 7. When residence not lost by reason of absence. No elector shall be deemed to have lost his residence in the state, by reason of his absence on business of the United States, or of this state, or in the military or naval service of the United States.

Sec. 8. Soldiers stationed in state not considered residents. No soldier, seaman, or marine in the army or navy of the United States shall be deemed a resident of this state in consequence of his being stationed therein.

Sec. 9. Educational qualifications of electors. No person shall have the right to vote who shall not be able to read the constitution of this state. The provisions of this section shall not apply to any person prevented by physical disability from complying with its requirements.

*The Federal Voting Rights Act Amendments of 1970 prevent the use of a test or device as a condition to voting.

Sec. 10. Alien suffrage. Nothing herein contained shall be construed to deprive any person of the right to vote who has such right at the time of the adoption of this constitution, unless disqualified by the restrictions of section six of this article. After the expiration of five (5) years from the time of the adoption of this constitution, none but citizens of the United States shall have the right to vote.

Sec. 11. Manner of holding elections. All elections shall be by ballot. The legislature shall provide by law that the names of all candidates for the same office, to be voted for at any election, shall be printed on the same ballot, at public expense, and on election day be delivered to the voters within the polling place by sworn public officials, and only such ballots so delivered shall be received and counted. But no voter shall be deprived the privilege of writing upon the ballot used the name of any other candidate. All voters shall be guaranteed absolute privacy in the preparation of their ballots, and the secrecy of the ballot shall be made compulsory.

Sec. 12. Registration of voters required. No person qualified to be an elector of the State of Wyoming, shall be allowed to vote at any general or special election hereafter to be holden in the state, until he or she shall have registered as a voter according to law, unless the failure to register is caused by sickness or absence, for which provisions shall be made by law. The legislature of this state shall enact such laws as will carry into effect the provisions of this section, which enactment shall be subject to amendment, but shall never be repealed; but this section shall not apply to the first election held under this constitution.

Sec. 13. Purity of elections to be provided for. The legislature shall pass laws to secure the purity of elections, and guard against abuses of the elective franchise.

Sec. 14. Election contests. The legislature shall, by general law, designate the courts by which the several classes of election contests not otherwise provided for, shall be tried, and regulate the manner of trial and all matters incident thereto; but no such law shall apply to any contest arising out of an election held before its passage.

Sec. 15. Qualifications for office. No person except a qualified elector shall be elected or appointed to any civil or military office in the state. "Military office" shall be limited to the offices of adjutant general, assistant adjutant general for the army national guard and assistant adjutant general for the air national guard.

Sec. 16. When officers to hold over; suspension of officers. Every person holding any civil office under the state or any municipality therein shall, unless removed according to law, exercise the duties of such office until his successor is duly qualified, but this shall not apply to members of the legislature, nor to members of any board or assembly, two or more of whom are elected the same time. The legislature may by law provide for suspending any officer in his functions, pending impeachment or prosecution for misconduct in office.

Sec. 17. Time of holding general and special elections; when elected officers to enter upon duties.
All general elections for state and county officers, for members of the house of representatives and the senate of the State of Wyoming, and representatives to the congress of the United States, shall be held on the Tuesday next following the first Monday in November of each even year. Special elections may be held as now, or may hereafter be provided by law. All state and county officers elected at a general election shall enter upon their respective duties on the first Monday in January next following the date of their election, or as soon thereafter as may be possible.

Sec. 18. Method of selecting officers whose election is not provided for. All officers, whose election is not provided for in this constitution, shall be elected or appointed as may be directed by law.

Sec. 19. Dual office holding. No member of congress from this state, nor any person holding or exercising any office or appointment of trust or profit under the United States, shall at the same time hold or exercise any office in this state to which a salary, fees or perquisites shall be attached. The legislature may by law declare what offices are incompatible.

Sec. 20. Oath of office; form. Senators and representatives and all judicial, state and county officers shall, before entering on the duties of their respective offices, take and subscribe the following oath or affirmation: "I do solemnly swear (or affirm) that I will support, obey and defend the constitution of the United States, and the constitution of this state, and that I will discharge the duties of my office with fidelity; that I have not paid or contributed, or promised to pay or contribute, either directly or indirectly, any money or other valuable thing, to procure my nomination or election, (or appointment) except for necessary and proper expenses expressly authorized by law; that I have not, knowingly, violated any election law of the state, or procured it to be done by others in my behalf; that I will not knowingly receive, directly or indirectly, any money or other valuable thing for the performance or nonperformance of any act or duty pertaining to my office, other than the compensation allowed by law."

Sec. 21. Oath of office; how administered. The foregoing oath shall be administered by some person authorized to administer oaths, and in the case of state officers and judges of the supreme court shall be filed in the office of the secretary of state, and in the case of other judicial and county officers in the office of the clerk of the county in which the same is taken; any person refusing to take said oath or affirmation shall forfeit his office, and any person who shall be convicted of having sworn or affirmed falsely, or of having violated said oath or affirmation, shall be guilty of perjury, and be forever disqualified from holding any office of trust or profit within this state. The oath to members of the senate and house of representatives shall be administered by one of the judges of the supreme court or a justice of the peace, in the hall of the house to which the members shall be elected.

Sec. 22. Absent voter ballots, voting and registration. The provisions of section 11 of article 6 of this constitution, which provides that the ballots therein mentioned shall be delivered on election day to the voters within the polling place by sworn public officials, and that only such ballots so delivered shall be received and counted, shall not be applicable to, affect or invalidate absent voter ballots and voting thereof and registration therefor, as provided by article 14, of chapter 36, Wyoming Revised Statutes, 1931.

and other acts of the legislature of the State of Wyoming, amendatory thereof or related thereto, whether heretofore or hereafter enacted.

This section was added by an amendment proposed at the 1944 special session of the legislature, ratified by a vote of the people at the general election held November 7, 1944, and proclaimed in effect December 6, 1944.

ARTICLE 7

EDUCATION; STATE INSTITUTIONS; PROMOTION OF HEALTH AND MORALS; PUBLIC BUILDINGS

Sec. 1. Legislature to provide for public schools. The legislature shall provide for the establishment and maintenance of a complete and uniform system of public instruction, embracing free elementary schools of every needed kind and grade, a university with such technical and professional departments as the public good may require and the means of the state allow, and such other institutions as may be necessary.

Sec. 2. School revenues. The following are declared to be perpetual funds for school purposes, of which the annual income only can be appropriated, to-wit: Such per centum as has been or may hereafter be granted by congress on the sale of lands in this state; all moneys arising from the sale or lease of sections number sixteen and thirty-six in each township in the state, and the lands selected or that may be selected in lieu thereof; the proceeds of all lands that have been or may hereafter be granted to this state, where by the terms and conditions of the grant, the same are not to be otherwise appropriated; the net proceeds of lands and other property and effects that may come to the state by escheat or forfeiture, or from unclaimed dividends or distributive shares of the estates of deceased persons; all moneys, stocks, bonds, lands and other property now belonging to the common school funds. Provided, that the rents for the ordinary use of said lands shall be applied to the support of public schools and, when authorized by general law, not to exceed thirty-three and one-third (33 1/3) per centum of oil, gas, coal, or other mineral royalties arising from the lease of any said school lands may be so applied.

This section was amended by a resolution adopted by the 1923 legislature, ratified by a vote of the people at the general election held November 4, 1924, and proclaimed in effect December 10. 1924. The amendment added the proviso clause.

Sec. 3. Other sources of school revenues. To the sources of revenue above mentioned shall be added all other grants, gifts and devises that have been or may hereafter be made to this state and not otherwise appropriated by the terms of the grant, gift or devise.

Sec. 4. Restriction in use of revenues. All money, stocks, bonds, lands and other property belonging to a county school fund, except such moneys and property as may be provided by law for current use in aid of public schools, shall belong to and be invested by the several counties as a county public school fund, in such manner as the legislature shall by law provide, the income of which shall be appropriated exclusively to the use and support of free public schools in the several counties of the state.

This section was amended by a resolution adopted by the 1969 legislature, ratified by a vote of the people at the general election held November 3, 1970, and proclaimed in effect on December 3, 1970.

Sec. 5. Fines and penalties to belong to public school fund. All fines and penalties under general laws of the state shall belong to the public school fund of the respective counties and be paid over to the custodians of such funds for the current support of the public schools therein.

Sec. 6. State to keep school funds; investment. All funds belonging to the state for public school purposes, the interest and income of which only are to be used, shall be deemed trust funds in the care of the state, which shall keep them for the exclusive benefit of the public schools. The legislature shall provide by law for the investment of such trust funds.

This section was amended by resolutions adopted by the 1915 and 1969 legislatures. The latest amendment was ratified by a vote of the people at the general election held November 3, 1970, and proclaimed in effect on December 3, 1970.

Sec. 7. Application of school funds. The income arising from the funds mentioned in the preceding section, together with all the rents of the unsold school lands and such other means as the legislature may provide, shall be exclusively applied to the support of free schools in every county in the state.

Sec. 8. Distribution of school funds. Provision shall be made by general law for the equitable allocation of such income among all school districts in the state. But no appropriation shall be made from said fund to any district for the year in which a school has not been maintained for at least three (3) months; nor shall any portion of any public school fund ever be used to support or assist any private school, or any school, academy, seminary, college or other institution of learning controlled by any church or sectarian organization or religious denomination whatsoever.

This section was amended by a resolution adopted by the 1978 legislature, ratified by a vote of the people at the general election held on November 7, 1978, and proclaimed in effect on November 25, 1978.

Sec. 9. Taxation for schools. The legislature shall make such further provision by taxation or otherwise, as with the income arising from the general school fund will create and maintain a thorough and efficient system of public schools, adequate to the proper instruction of all youth of the state, between the ages of six and twenty-one years, free of charge; and in view of such provision so made, the legislature shall require that every child of sufficient physical and mental ability shall attend a public school durin[g] the period between six and eighteen years for a time equivalent to three years, unless educated by other means.

Sec. 10. No discrimination between pupils. In none of the public schools so established and maintained shall distinction or discrimination be made on account of sex, race or color.

Sec. 11. Textbooks. Neither the legislature nor the superintendent of public instruction shall have power to prescribe text book to be used in the public schools.

Sec. 12. Sectarianism prohibited. No sectarian instruction, qualifications or tests shall be imparted, exacted, applied or in any manner tolerated in the schools of any grade or character controlled by the state, nor shall attendance be required at any religious service therein, nor shall any sectarian tenets or doctrines be taught or favored in any public school or institution that may be established under this constitution.

Sec. 13. Land commissioners. [Superseded by Article 18, Section 3 as amended 1922.]

Sec. 14. Supervision of schools entrusted to state superintendent of public instruction. The general supervision of the public schools shall be entrusted to the state superintendent of public instruction, whose powers and duties shall be prescribed by law.

Sec. 15. Establishment of university confirmed. The establishment of the University of Wyoming is hereby confirmed, and said institution, with its several departments, is hereby declared to be the University of the State of Wyoming. All lands which have been heretofore granted or which may be granted hereafter by congress unto the university as such, or in aid of the instruction to be given in any of its departments, with all other grants, donations, or devises for said university, or for any of its departments, shall vest in said university, and be exclusively used for the purposes for which they were granted, donated or devised. The said lands may be leased on terms approved by the land commissioners, but may not be sold on terms not approved by congress.

Sec. 16. Tuition free. The university shall be equally open to students of both sexes, irrespective of race or color; and, in order that the instruction furnished may be as nearly free as possible, any amount in addition to the income from its grants of lands and other sources above mentioned, necessary to its support and maintenance in a condition of full efficiency shall be raised by taxation or otherwise, under provisions of the legislature.

Sec. 17. Government of university. The legislature shall provide by law for the management of the university, its lands and other property by a board of trustees, consisting of not less than seven members, to be appointed by the governor by and with the advice and consent of the senate, and the president of the university, and the superintendent of public instruction, as members ex officio, as such having the right to speak, but not to vote. The duties and powers of the trustees shall be prescribed by law.

Sec. 18. Establishment of institutions. Such charitable, reformatory and penal institutions as the claims of humanity and the public good may require, shall be established and supported by the state in such manner as the legislature may prescribe. They shal[l] be supervised as prescribed by law.

Sec. 19. Territorial institutions pass to state. The property of all charitable and penal institutions belonging to the Territory o[f] Wyoming shall, upon the adoption of this constitution, become the property of the State of Wyoming, and such of said institutions a[s] are then in actual operation, shall thereafter have the supervision of the board of charities and reform as provided in the last preceding section of this article, under provisions of the legislature.

Sec. 20. Duty of legislature to protect and promote health and morality of people. As the health and morality of the people are essential to their well-being, and to the peace and permanence of the state, it shall be the duty of the legislature to protect and promote these vital interests by such measures for the encouragement of temperance and virtue, and such restrictions upon vice and immorality of every sort, as are deemed necessary to the public welfare.

Sec. 21. Buildings and property of territory pass to state. All public buildings and other property, belonging to the territory shall, upon the adoption of this constitution, become the property of the State of Wyoming.

Sec. 22. Construction and supervision. The construction, care and preservation of all public buildings of the state not under the control of the board or officers of public institutions by authority of law shall be entrusted to such officers or boards, and under such regulations as shall be prescribed by law.

Sec. 23. Permanent location. The legislature shall have no power to change or to locate the seat of government, the state university, or state hospital, but may provide by law for submitting the question of the permanent locations thereof respectively, to the qualified electors of the state, at some general election, and a majority of all votes upon said question cast at said election, shall be necessary to determine the location thereof; but until the same are respectively and permanently located, as herein provided, the location of the seat of government and said institutions shall be as follows: The seat of government shall be located at the City of Cheyenne, in the County of Laramie. The state university shall be centered at the City of Laramie, in the County of Albany. The state hospital shall be located at or near the City of Evanston, in the County of Uinta. A penitentiary shall be located at or near the City of Rawlins, in the County of Carbon. The legislature may provide by law the location of other public institutions, including correctional facilities.

This section was amended by a resolution adopted by the 1978 legislature, ratified by a vote of the people at the general election held on November 7, 1978, and proclaimed in effect on November 25, 1978.

ARTICLE 8

IRRIGATION AND WATER RIGHTS

Sec. 1. Water is state property. The water of all natural streams, springs, lakes or other collections of still water, within the boundaries of the state, are hereby declared to be the property of the state.

Sec. 2. **Board of control.** There shall be constituted a board of control, to be composed of the state engineer and superintendents of the water divisions; which shall, under such regulations as may be prescribed by law, have the supervision of the waters of the state and of their appropriation, distribution and diversion, and of the various officers connected therewith. Its decisions to be subject to review by the courts of the state.

Sec. 3. **Priority of appropriation.** Priority of appropriation for beneficial uses shall give the better right. No appropriation shall be denied except when such denial is demanded by the public interests.

Sec. 4. **Water divisions.** The legislature shall by law divide the state into four (4) water divisions, and provide for the appointment of superintendents thereof.

Sec. 5. **State engineer.** There shall be a state engineer who shall be appointed by the governor of the state and confirmed by the senate; he shall hold his office for the term of six (6) years, or until his successor shall have been appointed and shall have qualified. He shall be president of the board of control, and shall have general supervision of the waters of the state and of the officers connected with its distribution. No person shall be appointed to this position who has not such theoretical knowledge and such practical experience and skill as shall fit him for the position.

ARTICLE 9

MINES AND MINING

Sec. 1. **Inspector of mines.** There shall be established and maintained the office of inspector of mines, the duties of which shall be prescribed by law.

This section was amended by a resolution adopted by the 1989 legislature, ratified by a vote of the people at the general election held on November 6, 1990, and proclaimed in effect on November 28, 1990.

Sec. 2. **Legislature to enact regulatory laws.** The legislature shall provide by law for the proper development, ventilation, drainage and operation of all mines in this state.

Sec. 3. **Restrictions on employment in mines.** [Repealed November 7, 1978.]

Sec. 4. **Right of action for injuries.** For any injury to person or property caused by wilful failure to comply with the provisions of this article, or laws passed in pursuance hereof, a right of action shall accrue to the party injured, for the damage sustained thereby, and in all cases in this state, whenever the death of a person shall be caused by wrongful act, neglect or default, such as would, if death had not ensued, have entitled the party injured to maintain an action to recover damages in respect thereof, the person who, or the corporation which would have been liable, if death had not ensued, shall be liable to an action for damages notwithstanding the death of the person injured, and the legislature shall provide by law at its first session for the manner in which the right of action in respect thereto shall be enforced.

Sec. 5. **School of mines.** The legislature may provide that the science of mining and metallurgy be taught in one of the institutions of learning under the patronage of the state.

Sec. 6. **State geologist.** [Repealed.]

This section was amended by a resolution adopted by the 1989 legislature, ratified by a vote of the people at the general election held on November 6, 1990, and proclaimed in effect on November 28, 1990.

ARTICLE 10

CORPORATIONS

Sec. 1. **Creation.** The legislature shall provide for the organization of corporations by general law. All laws relating to corporations may be altered, amended or repealed by the legislature at any time when necessary for the public good and general welfare, and all corporations doing business in this state may as to such business be regulated, limited or restrained by law not in conflict with the constitution of the United States.

Sec. 2. **Control by state.** All powers and franchises of corporations are derived from the people and are granted by their agent, the government, for the public good and general welfare, and the right and duty of the state to control and regulate them for these purposes is hereby declared. The power, rights and privileges of any and all corporations may be forfeited by willful neglect or abuse thereof. The police power of the state is supreme over all corporations as well as individuals.

Sec. 3. **Forfeited charters.** [Executed.]

Sec. 4. **Damages for personal injuries or death not to be limited; worker's compensation.** No law shall be enacted limiting the amount of damages to be recovered for causing the injury or death of any person. Any contract or agreement with any employee waiving any right to recover damages for causing the death or injury of any employee shall be void. As to all extrahazardous employments the legislature shall provide by law for the accumulation and maintenance of a fund or funds out of which shall be paid compensation as may be fixed by law according to proper classifications to each person injured in such employment or to the dependent families of such as die as the result of such injuries, except in case of injuries due solely to the culpable negligence of the injured employee. The fund or funds shall be accumulated, paid into the state treasury and maintained in such manner as may be provided by law. Monies in the fund shall be expended only for compensation authorized by this section, for administration and management of the Worker's Compensation Act, debt service related to the fund and for workplace safety programs conducted by the state as authorized by law. The right of each employee to compensation from the fund shall be in lieu of and shall take the place of any and all rights of action against any employer contributing as required by law to the fund in favor of any person or persons by reason of the injuries or death.   Subject to conditions specified by law, the legislature may allow employments not designated extra hazardous to be covered by the state fund at the option of the employer.   To the extent an employer elects to be covered by the state fund and contributes to the fund as required by law, the employer shall enjoy the same immunity as provided for extrahazardous employments.

This section was amended by a resolution adopted by the 1986 special session legislature, ratified by a vote of the people at the general election held November 4, 1986, and proclaimed in effect November 18, 1986.

Sec. 5.   Acceptance of constitution. No corporation organized under the laws of Wyoming Territory or any other jurisdiction than this state, shall be permitted to transact business in this state until it shall have accepted the constitution of this state and filed such acceptance in accordance with the laws thereof.

Sec. 6.   Engaging in more than one line of business. Corporations shall have power to engage in such and as many lines or departments of business as the legislature shall provide.

This section was amended by a resolution adopted by the 1959 legislature, ratified by a vote of the people at the general election held November 8, 1960, and proclaimed in effect December 2, 1960.   Prior to this amendment, corporations were limited to one general line of department of business.

Sec. 7.   What corporations are common carriers. All corporations engaged in the transportation of persons, property, mineral oils, and minerals products, news or intelligence, including railroads, telegraphs, express companies, pipe lines and telephones, are declared to be common carriers.

Sec. 8.   Trusts prohibited. There shall be no consolidation or combination of corporations of any kind whatever to prevent competition, to control or influence productions or prices thereof, or in any other manner to interfere with the public good and general welfare.

Sec. 9.   Eminent domain. The right of eminent domain shall never be so abridged or construed as to prevent the legislature from taking property and franchises of incorporated companies and subjecting them to public use the same as the property of individuals.

Sec. 10.   Mutual and co-operative associations. The legislature shall provide by suitable legislation for the organization of mutual and co-operative associations or corporations.

Sec. 11.   Powers and rights of railroads. Any railroad corporation or association organized for the purpose, shall have the right to construct and operate a railroad between any points within this state and to connect at the state line with railroads of other states. Every railroad shall have the right with its road to intersect, connect with or cross any other railroad, and all railroads shall receive and transport each other's passengers, and tonnage and cars, loaded or empty, without delay or discrimination.

Sec. 12.   Discrimination by railroads and telegraph lines forbidden. Railroad and telegraph lines heretofore constructed or that may hereafter be constructed in this state are hereby declared public highways and common carriers, and as such must be made by law to extend the same equality and impartiality to all who use them, excepting employees and their families and ministers of the gospel, whether individuals or corporations.

Sec. 13.   Railroads to make annual reports to state auditor. Every railroad corporation or association operating a line of railroad within this state shall annually make a report to the auditor of state of its business within this state, in such form as the legislature may prescribe.

Sec. 14.   Eminent domain. Exercise of the power and right of eminent domain shall never be so construed or abridged as to prevent the taking by the legislature of property and franchises of incorporated companies and subjecting them to public use the same as property of individuals.

Sec. 15.   Aid to railroads and telegraph lines prohibited. Neither the state, nor any county, township, school district or municipality shall loan or give its credit or make donations to or in aid of any railroad or telegraph line; provided, that this section shall not apply to obligations of any county, city, township or school district, contracted prior to the adoption of this constitution.

Sec. 16.   Acceptance of constitution by existing railroad, transportation and telegraph companies. No railroad or other transportation company or telegraph company in existence upon the adoption of this constitution shall derive the benefit of any future legislation without first filing in the office of the secretary of state an acceptance of the provisions of this constitution.

Sec. 17.   Rights of telegraph companies. Any association, corporation or lessee of the franchises thereof organized for the purpose shall have the right to construct and maintain lines of telegraph within this state, and to connect the same with other lines.

Sec. 18.   Foreign railroad or telegraph company must have agent for service of process. No foreign railroad or telegraph line shall do any business within this state without having an agent or agents within each county through which such railroad or telegraph line shall be constructed upon whom process may be served.

Sec. 19.   Location of depots. No railroad company shall construct or operate a railroad within four (4) miles of any existing town or city without providing a suitable depot or stopping place at the nearest practicable point for the convenience of said town or city, and stopping all trains doing local business at said stopping place. No railroad company shall deviate from the most direct practicable line in constructing a railroad for the purpose of avoiding the provisions of this section.

ARTICLE 11

BOUNDARIES

Sec. 1. State boundaries. The boundaries of the State of Wyoming shall be as follows: Commencing at the intersection of the twenty-seventh meridian of longitude west from Washington with the forty-fifth degree of north latitude, and running thence west to the thirty-fourth meridian of west longitude, thence south to the forty-first degree of north latitude, thence east to the twenty-seventh meridian of west longitude, and thence north to the place of beginning.

ARTICLE 12

COUNTY ORGANIZATION

Sec. 1. Existing counties remain such. The several counties in the Territory of Wyoming as they shall exist at the time of the admission of said territory as a state, are hereby declared to be counties of the State of Wyoming.

Sec. 2. Organization of new counties. The legislature shall provide by general law for organizing new counties, locating the county seats thereof temporarily and changing county lines. But no new county shall be formed unless it shall contain within the limits thereof property of the valuation of two million dollars, as shown by last preceding tax returns, and not then unless the remaining portion of the old county or counties shall each contain property of at least three million dollars of assessable valuation; and no new county shall be organized nor shall any organized county be so reduced as to contain a population of less than one thousand five hundred bona fide inhabitants, and in case any portion of an organized county or counties is stricken off to form a new county, the new county shall assume and be holden for an equitable proportion of the indebtedness of the county or counties so reduced. No county shall be divided unless a majority of the qualified electors of the territory proposed to be cut off voting on the proposition shall vote in favor of the division.

Sec. 3. Changing county seats. The legislature shall provide by general law for changing county seats in organized counties, but it shall have no power to remove the county seat of any organized county.

Sec. 4. Township organization. The legislature shall provide by general law for a system of township organization and government, which may be adopted by any county whenever a majority of the citizens thereof voting at a general election shall so determine.

Sec. 5. County officers. The legislature shall provide by law for the election of such county officers as may be necessary.

ARTICLE 13

MUNICIPAL CORPORATIONS

Sec. 1. Incorporation; alteration of boundaries; merger; consolidation; dissolution; determination of local affairs; classification; referendum; liberal construction.

(a)   The legislature shall provide by general law, applicable to all cities and towns,

  (i)   For the incorporation of cities,

  (ii)   For the methods by which city and town boundaries may be altered, and

  (iii)   For the procedures by which cities and towns may be merged, consolidated or dissolved; provided that existing laws on such subjects and laws pertaining to civil service, retirement, collective bargaining, the levying of taxes, excises, fees, or any other charges, whether or not applicable to all cities and towns on the effective date of this amendment, shall remain in effect until superseded by general law and such existing laws shall not be subject to charter ordinance.

(b)   All cities and towns are hereby empowered to determine their local affairs and government as established by ordinance passed by the governing body, subject to referendum when prescribed by the legislature, and further subject only to statutes uniformly applicable to all cities and towns, and to statutes prescribing limits of indebtedness. The levying of taxes, excises, fees, or any other charges shall be prescribed by the legislature. The legislature may not establish more than four (4) classes of cities and towns. Each city and town shall be governed by all other statutes, except as it may exempt itself by charter ordinance as hereinafter provided.

(c)   Each city or town may elect that the whole or any part of any statute, other than statutes uniformly applicable to all cities and towns and statutes prescribing limits of indebtedness, may not apply to such city or town. This exemption shall be by charter ordinance passed by a two-thirds (2/3) vote of all members elected to the governing body of the city or town. Each such charter ordinance shall be titled and may provide that the whole or any part of any statute, which would otherwise apply to such city or town as specifically designated in the ordinance shall not apply to such city or town. Such ordinance may provide other provisions on the same subject. Every charter ordinance shall be published once each week for two consecutive weeks in the official city or town newspaper, if any, otherwise in a newspaper of general circulation in the city or town. No charter ordinance shall take effect until the sixtieth (60th) day after its final publication. If prior thereto, a petition, signed by a number of qualified electors of the city or town, equaling at least ten per cent (10%) of the number of votes cast at the last general municipal election, shall be filed in the office of the clerk of such city or town, demanding that such ordinance be submitted to referendum, then the ordinance shall not take effect unless approved by a majority of the electors voting thereon. Such referendum election shall be called within thirty (30) days and held within ninety (90) days after the petition is filed. An ordinance establishing procedures, and fixing the date of such election shall be passed by the governing body and published once each week for three (3) consecutive weeks in the official city or town newspaper, if any, otherwise in a newspaper of general circulation in the city or town. The question on the ballot shall be: "Shall Charter Ordinance No. .... Entitled (stating the title of the ordinance) take effect?". The governing body may submit, without a petition, any charter ordinance to referendum election under the procedures as previously set out. The charter ordinance shall take effect if approved by a majority of the electors voting thereon. An approved charter ordinance, after becoming effective, shall be recorded by the clerk in a book maintained for that purpose with a certificate of the procedures of adoption. A certified copy of the ordinance shall be filed with the secretary of state, who shall keep an index of such ordinances. Each charter ordinance enacted shall prevail over any prior act of the governing body of the city or town, and may be repealed or amended only by subsequent charter ordinance, or by enactments of the legislature applicable to all cities and towns.

(d) The powers and authority granted to cities and towns, pursuant to this section, shall be liberally construed for the purpose of giving the largest measure of self-government to cities and towns.

Sec. 2. Consent of electors necessary. No municipal corporation shall be organized without the consent of the majority of the electors residing within the district proposed to be so incorporated, such consent to be ascertained in the manner and under such regulations as may be prescribed by law.

Sec. 3. Restriction on powers to levy taxes and contract debts. The legislature shall restrict the powers of such corporations to levy taxes and assessments, to borrow money and contract debts so as to prevent the abuse of such power, and no tax or assessment shall be levied or collected or debts contracted by municipal corporations except in pursuance of law for public purposes specified by law.

Sec. 4. Franchises. No street passenger railway, telegraph, telephone or electric light line shall be constructed within the limits of any municipal organization without the consent of its local authorities.

Sec. 5. Acquisition of water rights. Municipal corporations shall have the same right as individuals to acquire rights by prior appropriation and otherwise to the use of water for domestic and municipal purposes, and the legislature shall provide by law for the exercise upon the part of incorporated cities, towns and villages of the right of eminent domain for the purpose of acquiring from prior appropriators upon the payment of just compensation, such water as may be necessary for the well being thereof and for domestic uses.

ARTICLE 14

PUBLIC OFFICERS

Sec. 1. Stated salaries to be paid. All state, city, county, town and school officers, (excepting justices of the peace and constables in precincts having less than fifteen hundred population, and excepting court commissioners, boards of arbitration and notaries public) shall be paid fixed and definite salaries. The legislature shall, from time to time, fix the amount of such salaries as are not already fixed by this constitution, which shall in all cases be in proportion to the value of the services rendered and the duty performed.

Sec. 2. Fees. The legislature shall provide by law the fees which may be demanded by justices of the peace and constables in precincts having less than fifteen hundred population, and of court commissioners, boards of arbitration and notaries public, which fees the said officers shall accept as their full compensation. But all other state, county, city, town and school officers shall be required by law to keep a true and correct account of all fees collected by them, and to pay the same into the proper treasury when collected, and the officer whose duty it is to collect such fees shall be held responsible, under his bond, for neglect to collect the same.

Sec. 3. Legislature to designate county offices and fix salaries of county officers. The legislature shall by law designate county offices and shall, from time to time, fix the salaries of county officers, which shall in all cases be in proportion to the value of the services rendered and the duties performed.

Sec. 4. Deputies. The legislature shall provide by general law for such deputies as the public necessities may require, and shall fix their compensation.

Sec. 5. Who are county officers referred to by section 3. Any county officers performing the duties usually performed by the officers named in this article shall be considered as referred to by section 3 of this article, regardless of the title by which their offices may hereafter be designated.

Sec. 6. Consolidation of offices. Whenever practicable the legislature may, and whenever the same can be done without detriment to the public service, shall consolidate offices in state, county and municipalities respectively, and whenever so consolidated, the duties of such additional office shall be performed under an ex officio title.

ARTICLE 15

TAXATION AND REVENUE

Sec. 1. Assessment of lands and improvements thereon. All lands and improvements thereon shall be listed for assessment, valued for taxation and assessed separately.

Sec. 2. Assessment of coal lands. All coal lands in the state from which coal is not being mined shall be listed for assessment, valued for taxation and assessed according to value.

Sec. 3. Taxation of mines and mining claims. All mines and mining claims from which gold, silver and other precious metals, soda, saline, coal, mineral oil or other valuable deposit, is or may be produced shall be taxed in addition to the surface improvements, and in lieu of taxes on the lands, on the gross product thereof, as may be prescribed by law; provided, that the product of all mines shall be taxed in proportion to the value thereof.

Sec. 4. State levy limited. For state revenue, there shall be levied annually a tax not to exceed four mills on the dollar of the assessed valuation of the property in the state except for the support of state educational and charitable institutions, the payment of the state debt and the interest thereon.

Sec. 5. County levies limited. For county revenue, there shall be levied annually a tax not to exceed twelve mills on the dollar for all purposes including general school tax, exclusive of state revenue, except for the payment of its public debt and the interest thereon.

Sec. 6. City levies limited. No incorporated city or town shall levy a tax to exceed eight mills on the dollar in any one year, except for the payment of its public debt and the interest thereon.

Sec. 7. Depositories for public moneys. All money belonging to the state or to any county, city, town, village or other subdivision therein, except as herein otherwise provided, shall, whenever practicable, be deposited in a national bank or banks or in a bank or banks incorporated under the laws of this state; provided, that the bank or banks in which such money is deposited shall furnish security to be approved as provided by law; and provided further, that such bank or banks shall pay the same rate of interest on any money so deposited therein on time certificates of deposit by the legal custodian or custodians of any such public moneys as such bank or banks pay on time certificates of deposit of private depositors, and the custodian or custodians of any such public moneys shall be authorized to deposit same under time certificates of deposit as may be provided by law. Such interest shall accrue to the fund from which it is derived.

Sec. 8. Profit making from public funds prohibited. The making of profit, directly or indirectly, out of state, county, city, town or school district money or other public fund, or using the same for any purpose not authorized by law, by any public officer, shall be deemed a felony, and shall be punished as provided by law.

Sec. 9. Legislature to provide for state board of equalization. The legislature shall provide by law for a state board of equalization.

Sec. 10. Duties of state board of equalization. The duties of the state board shall be to equalize the valuation on all property in the several counties and such other duties as may be prescribed by law.

Sec. 11. Uniformity of assessment required.

(a) All property, except as in this constitution otherwise provided, shall be uniformly valued at its full value as defined by the legislature, in three (3) classes as follows:

(i) Gross production of minerals and mine products in lieu of taxes on the land where produced;

(ii) Property used for industrial purposes as defined by the legislature; and

(iii) All other property, real and personal.

(b) The legislature shall prescribe the percentage of value which shall be assessed within each designated class. All taxable property shall be valued at its full value as defined by the legislature except agricultural and grazing lands which shall be valued according to the capability of the land to produce agricultural products under normal conditions. The percentage of value prescribed for industrial property shall not be more than forty percent (40%) higher nor more than four (4) percentage points more than the percentage prescribed for property other than minerals.

(c) The legislature shall not create new classes or subclasses or authorize any property to be assessed at a rate other than the rates set for authorized classes.

(d) All taxation shall be equal and uniform within each class of property. The legislature shall prescribe such regulations as shall secure a just valuation for taxation of all property, real and personal.A

Sec. 12. Exemptions from taxation. The property of the United States, the state, counties, cities, towns, school districts and municipal corporations, when used primarily for a governmental purpose, and public libraries, lots with the buildings thereon used exclusively for religious worship, church parsonages, church schools and public cemeteries, shall be exempt from taxation, and such other property as the legislature may by general law provide.

Sec. 13. Tax must be authorized by law; law to state object. No tax shall be levied, except in pursuance of law, and every law imposing a tax shall state distinctly the object of the same, to which only it shall be applied.

Sec. 14. Surrender of taxing power prohibited. The power of taxation shall never be surrendered or suspended by any grant or contract to which the state or any county or other municipal corporation shall be a party.

Sec. 15. State tax for support of public schools. For the support of the public schools in the state there may be levied each year a state tax not exceeding twelve mills on the dollar of the assessed valuation of the property in the state.

Sec. 16. Disposition of fees, excises and license taxes on vehicles and gasoline. No moneys derived from fees, excises, or license taxes levied by the state and exclusive of registration fees and licenses or excise taxes imposed by a county or municipality, relating to registration, operation or use of vehicles on public highways, streets or alleys, or to fuels used for propelling such vehicles, shall be expended for other than cost of administering such laws, statutory refunds and adjustments allowed therein, payment of highway obligations, costs for construction, reconstruction, maintenance and repair of public highways, county roads, bridges, and streets, alleys and bridges in cities and towns, and expense of enforcing state traffic laws.

Sec. 17. County levy for support and maintenance of public schools. There shall be levied each year in each county of the state a tax of not to exceed six mills on the dollar of the assessed valuation of the property in each county for the support and maintenance of the public schools. This tax shall be collected by the county treasurer and disbursed among the school districts within the county as the legislature shall provide. The legislature may authorize boards of trustees of school districts to levy a special tax on the property of the district. The legislature may also provide for the distribution among one or more school districts of not more than three-fourths of any revenue from the special school district property tax in excess of a state average yield, which shall be calculated each year, per average daily membership.

Sec. 18. Full tax credit allowed against any liability arising from a tax on income. No tax shall be imposed upon income without allowing full credit against such tax liability for all sales, use, and ad valorem taxes paid in the taxable year by the same taxpayer to any taxing authority in Wyoming.

Sec. 19. Mineral excise tax; distribution. The Legislature shall provide by law for an excise tax on the privilege of severing or extracting minerals, of one and one-half percent (1 1/2%) on the value of the gross product extracted. The minerals subject to such excise tax shall be coal, petroleum, natural gas, oil shale, and such other minerals as may be designated by the Legislature.

Such tax shall be in addition to any other excise, severance or ad valorem tax. The proceeds from such tax shall be deposited in the Permanent Wyoming Mineral Trust Fund, which fund shall remain inviolate. The monies in the fund shall be invested as prescribed by the Legislature and all income from fund investments shall be deposited by the State Treasurer in the general fund on an annual basis. The Legislature may also specify by law, conditions and terms under which monies in the fund may be loaned to political subdivisions of the state.

ARTICLE 16

PUBLIC INDEBTEDNESS

Sec. 1.   Limitation on state debt. The State of Wyoming shall not, in any manner, create any indebtedness exceeding one per centum on the assessed value of the taxable property in the state, as shown by the last general assessment for taxation, preceding; except to suppress insurrection or to provide for the public defense.

Sec. 2.   Creation of state debt in excess of taxes for current year. No debt in excess of the taxes for the current year, shall in any manner be created in the State of Wyoming, unless the proposition to create such debt shall have been submitted to a vote of the people and by them approved; except to suppress insurrection or to provide for the public defense.

Sec. 3.   Limitation on county debt. No county in the State of Wyoming shall in any manner create any indebtedness, exceeding two per centum on the assessed value of taxable property in such county, as shown by the last general assessment, preceding; provided, however, that any county, city, town, village or other subdivision thereof in the State of Wyoming, may bond its public debt existing at the time of the adoption of this constitution, in any sum not exceeding four per centum on the assessed value of the taxable property in such county, city, town, village or other subdivision, as shown by the last general assessment for taxation.

Sec. 4.   Creation of county or municipal debt in excess of taxes for current year. No debt in excess of the taxes for the current year shall, in any manner, be created by any county or subdivision thereof, or any city, town or village, or any subdivision thereof in the State of Wyoming, unless the proposition to create such debt shall have been submitted to a vote of the people thereof and by them approved.

Sec. 5.   Limitation on municipal, county or school district debt. No city or town shall in any manner create any indebtedness exceeding four per cent (4%) of the assessed value of the taxable property therein, except that an additional indebtedness of four per cent (4%) of the assessed value of the taxable property therein may be created for sewage disposal systems. Indebtedness created for supplying water to cities or towns is excepted from the limitation herein.

No county shall in any manner create any indebtedness exceeding two per cent (2%) of the taxable property therein.

No school district shall in any manner create any indebtedness exceeding ten per cent (10%) on the assessed value of the taxable property therein for the purpose of acquiring land, erection, enlarging and equipping of school buildings. All limitations herein shall refer to the last preceding general assessment.

This section was amended by a resolution adopted by the 1919, 1953, and 1961 legislatures. The latest amendment was voted by a vote of the people at the general election held November 6, 1962.

Sec. 6.   Loan of credit; donations prohibited; works of internal improvement. Neither the state nor any county, city, township, town, school district, or any other political subdivision, shall loan or give its credit or make donations to or in aid of any individual, association or corporation, except for necessary support of the poor, nor subscribe to or become the owner of the capital stock of any association or corporation, except that funds of public employee retirement systems and the permanent funds of the state of Wyoming may be invested in such stock under conditions the legislature prescribes. The state shall not engage in any work of internal improvement unless authorized by a two-thirds (2/3) vote of the people.

This section was amended by a resolution adopted by the 1984 legislature, ratified by a vote of the people at the general election held November 6, 1984, and proclaimed in effect on November 14, 1984.

Sec. 7.   Payments of public money. No money shall be paid out of the state treasury except upon appropriation by law and on warrant drawn by the proper officer, and no bills, claims, accounts or demands against the state, or any county or political subdivision, shall be audited, allowed or paid until a full itemized statement in writing, certified to under penalty of perjury, shall be filed with the officer or officers whose duty it may be to audit the same.

This section was amended by a resolution adopted by the 1969 legislature, ratified by a vote of the people at the general election held November 6, 1984, and proclaimed in effect on December 3, 1970.

Sec. 8.   Endorsements required on bonds and other evidences of indebtedness. No bond or evidence of indebtedness of the state shall be valid unless the same shall have endorsed thereon a certificate signed by the auditor and secretary of state that the bond or evidence of debt is issued pursuant to law and is within the debt limit. No bond or evidence of debt of any county, or bond of any township or other political subdivision, shall be valid unless the same [shall] have endorsed thereon a certificate signed by the county auditor or other officer authorized by law to sign such certificate, stating that said bond or evidence of debt is issued pursuant to law and is within the debt limit.

Sec. 9.   Construction and improvement of public roads and highways. The provision of section 6 of article 16 of this constitution prohibiting the state from engaging in any work of internal improvement unless authorized by a two-thirds vote of the people shall not apply to or affect the construction or improvement of public roads and highways; but the legislature shall have power to provide for the construction and improvement of public roads and highways in whole or in part by the state, either directly or by extending aid to counties; and, notwithstanding said inhibition as to works of internal improvement, whenever grants of land or other property shall have been made to the state, especially dedicated by the grant to particular works of internal improvement, the state may carry on such particular works and shall devote thereto the avails of such grants, and may pledge or appropriate the revenues derived from such works in the aid of their completion.

This section was amended by a resolution adopted by the 1915 legislature, ratified by a vote of the people at the general election held November 7, 1916, and proclaimed in effect December 22, 1916.

Sec. 10. Construction and improvement of works for conservation and utilization of water. The provisions of section 6 of article 16 of this constitution prohibiting the state from engaging in any work of internal improvements, unless authorized by a two-thirds vote of the people, shall not apply to or affect the construction or improvement of any works designed, constructed or operated for the purposes of conservation or utilization of water, but the legislature shall have the power to provide for the construction or improvement in whole or in part, of any works designed, constructed or operated for the purposes of conservation or utilization of water, either directly or by extending aid to legal subdivisions of the State of Wyoming, duly organized irrigation, drainage, soil conservation, and public irrigation and power districts, and any public corporation legally organized for the purposes of the conservation, distribution or utilization of water or soil; and notwithstanding said inhibition as to works of internal improvement, whenever grants of land or other property shall be made to the state, especially dedicated by the grant to particular works of internal improvement, the state may carry on such particular works of internal improvement and shall devote thereto the avails of such grants, and may likewise pledge or appropriate the revenues derived from such works in aid of their completion.

This section was added by an amendment proposed by the 1939 legislature and adopted by a vote of the people at the general election held November 5, 1940.

Sec. 11. Construction, maintenance and improvement of public airports, aircraft landing strips and related facilities. The provisions of section 6 of article XVI of this constitution prohibiting the state from engaging in any work of internal improvement unless authorized by a two-thirds vote of the people, shall not apply to or affect the construction, maintenance or improvement of public airports, aircraft landing strips and related facilities but the legislature shall have power to provide for the construction, maintenance and improvement of public airports, aircraft landing strips and related facilities, in whole or in part by the state, either directly or by extending aid to its political subdivisions and, notwithstanding said inhibition as to works of internal improvement, whenever grants of land or other property shall have been made to the state, especially dedicated by the grant to particular works of internal improvement, the state may carry on such particular works and shall devote thereto the avails of such grants, and may pledge or appropriate the revenues derived from such works in the aid of their completion and maintenance.

This section was added by an amendment proposed by the 1947 legislature and adopted by a vote of the people at the general election held November 2, 1948, and proclaimed in effect December 1, 1948.

Sec. 12. Economic development loan fund.
(a) Notwithstanding Article 3, Section 36 and Article 16, Sections 1, 2 and 6 of this Constitution, the legislature, by a two-thirds (2/3) vote of all the members of each of the two (2) houses voting separately, may appropriate monies in an amount not exceeding one percent (1%) times the assessed value of the taxable property in the state as shown by the last preceding general assessment for taxation, to provide a revolving investment fund to be used to promote and aid the economic development of the state.
(b) The investment fund created by this section shall be used to provide fully-funded loan guarantees or loans to proposed or existing enterprises which will employ people within the state, provide services within the state, use resources within the state or otherwise add economic value to goods, services or resources within the state.
(c) Monies within the revolving investment fund shall be loaned or used to guarantee loans under such terms and conditions as the legislature may by law direct.
(d) The cumulative total of monies appropriated to provide a revolving investment fund shall never exceed one percent (1%) on the assessed value of the taxable property in the state as shown by the last preceding general assessment for taxation.
(e) Notwithstanding the limitation of subsection (d) of this section, earnings on the revolving investment fund shall be added to the revolving investment fund and shall be invested as provided in this section.

This section was added by an amendment proposed by the 1986 legislature and adopted by a vote of the people at the general election held November 4, 1986, and proclaimed in effect November 18, 1986.

ARTICLE 17

STATE MILITIA

Sec. 1. Of whom militia constituted. The militia of the state shall consist of all able-bodied qualified residents of the state, and those nonresidents who are accepted into service, between the ages of seventeen (17) and seventy (70) years; except those exempted by the law of the United States or of the state. But all residents having scruples of conscience averse to bearing arms shall be excused therefrom upon conditions as shall be prescribed by law.

Sec. 2. Legislature to provide for enrollment, equipment and discipline. The legislature shall provide by law for the enrollment, equipment and discipline of the militia to conform as nearly as practicable to the regulations for the government of the armies of the United States.

Sec. 3. How officers commissioned. All militia officers shall be commissioned by the governor, the manner of their selection to be provided by law, and may hold their commission for such period of time as the legislature may provide.

Sec. 4. Flags. No military organization under the laws of the state shall carry any banner or flag representing any sect or society or the flag of any nationality but that of the United States.

Sec. 5. Governor to be commander-in-chief; powers. The governor shall be commander-in-chief of all the military forces of the state, and shall have power to call out the militia to preserve the public peace, to execute the laws of the state, to suppress insurrection or repel invasion.

ARTICLE 18
PUBLIC LANDS AND DONATIONS

Sec. 1. Acceptance of lands from United States; sale of such lands. The State of Wyoming hereby agrees to accept the grants of lands heretofore made, or that may hereafter be made by the United States to the state, for educational purposes, for public buildings and institutions and for other objects, and donations of money with the conditions and limitations that may be imposed by the act or acts of congress, making such grants or donations. Such lands shall be disposed of only at public auction to the highest responsible bidder, after having been duly appraised by the land commissioners, at not less than three-fourths the appraised value thereof, and for not less than $10 per acre; provided, that in the case of actual and bona fide settlement and improvement thereon at the time of the adoption of this constitution, such actual settler shall have the preference right to purchase the land whereon he may have settled, not exceeding 160 acres at a sum not less than the appraised value thereof, and in making such appraisement the value of improvements shall not be taken into consideration. If, at any time hereafter, the United States shall grant any arid lands in the state to the state, on the condition that the state reclaim and dispose of them to actual settlers, the legislature shall be authorized to accept such arid lands on such conditions, or other conditions, if the same are practicable and reasonable.

Sec. 2. Application of proceeds of sale or rental. The proceeds from the sale and rental of all lands and other property donated, granted or received, or that may hereafter be donated, granted or received, from the United States or any other source, shall be inviolably appropriated and applied to the specific purposes specified in the original grant or gifts.

Sec. 3. Board of land commissioners. The governor, secretary of state, state treasurer, state auditor and superintendent of public instruction shall constitute a board of land commissioners, which under direction of the legislature as limited by this constitution, shall have direction, control, leasing and disposal of lands of the state granted, or which may be hereafter granted for the support and benefit of public schools, subject to the further limitations that the sale of all lands shall be at public auction, after such delay (not less than the time fixed by congress) in portions at proper intervals of time, and at such minimum prices (not less than the minimum fixed by congress) as to realize the largest possible proceeds. And said board, subject to the limitations of this constitution and under such regulations as may be provided by law shall have the direction, control, disposition and care of all lands that have been heretofore or may hereafter be granted to the state.

This section was amended by a resolution adopted by the 1921 legislature, ratified by a vote of the people at the general election held November 7, 1922, and proclaimed in effect December 20, 1922.

Sec. 4. Legislature to provide for disposition of lands. The legislature shall enact the necessary laws for the sale, disposal, leasing or care of all lands that have been or may hereafter be granted to the state, and shall, at the earliest practicable period, provide by law for the location and selection of all lands that have been or may hereafter be granted by congress to the state, and shall pass laws for the suitable keeping, transfer and disbursement of the land grant funds, and shall require all officers charged with the same or the safekeeping thereof to give ample bonds for all moneys and funds received by them.

Sec. 5. Special privileges prohibited. Except a preference right to buy as in this constitution otherwise provided, no law shall ever be passed by the legislature granting any privileges to persons who may have settled upon any of the school lands granted to the state subsequent to the survey thereof by the general government, by which the amount to be derived by the sale or other disposition of such lands, shall be diminished directly or indirectly.

Sec. 6. Disposition of unexpended income of perpetual school fund. If any portion of the interest or income of the perpetual school fund be not expended during any year, said portion shall be added to and become a part of the said school fund.

ARTICLE 19
MISCELLANEOUS

Sec. 1. Legislature to provide for protection of livestock and stock owners. The legislature shall pass all necessary laws to provide for the protection of livestock against the introduction or spread of pleuro-pneumonia, glanders, splenetic or Texas fever, and other infectious or contagious diseases. The legislature shall also establish a system of quarantine, or inspection, and such other regulations as may be necessary for the protection of stock owners, and most conducive to the stock interests within the state.

Labor

Sec. 2. Day's work. Eight (8) hours actual work shall constitute a lawful day's work in all mines, and on all state and municipal works.

Labor on Public Works

Sec. 3. Who shall not be employed on public works. No person not a citizen of the United States or who has not declared his intention to become such, shall be employed upon or in connection with any state, county or municipal works or employment.

Sec. 4. Legislature to provide for enforcement of section 3. The legislature shall, by appropriate legislation, see that the provisions of the foregoing section are enforced.

Board of Arbitration

Sec. 5. Legislature to establish courts of arbitration; duties. [Repealed by Laws 1965.]

Police Powers

Sec. 6. Importing armed bodies to suppress violence prohibited; exception. No armed police force, or detective agency, or armed body, or unarmed body of men, shall ever be brought into this state, for the suppression of domestic violence, except upon the application of the legislature, or executive, when the legislature cannot be convened.

Labor Contracts

Sec. 7. Contract exempting employer from liability for personal injuries prohibited. It shall be unlawful for any person, company or corporation, to require of its servants or employes as a condition of their employment, or otherwise, any contract or agreement whereby such person, company or corporation shall be released or discharged from liability or responsibility, on account of personal injuries received by such servants or employees, while in the service of such person, company or corporation, by reason of the negligence of such person, company or corporation, or the agents or employes thereof, and such contracts shall be absolutely null and void.

Arbitration

Sec. 8. Legislature to provide for voluntary submission of differences to arbitrators. The legislature may provide by law for the voluntary submission of differences to arbitrators for determination and said arbitrators shall have such powers and duties as may be prescribed by law; but they shall have no power to render judgment to be obligatory on parties; unless they voluntarily submit their matters of difference and agree to abide the judgment of such arbitrators.

Homesteads

Sec. 9. Exemption of homestead. A homestead as provided by law shall be exempt from forced sale under any process of law, and shall not be alienated without the joint consent of husband and wife, when that relation exists; but no property shall be exempt from sale for taxes, or for the payment of obligations contracted for the purchase of said premises, or for the erection of improvements thereon.

Intoxicating Liquors

Sec. 10. Intoxicating liquors. On and after the first day of March, 1935, the manufacture, sale and keeping for sale of malt, vinous or spirituous liquors, wine, ale, porter, beer or any intoxicating drink, mixture or preparation of like nature may be permitted in the State of Wyoming under such regulation as the legislature may prescribe.

In 1917 the Prohibition amendment was passed and in 1933 this amendment which repealed Prohibition was approved.

Sec. 11. Use of monies in public employee retirement funds restricted. All monies from any source paid into any public employee retirement system created by the laws of this state shall be used only for the benefit of the members, retirees and beneficiaries of that system, including the payment of system administrative costs.

ARTICLE 20

AMENDMENTS

Sec. 1. How amendments proposed by legislature and submitted to people. Any amendment or amendments to this constitution may be proposed in either branch of the legislature, and, if the same shall be agreed to by two-thirds of all the members of each of the two houses, voting separately, such proposed amendment or amendments shall, with the yeas and nays thereon, be entered on their journals, and it shall be the duty of the legislature to submit such amendment or amendments to the electors of the state at the next general election, and cause the same to be published without delay for at least twelve (12) consecutive weeks, prior to said election, in at least one newspaper of general circulation, published in each county, and if a majority of the electors shall ratify the same, such amendment or amendments shall become a part of this constitution.

Sec. 2. How two or more amendments voted on. If two or more amendments are proposed, they shall be submitted in such manner that the electors shall vote for or against each of them separately.

Sec. 3.   Constitutional convention. Whenever two-thirds of the members elected to each branch of the legislature shall deem necessary to call a convention to revise or amend this constitution, they shall recommend to the electors to vote at the next general election for or against a convention, and if a majority of all the electors voting at such election shall have voted for a convention, legislature shall at the next session provide by law for calling the same; and such convention shall consist of a number of members not less than double that of the most numerous branch of the legislature.

Sec. 4.   Constitution adopted by convention to be submitted to people. Any constitution adopted by such convention shall have no validity until it has been submitted to and adopted by the people.

ARTICLE 21

SCHEDULE

Sec. 1.   Acquired rights continue. That no inconvenience may arise from a change of the territorial government to a permanent state government, it is declared that all writs, actions, prosecutions, claims, liabilities and obligations against the Territory of Wyoming, of whatever nature, and rights of individuals, and of bodies corporate, shall continue as if no change had taken place in this government, and all process which may, before the organization of the judicial department under this constitution, be issued under the authority of the Territory of Wyoming, shall be as valid as if issued in the name of the state.

Sec. 2.   Territorial property vested in state. All property, real and personal, and all moneys, credits, claims and choses in action, belonging to the Territory of Wyoming, at the time of the adoption of this constitution, shall be vested in and become the property of the State of Wyoming.

Sec. 3.   Territorial laws become state laws. All laws now in force in the Territory of Wyoming, which are not repugnant to constitution, shall remain in force until they expire by their own limitation, or be altered or repealed by the legislature.

Sec. 4.   Accrued fines go to state. All fines, penalties, forfeitures and escheats, accruing to the Territory of Wyoming, shall accrue to the use of the state.

Sec. 5.   State to sue on bonds and prosecute crimes. All recognizances, bonds, obligations or other undertakings heretofore taken, or which may be taken before the organization of the judicial department under this constitution shall remain valid, and shall pass over to and may be prosecuted in the name of the state, and all bonds, obligations or other undertakings executed to this territory, or to any officer in his official capacity, shall pass over to the proper state authority and to their successors in office, for the uses therein respectively expressed, and may be sued for and recovered accordingly. All criminal prosecutions and penal actions which have arisen or which may arise before the organization of the judicial department under this constitution, and which shall then be pending, may be prosecuted to judgment and execution in the name of the state.

Sec. 6.   Territorial officers to hold over. All officers, civil and military, holding their offices and appointments in this territory under the authority of the United States or under the authority of this territory, shall continue to hold and exercise their respective offices and appointments until suspended under this constitution.

Sec. 7.   Submission of constitution. This constitution shall be submitted for adoption or rejection to a vote of the qualified electors of this territory, at an election to be held on the first Tuesday in November, A. D. 1889. Said election, as nearly as may be shall be conducted in all respects in the same manner as provided by the laws of the territory for general elections, and the returns thereof shall be made to the secretary of said territory, who with the governor and chief justice thereof, or any two of them, shall canvass the same, and if a majority of the legal votes cast shall be for the constitution the governor shall certify the result to the president of the United States, together with a statement of the votes cast thereon and a copy of said constitution, articles, propositions and ordinances. At the said election the ballots shall be in the following form: "For the constitution--Yes. No." And as a heading to each of said ballots, shall be printed on each ballot the following instructions to voters: "All persons who desire to vote for constitution may erase the word 'No.' All persons who desire to vote against the constitution may erase the word 'Yes.'" Any person may have printed or written on his ballot only the words: "For the Constitution," or "Against the Constitution," and such ballots shall be counted for or against the constitution accordingly.

Sec. 8.   When constitution takes effect. This constitution shall take effect and be in full force immediately upon the admission of the territory as a state.

Sec. 9.   First state election; time of holding; proclamation. Immediately upon the admission of the territory as a state, the governor of the territory, or in case of his absence or failure to act, the secretary of the territory, or in case of his absence or failure to act, the president of this convention, shall issue a proclamation, which shall be published and a copy thereof mailed to the chairman of the board of county commissioners of each county, calling an election by the people for all state, district and other officers, created and made elective by this constitution, and fixing a day for such election, which shall not be less than forty days after the date such proclamation nor more than ninety days after the admission of the territory as a state.

Sec. 10.   First state election; duty of county commissioners; who may vote; conduct of election. The board of commissioners of the several counties shall thereupon order such election for said day, and shall cause notice thereof to be given, in the manner and for the length of time provided by the laws of the territory in cases of general elections for delegate to congress, and county and other officers. Every qualified elector of the territory at the date of said election shall be entitled to vote thereat. Said election shall be conducted in all respects in the same manner as provided by the laws of the territory for general elections, and the returns thereof shall be made to the canvassing board hereinafter provided for.

Sec. 11.   First state election; board of canvassers. The governor, secretary of the territory and president of this convention, a majority of them, shall constitute a board of canvassers to canvass the vote of such election for member of congress, all state and district officers and members of the legislature. The said board shall assemble at the seat of government of the territory on the third

eth day after the day of such election (or on the following day if such day fall on Sunday) and proceed to canvass the votes for all state and district officers and members of the legislature, in the manner provided by the laws of the territory for canvassing the vote for delegate to congress, and they shall issue certificates of election to the persons found to be elected to said offices, severally, and shall make and file with the secretary of the territory an abstract certified by them of the number of votes cast for each person, for each of said offices, and of the total number of votes cast in each county.

Sec. 12. When officers shall qualify; oaths; bonds. All officers elected at such election, except members of the legislature, shall, within thirty days after they have been declared elected, take the oath required by this constitution, and give the same bond required by law of the territory to be given in case of like officers of the territory or district, and shall thereupon enter upon the duties of their respective offices; but the legislature may require by law all such officers to give other or further bonds as a condition of their continuance in office.

Sec. 13. First state legislature. The governor elect of the state, immediately upon his qualifying and entering upon the duties of his office, shall issue his proclamation convening the legislature of the state at the seat of government, on a day to be named in said proclamation, and which shall not be less than thirty nor more than sixty days after the date of such proclamation. Within ten days after the organization of the legislature, both houses of the legislature, in joint session, shall then there proceed to elect, as provided by law, two senators of the United States for the State of Wyoming. At said election the two persons who shall receive the majority of all the votes cast by said senators and representatives shall be elected as such United States senators, and shall be so declared by the presiding officers of said joint session. The presiding officers of the senate and house shall issue a certificate to each of said senators, certifying his election, which certificates shall also be signed by the governor and attested by the secretary of state.

Sec. 14. Laws to be passed. The legislature shall pass all necessary laws to carry into effect the provisions of this constitution.

Sec. 15. Transfer of pending causes, records and seal of courts. Whenever any two of the judges of the supreme court of the state, elected under the provisions of this constitution, shall have qualified in their offices, the causes then pending in the supreme court of the territory, and the papers, records and proceedings of said court, and the seal and other property pertaining thereto, shall pass into the jurisdiction and possession of the supreme court of the state; and until so superseded the supreme court of the territory and the judges thereof shall continue with like powers and jurisdiction, as if this constitution had not been adopted. Whenever the judge of the district court of any district, elected under the provisions of this constitution, shall have qualified in office, the several causes then pending in the district court of the territory, within any county in such district, and the records, papers and proceedings of said district court and the seal and other property pertaining thereto, shall pass into the jurisdiction and possession of the district court of the state for such county; and until the district courts of this territory shall be superseded in the manner aforesaid, the said district courts and the judges thereof shall continue with the same jurisdiction and power to be exercised in the same judicial districts respectively as heretofore constituted under the laws of the territory.

Sec. 16. Court seals. Until otherwise provided by law the seals now in use in the supreme and district courts of this territory are hereby declared to be the seals of the supreme and district courts, respectively, of the state.

Sec. 17. Transfer of causes and records from probate courts to district courts. Whenever this constitution shall go into effect, records and papers and proceedings of the probate court in each county, and all causes and matters of administration and other matters pending therein, shall pass into the jurisdiction and possession of the district court of the same county, and the said district court shall proceed to final decree or judgment order or other determination in the said several matters and causes, as the said probate court might have done if this constitution had not been adopted.

Sec. 18. How legislature chosen. Senators and members of the house of representatives shall be chosen by the qualified electors of the several senatorial and representative districts as established in this constitution, until such districts shall be changed by law, and thereafter by the qualified electors of the several districts as the same shall be established by law.

Sec. 19. Duration of terms of territorial county and precinct officers. All county and precinct officers who may be in office at the time of the adoption of this constitution, shall hold their respective offices for the full time for which they may have been elected, and until such time as their successors may be elected and qualified, as may be provided by law, and the official bonds of all such officers shall continue in full force and effect as though this constitution had not been adopted.

Sec. 20. Terms of state officers first elected. Members of the legislature and all state officers, district and supreme judges elected at the first election held under this constitution shall hold their respective offices for the full term next ensuing such election, in addition to the period intervening between the date of their qualification and the commencement of such full term.

Sec. 21. Regular session of legislature following first session. If the first session of the legislature under this constitution shall be concluded within twelve months of the time designated for a regular session thereof, then the next regular session following said special session shall be omitted.

Sec. 22. Regular election following first session of legislature to be omitted. The first regular election that would otherwise occur following the first session of the legislature, shall be omitted, and all county and precinct officers elected at the first election held under this constitution shall hold their office for the full term thereof, commencing at the expiration of the term of the county and precinct officers then in office, or the date of their qualification.

Sec. 23. Why constitution framed. This convention does hereby declare on behalf of the people of the Territory of Wyoming, that this constitution has been prepared and submitted to the people of the Territory of Wyoming for their adoption or rejection, with no purpose of setting up or organizing a state government until such time as the congress of the United States shall enact a law for the admission of the Territory of Wyoming as a state under its provisions.

Ordinances

Sec. 24. State part of United States. The State of Wyoming is an inseparable part of the federal union and the constitution of the United States is the supreme law of the land.

Sec. 25. Religious liberty. Perfect toleration of religious sentiment shall be secured, and no inhabitant of this state shall ever be molested in person or property on account of his or her mode of religious worship.

Sec. 26. Ownership of certain lands disclaimed; restriction on taxation of nonresidents. The people inhabiting this state do agree and declare that they forever disclaim all right and title to the unappropriated public lands lying within the boundaries thereof, and to all lands lying within said limits owned or held by any Indian or Indian tribes, and that until the title thereto shall have been extinguished by the United States, the same shall be and remain subject to the disposition of the United States and that said Indian lands shall remain under the absolute jurisdiction and control of the congress of the United States; that the lands belonging to the citizens of the United States residing without this state shall never be taxed at a higher rate than the lands belonging to residents of this state; that no taxes shall be imposed by this state on lands or property therein, belonging to, or which may hereafter be purchased by the United States, or reserved for its use. But nothing in this article shall preclude this state from taxing as other lands are taxed, any lands owned or held by any Indian who has severed his tribal relations, and has obtained from the United States or from any person a title thereto, by patent or other grant, save and except such lands as have been or may be granted to any Indian or Indians under any acts of congress containing a provision exempting the lands thus granted from taxation, which last mentioned lands shall be exempt from taxation so long, and to such an extent, as is, or may be provided in the act of congress granting the same.

Sec. 27. Territorial liabilities assumed. All debts and liabilities of the Territory of Wyoming shall be assumed and paid by this state.

Sec. 28. Legislature to provide for public schools. The legislature shall make laws for the establishment and maintenance of systems of public schools which shall be open to all the children of the state and free from sectarian control.

Attested:

MELVILLE C. BROWN,
President,

GEO. W. BAXTER,
A. C. CAMPBELL,
J. A. CASEBEER,
C. D. CLARK,
HENRY A. COFFEEN,
ASBURY B. CONAWAY,
HENRY S. ELLIOTT,
MORTIMER N. GRANT,
HENRY G. HAY,
FREDERICK H. HARVEY,
MARK HOPKINS,
JOHN W. HOYT,
WM. C. IRVINE,
JAMES A. JOHNSTON,
JESSE KNIGHT,
ELLIOTT N. MORGAN,
EDWARD J. MORRIS,
JOHN M. MCCANDLISH,
HERMAN F. MENOUGH,
CALEB P. ORGAN,
LOUIS J. PALMER,
C. W. HOLDEN.

JOHN K. JEFFREY,
Secretary,

H. G. NICKERSON,
A. L. SUTHERLAND,
W. E. CHAPLIN,
JONATHAN JONES,
JOHN L. RUSSELL,
GEO. W. FOX,
FRANK M. FOOTE,
CHAS. H. BURRITT,
CHAS. N. POTTER,
D. A. PRESTON,
JOHN A. RINER,
GEO. C. SMITH
H. E. TESCHEMACHER,
C. L. VAGNER,
THOS. R. REID,
ROBT. C. BUTLER,
C. W. BURDICK,
DE FOREST RICHARDS,
MEYER FRANK,
M. C. BARROW,
RICHARD H. SCOTT,